The Teacher of
Brain-Injured Children

The Teacher of Brain-Injured Children

A DISCUSSION OF THE BASES FOR COMPETENCY

WILLIAM M. CRUICKSHANK

EDITOR

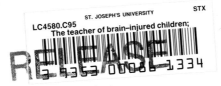
SYRACUSE UNIVERSITY PRESS

Syracuse University Special Education
and Rehabilitation Monograph Series 7

WILLIAM M. CRUICKSHANK
E D I T O R

Library of Congress
Catalog Card Number: 66-20050

Manufactured in the United States of America

Preface

The contents of this book are unique. It is not often that professional people have the opportunity to attack a problem leisurely without the necessity of acknowledging tradition, precedent, or legal strictures. This is what has happened in the development of the materials which constitute this book, and in the process, as one participant in the Seminar observed, some shattering blows to the "generic basis" of teacher education have been struck. Because of the uniqueness of the procedures which have been employed herein, this preface will consist of an account of how the project developed.

The need for qualified teachers of brain-injured children is apparent to parents and to those in many professions. Indeed, the need is so pressing that the word "apparent" is certainly inadequate. However, confusion exists on all sides in the profession as to the procedures to be used in preparing qualified teachers—and others—to work with brain-injured children. In the face of the need and of the confusion, a request was made by the editor to a foundation for sufficient funds to examine the problem fully. These funds were immediately granted.

From this writer's experience with brain-injured children and through conferences with others, areas of competency for teachers of brain-injured children were identified. With a list of competencies available, a second list of persons qualified to consider an individual topic was drawn up. Advice on the ability of individuals to deal with a given topic as well as suggestions for personnel were solicited from several national sources.

Invitations were sent to eighteen individuals inviting them to prepare a working paper on a topic to be indicated later and also inviting them to participate subsequently in a lengthy seminar in Washington, D.C., to discuss these papers. Sixteen acceptances were received; two persons were unable to participate, but they suggested other highly qualified individuals both of whom, upon invitation, immediately accepted. The fact that eighteen leading professional persons responded so favorably and so quickly is indeed an indication in itself of the pressure being felt regarding this problem. Many of their replies voiced a feeling of urgency to solve the matter at hand.

It should be stressed that qualified persons were sought who were, by reason of experience and interests, authoritative in working with some aspect of the growth and development of brain-injured children. There was no attempt to select persons on a geographical, political, or professional basis. Competency was the essential criterion. Quite naturally, for example, when dealing with a problem of neurological concern, educators were not considered. In selecting the neurologist, however, great care was taken to locate one whose experience and reputation carried him into areas of activity with brain-injured children outside his own professional specialty and to select one whose interests and perspectives were universal rather than parochial to neurology.

With areas of competency determined and with participants agreeing to assume an obligation, there remained the assignment of topics to each of the latter. This was done in May 1965 with the request that the working paper be prepared and submitted no later than September 1, 1965. Upon receipt, the papers were immediately duplicated and sent to each of the eighteen participants. The participants were then asked to read each paper carefully, not from the point of view of criticism, but from the point of view of critique and with the goal of strengthening what was already assumed to be a good statement.

On October 28 and 29, 1965, the eighteen participants, joined by others to be mentioned, met in Washington for two days consisting of five lengthy sessions to discuss the papers and to try to arrive at some consensus. The goal of the Seminar, however, was not necessarily to achieve unanimity, but, again, to strengthen by discussion the papers which had been presented. The authors, although listed in the table of contents, are included here for convenience to the reader:

WILLIAM C. ADAMSON, M.D., The Pathway School, Jeffersonville, Pennsylvania

RAY H. BARSCH, Ph.D., University of Wisconsin, Madison

ELIZABETH S. FREIDUS, Teachers College, Columbia University, New York

MARIANNE FROSTIG, Ph.D., Marianne Frostig Center for Educational Therapy, Los Angeles, California

WILLIAM H. GADDES, Ph.D., University of Victoria, British Columbia

JAMES J. GALLAGHER, Ed.D., University of Illinois, Urbana

RILEY W. GARDNER, Ph.D., The Menninger Foundation, Topeka, Kansas

GERALD GETMAN, O.D., Luverne, Minnesota

HERBERT J. GROSSMAN, M.D., University of Illinois Medical Center, Chicago

MIRIAM PAULS HARDY, Ph.D., Johns Hopkins University Medical Center, Baltimore, Maryland

HOMER HENDRICKSON, O.D., Temple City, California

NEWELL C. KEPHART, Ph.D., Purdue University, Lafayette, Indiana

PETER KNOBLOCK, Ph.D., Syracuse University, New York
WILLIAM C. MORSE, Ph.D., University of Michigan, Ann Arbor
SHELDON R. RAPPAPORT, Ph.D., The Pathway School, Jeffersonville, Pennsylvania.
RALPH M. REITAN, Ph.D., University of Indiana Medical Center, Indianapolis
CHARLES R. STROTHER, Ph.D., University of Washington, Seattle
MIRIAN TANNHAUSER, Montgomery County Board of Education, Maryland

To the above list of participants, a group of observers was added. The observers represented national organizations which for the most part maintained an interest in the education of brain-injured children. It was hoped that observers would not only contribute to the Washington Seminar discussions, but would serve as channels for feedback to their organizations and thus would sensitize professional groups as quickly as possible to the nature of the activity which was taking place. The observers consisted of the following persons:

SAM CLEMENTS, Ph.D., Child Guidance Clinic, University of Arkansas Medical Center, Fayetteville. Dr. Clements was invited because of his responsibilities as Project Director of Task Force One of a three-phase study of minimal brain dysfunction in children co-sponsored by the National Institute of Neurological Diseases and Blindness and the National Society for Crippled Children and Adults, Inc.
SUE DAVIS, representing the Council of Administrators of Special Education of the Council for Exceptional Children.
LOUIS A. FLIEGLER, Ph.D., representing the Division on Teacher Education of the Council for Exceptional Children.
JUNE JORDAN, Ed.D., representing the Council for Exceptional Children, National Education Association.
WILLIAM MEYER, Ph.D., Professor of Psychology, Syracuse University, New York.
GERALDINE T. SCHOLL, Ed.D., representing the United States Office of Education.
RAPHAEL SIMCHES, representing the National Association of State Directors of Special Education.

This book is the result of the individually prepared working papers and the discussions of them. Each chapter comprises three elements: (1) brief editorial comment, noted each time as such, to provide a unifying thread for the total study; (2) the final paper revised for publication by the author; and (3) in certain chapters, some pertinent comments related to each paper lifted bodily from a complete stenotype record of the Seminar. These latter statements are not edited except for syntax. Their authorship is indicated in every instance. The comments (often by the author) are included because the new points added, together with the paper, expand upon an idea, or because they provide explanation, as the result of interchange between an author and Seminar participants, of an author's ideas.

This exercise in professional thought has proven fruitful. It pertains only to the teaching profession. The interdisciplinary concepts which are stressed throughout the individual papers point up the necessity of examining the preparation of other types of personnel who will work with brain-injured children from the same thoughtful perspective.

WILLIAM M. CRUICKSHANK

Syracuse University
April 1966

Acknowledgments

While all the authors and observers who have engaged in this experience have acknowledged that they as individuals profited from the many contributions of other authors, I must recognize the great cooperation, thoughtful effort, and enthusiastic actions of those who prepared papers and of those who participated in the Seminar itself. Some of the authors, recognizing the significance of their efforts for the education of brain-injured children, have submitted several "final drafts" of their papers. All have prepared them with the recognition that they would have value to the profession in the preparation of teachers who would ultimately work with brain-injured children. The profession owes these people great gratitude.

To the group of citizens who made funds available to support this project—men and women of good will whose interests are for all children and in particular for brain-injured children—the profession must acknowledge its debt. This is the role of private funds—to stimulate and to create—and these monies have been gratefully received and used in the creation of an idea which in turn will stimulate teacher education to new directions.

Certain persons have assisted me throughout. Mrs. Edith Shafer, my Administrative Secretary, both at Syracuse and in Washington, provided the structure needed to make the project a success. Dr. Eva Woolfolk, Assistant Professor of Special Education at Syracuse University, was asked to assume a major role in bringing the manuscripts to the point of publication. Messrs. James L. Paul and John E. Garrett, both Fellows at Syracuse University, worked with Dr. Woolfolk on the manuscript preparation and with her functioned as observers during the Washington Seminar. To these four very capable people my personal thanks are gladly given. Mrs. Dorothy W. Cruickshank has served in numerous capacities both in Washington during the Seminar and in Syracuse to bring this project to its conclusion, and thanks in this direction cannot really be put into appropriate words. The officers of the Syracuse University Research Institute have in their capacity and responsibility made significant contributions to this work.

W.M.C.

Contents

Part II. Educational Competencies

Part III. Cognitive, Perceptual, and Motor Competencies

Part V. Interdisciplinary Competencies

PART I
INTRODUCTION

Chapter 1

An Introductory Overview

WILLIAM M. CRUICKSHANK, Ph.D.

DR. WILLIAM M. CRUICKSHANK is Professor of Education and Psychology in the School of Education, Syracuse University, Syracuse, New York. He has served and continues to serve in numerous advisory roles to organizations and school systems that are concerned with brain-injured children. His research interests in the past several years have all related to the psychopathology and education of various types of children with central nervous system disorders. He is the editor, author, or co-author of numerous books and articles dealing with exceptional children, and in particular brain-injured children.

Chapter 1

An Introductory Overview
WILLIAM M. CRUICKSHANK, Ph.D.

The professional field of special education is 150 years old in the United States, if one considers the concerns of Rev. Thomas Gallaudet in 1815 for a few deaf children in his parish as the beginning of professional planning. In the intervening years research, service programs, and the insights of thoughtful people have together developed a complex and nation-wide program for physically, mentally, socially, and emotionally handicapped children. True, the quality of the programs varies from state to state and from locality to locality, but a responsible recognition of society's obligation exists and the goal of services to all children as they need them is well within the grasp of parents, professional people, and the children themselves.

Over the past thirty years, it is rare that the professions have been challenged to the degree they have been recently by a single type or group of problems such as are presented by the brain-injured child. The professions have been comfortable with the traditional classifications of disability: the deaf, the hard of hearing, the blind, the crippled, the mentally retarded, and others. While terminology differed on occasion from one profession to another, it in reality took little time to obtain a meeting of the minds when such differences did occur. The professions moved along rather easily, each developing its own techniques of habilitation, rehabilitation, or amelioration for the problem at hand. Occasionally professions joined to obtain a better understanding or working base, but this has not occurred as frequently as it probably should have.

All of a sudden, into the relative calm of the traditional classifications of disability was thrust a different problem. Not new, but different, and one which the traditional concepts and classifications were not prepared to assimilate. Over the years there had always been some mentally retarded children who did not seem to fit the pattern of mental retardation. Always there were reports of emotionally disturbed children who did not respond to the therapies and educational programs to which the majority of the children in the respective classifications responded well. Some blind children did not seem to be able to learn braille. These children perplexed educators and frustrated parents who were unable to cope with the unusual learning and behavior problems which their children demonstrated. Only in the field of speech pathology was some specialized recognition of this problem made. Here a classification of aphasia was developed to include certain types of receptive and expressive losses which now have become recognized as an aspect of a much broader problem.

In the United States the work of Heinz Werner and Alfred A. Strauss is generally credited with the initiation of interests in the brain-injured child on the part of educators and psychologists. Dr. Lauretta Bender, however, had also been working with children whose learning and adjustment problems stemmed from organic disturbances. The tremendously important role of Dr. Winthrop Morgan Phelps in alerting several professions to the needs of children with cerebral palsy also as a by-product caused many people to begin to see relationships between the problems of neurologically handicapped children with motor components and neurologically handicapped children without motor manifestations but often with similar patterns of learning and adjustment responses. Newell C. Kephart and this writer, as early associates of Werner and Strauss, were stimulated to carry out further programs of research and professional preparation with brain-injured children. To these innovators, since 1950, have been added a multitude of others from education, psychology, medicine, audiology, optometry, social work, speech pathology, and rehabilitation who have served to bring the profession to a relatively high level of sophistication.

It cannot be said that the problem of the brain-injured child is fully understood. This is a field of special education definitely in transition. More is now understood than is put into practice. Tens of thousands of brain-injured children wait for services which are still many years in the making. The knowledge of the existence of these children is at hand, although the number of children is yet to be determined with accuracy. The awareness of the needs of these children has been achieved, although more research in methods of meeting these needs still must be accomplished. An understanding based on some research and observation of methods of education of these children is in the literature, although a consensus as to method has not been fully achieved. The brain-injured child constitutes the frontier of special education.

QUALIFIED PERSONNEL NEEDED

Of fundamental importance to the ultimate solution of the problem of the brain-injured child is the matter of the preparation of fully competent professional persons from many disciplines. Two major theses run throughout the pages of this book, namely, the need for qualified professional people and the fact that under appropriate leadership these professional persons must function as an interdisciplinary entity.

It is recognized that many separate disciplines are required, each with its own focus, to provide the needed thrust for the solution of the problems of the brain-injured child. This book is concerned only with the profession of education. Similar approaches will be required in a study of the preparation of psychologists, pediatricians, neurologists, psychiatrists, ophthalmologists, optometrists, audiologists, speech pathologists, social workers, nurses, and others who must be brought into the spectrum of life planning for the child. It goes without saying, but is rarely implemented, that educational administrators, school principals, guidance personnel, and general elementary and secondary educators must at least be sensitized to the nature and needs of these children to assure that administration does not obstruct successful programming. Parents, those who have the most intimate and most constant contact with brain-injured children, must also be studied to ascertain what competencies they need over and above those assumed for all parents in order to provide security, parental direction, and healthy equilibrium to the child, to themselves, and to other children or relatives within the home. But in this book, the authors deal only with teachers. What competencies must teachers have in order to be able to deal optimally with the brain-injured child? This question and only this question is the concern of this book.

As was stated in the Preface, no effort at unanimity or consensus was sought in or among the papers which follow. The reader will be startled by the tremendous amount of spontaneous consensus, however, which is apparent in the chapters and in the discussions which relate to the individual chapters. Consensus on basic issues is present; minor differences of opinion on details of implementation are also present. The reader, however, will be rapidly convinced as he reads chapter after chapter that the minds of the people who are on "the cutting edge" of this problem, at least as represented in this group of authors, are essentially one. This is not a random trial-and-error approach to the problem. A group of leaders representing several separate disciplines are herein seen thinking closely alike. Where differences are real, they are apparent and pointed up as differences. This is, it appears to this writer, an important point, however. So often in teaching or research or in program planning, one feels himself to be isolated and alone in this vast and complicated problem area. The fact of the matter is, however, that on all sides there are individuals seriously attacking this problem, and their attack is with different tools from startlingly similar orientations. This is encouraging.

These children are present and they are in the schools. They are undoubtedly to be found in every elementary school in this country and they are likely to be found in almost every classroom. The professions are not dealing with isolated children. From one point of view this makes it easy to plan educationally for them, for administrative arrangements can be more readily developed for numbers of children without disrupting the total system. From other points of view, however, the suspected incidence and prevalence creates problems because the schools historically were assumed already to be serving all children. To create room for a new and greatly different clinical problem necessitates many new administrative approaches often not experienced previously in schools. Children will be served, however, and the capacity of the schools to adjust to new demands is one measure of their quality as agents of the society which created them.

GRADUATE TEACHERS A REQUISITE

To serve these children there must be qualified teachers. The children herein being considered are both the same and different from all other children. They are the same in that they have all the basic characteristics and needs of children generally, but they are different in that at some point in their neurophysiological development, prenatally, perinatally, or postnatally, they have experienced a neurological insult which has impaired one or more perceptive-motor systems, and thus their learning abilities deviate significantly from their normal peers. Externally, these children look no different. Location and extent of the insult are, of course, significant, but more significant is the fact that an insult has been experienced whether great or small, whether diffuse or specific. The location of the insult is of importance insofar as the manifestation of the learning problem is concerned, but the essential nature of the learning problem seems not to vary with location. The literature abounds with descriptions of these children, and it is not the intent of this volume to record them again. Suffice to say that the learning problems alluded to are of great magnitude and if unattended leave adjustment scars which will or may have lifetime significance to the individual. To meet this problem, skilled educators are needed as a part of the total interdisciplinary effort.

This is not a problem for the inexperienced or immature teacher. There is consensus within this group that this is a graduate type of preparation. Whatever form the graduate education takes, it must be based on a broad program of elementary education which includes much emphasis on individual differences and special education concepts. Hopefully, teachers of brain-injured children will have had experience in teaching normal children or some type of exceptional child before specialized preparation for teaching brain-injured children begins. Brain-injured children and the concomitant emotional problems which they have will demand the most of the best teacher. They will demand the most of a mature teacher. They will demand the most of a patient, creative, sensitive, understanding, and secure teacher.

The teacher of brain-injured children must understand normative development, normative perceptual processes, normative learning characteristics, and normative achievement rates. On this background of normative data, as Tannhauser in her chapter points out, he will be able to understand the unique differences which characterize brain-injured children. The educator with maturity and with background in the normative aspects of his profession will be able to understand why specialized teaching materials must be created by him for the child. He will understand how specialized settings and teaching materials are to be developed in terms of the unique psychopathology demonstrated by the child. He will understand how to function as an "ego bank" as Rappaport so ably discusses in his chapter. The skilled teacher with a background of sound preparation and experience will be able to implement Getman's concepts (Chapter 10) and understand the role of visuomotor training and perception with the brain-injured child as so ably described by Kephart. These facts and others which will be mentioned are not the province of the immature, the untested, or inexperienced teacher. These children possess such unique learning problems that to them must be brought the finest of the educational profession. Experience and graduate status alone will not accomplish the things which are expected of the educator of brain-injured children. Experience has illustrated to this writer that extremely careful selection based on a thorough evaluation of the personality characteristics and emotional adjustment of the prospective teacher is an absolute essential and is requisite to the beginning of specialized preparation. More teachers will probably be guided away from this specialization than are admitted to teacher education programs if college and university administrators are courageous and carry out their responsibilities with the interests of brain-injured children always in a foremost position. This is not an aspect of teacher education, nor indeed of professional education as a whole, in which all will succeed equally. These children are unique. Their teachers in their maturity, stability, insight, and educational daring must also be unique. To recruit and prepare this core of educators is the responsibility of a select number of institutions of higher education, each of which possesses faculty members who likewise are uniquely skilled in many facets of this complex problem. Quality is imperative at all levels: at the university level, at the administrative level, at the teacher level, and, as a result, at the program level that the teacher develops.

CREATIVE TEACHER EDUCATION

The reader of this volume will not find a recipe for teacher education. Nowhere in this volume will the reader find a curriculum outlined in detail nor, indeed, even in terms of major headings. Nowhere in this volume will the reader find a sequence of courses. Special education in the United States has too long been based on previous precedent and upon what Samuel A. Kirk has often referred to as a "cafeteria approach." What one university or college has previously done has served as the model for the development of a newer program. Often even identical course titles and university credits are assigned in a college on the basis of what a previous one has done. This is inbreeding of the most vicious sort. Only once has an attempt been made to ascertain competencies needed by teachers insofar as special education was concerned, but even in that national study adherence to tradition, fear of change, and maintenance of the status quo characterized much of what was ultimately published. There is a great danger in the present initial stages in which the education of brain-injured children finds itself that similar procedures are being followed. In one institution of higher education known to this writer, there are received, periodically and frequently, requests from other colleges and universities for courses of study, for curriculum guides, textbooks, bibliographies, and even for course examinations for "new programs" of teacher education being established without well-prepared faculty members in the latter institutions. The education of teachers of brain-injured children is too complex to trust this approach, which indeed is inexcusable for any field of education.

The thoughtful reader of this book will find the thinking of eighteen persons, each highly qualified in his own field. Each indicates in the brief space allotted to him the basis for essential competencies and knowledge and understanding which the teacher of brain-injured children should possess. The thrusts which are included in these eighteen essays are, as a totality, required of every teacher of brain-injured children. Indeed additional competencies are also often suggested or implied by the authors.

As has been stated, no attempt has been made to incorporate these into a pattern. The specialist in the college or university will take these basic requisites and weave them into a respectable graduate program—of one year or two years or of whatsoever length is required to produce a master teacher who in turn is capable of meeting the diverse needs of brain-injured children. Furthermore, it is not to be implied that each of the following eighteen papers constitutes the outline for eighteen separate courses of the traditional type. Some of the competencies described herein may have been achieved before the teacher begins his graduate preparation. Others must be acquired in interdisciplinary seminars where several facets, overlapping in nature, will be simultaneously stressed. Still others may require separate thrusts in the form of specialized courses which may last for the duration of the entire program. Teachers who are characterized by those qualities which are here stressed are the goal of this type of teacher education. How these programs are organized and the qualities transmitted is a matter left not to chance, but to the discretion of wise and insightful university leadership. The elements for the recipe are here; how they are blended to form a perfect educational product must be left to faculty which is also well-prepared for its responsibility.

Selected Centers

Not every college or university should assume this role in teacher education. As the reader assimilates what is included in this volume, it will shortly be obvious that only selected universities will have the capacity to become so organized that they can provide the base required. Several essentials are needed. First, competent faculty specific to the education of brain-injured children must be available. Secondly, ancillary faculty in pediatric clinical psychology, in pediatric psychiatry, in pediatric neurology, in general pediatrics, in speech pathology, in physiological psychology, in perceptual training, and in a variety of other disciplines must be easily accessible. Thus, broad programs of psychology and medicine must be available for instructional support. This requires ancillary professors who are at home when teaching in an educational setting and who can in time harmonize the vocabularies of two professions to the end that teachers will receive the understandings which are so necessary. Thirdly, clinical facilities and educational facilities for observation of diagnostic and educational procedures for brain-injured children constitute another basic essential. Lastly, important, but not so frequently utilized, will be the educational services of specialists in pharmacology, electroencephalography, pneumoencephalography, and often in endocrinology, ophthalmology, optometry, and pediatric cardiology. It is obvious from this brief description that the preparation of teachers of brain-injured children cannot or should not be carried out in the traditions of a college or school of education alone. The broad base of the university concept together with its medical and clinical centers will provide the interdisciplinary structure which is essential to this complex phase of teacher education. An educational problem dependent upon ancillary services of psychology, medicine, and many other disciplines is the issue before the readers of this book.

DEFINITION AND TERMINOLOGY: AN ESSAY ON CONFUSION

The Term

This writer enters with caution the morass of terms that are used in the literature to describe the children with which this volume is concerned. It is a problem which seemingly defies consensus, if by this a single term is meant to be employed as a descriptive tool with which professional people of different disciplines can communicate. Someone has commented that to seek a commonly accepted descriptive term and definition is a "logical impossibility." This writer does not share that pessimism.

The literature abounds with terminology, each term probably appropriate to the profession which has suggested it. Each term has meaning to certain professions or segments within professions. It is this writer's considered opinion that probably no single term can be developed which will fully satisfy the professions, and that ultimately an arbitrary selection of a term will be agreed upon, whether this term be completely accurate and meaningful or not. This should not be a major concern; there are others of greater magnitude which require our energies. There is precedent for an arbitrary decision which is accepted by both medical and educational professions and indeed by the community at large. What, for example, is a "hard-of-hearing" child? What is the exact meaning of this term? Does it describe a clinical entity accurately? Is it semantically accurate? Doubt regarding its appropriateness could be raised from many points of view. Yet, in spite of logical criticisms, the term continues to be used, is accepted, and has value because in general this term makes it possible for people to understand the clinical problem at hand. Always there is the necessity of describing exactly the specific characteristics of each "hard-of-hearing" child or adult for whom diagnostic procedures, clinical treatment, or educational therapy or rehabilitation is being planned. No one is concerned, however, that the term, hard-of-hearing, is accurate or inaccurate or that in itself it lacks the definitional structure to permit the communication of exactness. It is sufficient that it makes possible a professional meeting of minds.

It is with the above thinking in mind that this writer views the problem of terminology and definition in the area of the brain-injured child. It is for this reason that he has quickly reached a decision regarding the title of this book. Since it is not presently possible to find a term which definitionally reflects the total issue, let us accept a term which has general meaning as the basis of communication. The term, *brain-injured,* does this. It must be recognized that the term for the child being considered will always have to be defined, as Gallagher and Rappaport so ably point out in the paper and the subsequent comment of Chapter 2. In Chapter 4 Grossman points up limitations of the term, brain damage, from a medical point of view. Popular consensus, however, may well override these objections. Familiarity with the term undoubtedly will carry much weight insofar as future usage is concerned, limitations notwithstanding.

It is important, however, that there is placed before the reader the semantic jungle with which the student will be faced as he examines the literature and seeks to become oriented with it. The neophyte will quickly find himself immersed in terminology as he initially examines the publications which have appeared thus far, and shortly he will have before him, among others, the following list of terms:

Brain-injured children (minimal)
Brain-damaged children (minimal)
Minimal neurological handicap
Minimal cerebral (brain) dysfunction
Neurophysiological dysynchrony (immaturity)
"Organic" child
Perceptual handicap
Cognitive defect
Hyperactive child
Chronic brain syndrome
Dysfunctioning child
Developmental imbalance or developmental deviations
Learning disability or specific learning disability
Maturational lag
CNS (central nervous system) dysfunction or disorder
Hyperkinetic child
Child with language disorders

Task Force One of the joint study of the National Institute of Neurological Diseases and Blindness and the National Society for Crippled Children and Adults isolated thirty-eight terms which are used in the professional literature to identify the child which this group ultimately chose to call children with "minimal brain dysfunction." The American

Committee on Optics and Visual Physiology speaks of these children as children with dyslexia, thus placing the emphasis on reading—a symptom, not etiology. Legislation in the State of California is concerned with the "educationally handicapped child" as well as with the "neurologically handicapped child." Bateman says the "child with learning disabilities is perhaps best described as one who manifests an educationally significant discrepancy between his apparent capacity for language behavior and his actual level of language functioning." This definition utilizing language as the sole criterion suggests still another, albeit extraordinarily limited, dimension in conceptualizing the brain-injured child (Bateman, 1964).

It would be easy to become involved in a medieval-type argument as to the value of one of the terms as opposed to another. Each has logical value and each is appropriate to a particular orientation, point of view, or discipline system. No one term is applicable to all any more than is the term, hard-of-hearing, to which reference earlier has been made, applicable to all individuals with certain degrees of hearing loss. Certainly the group of authors assembled in this publication is not seeking another alternative to the list of terms which has been delineated here. Rather the authors are trying to focus their attention on the nature of children with certain characteristics and to understand these children and their needs from several different points of view and conceptual models.

Thus it appears to this writer that the term, brain-injured child, has value as a descriptive term. It is proposed that it be used generally. An arbitrary agreement is all that is necessary. Such an agreement recognizes that the term is deficient in certain dimensions and that it may not be accurate entirely in others. However, when the term, brain-injured child, is used, there is a degree of understanding possible immediately in spite of the infant nature of this professional area of concern. Stevens and Birch have suggested the term, Strauss Syndrome, be used to designate these children. This writer elsewhere has indicated the limitations of this term. It is true that Strauss did much to bring the brain-injured child to the attention of the professions, but others were contributing equally much earlier and also contemporaneously with the eminent Strauss, e.g., Bender and indeed Strauss' own longtime associate, Heinz Werner. As *Little's Disease* has more accurately become *cerebral palsy,* so the Strauss Syndrome may better and more accurately be referred to by what it is, brain injury.

Why has this writer chosen to use the word brain *injury* instead of minimal brain *dysfunction?* The brain is cellular. *Dysfunctions* of brain activity are the *result* of some disturbance to neurocellular tissue. The disturbance to brain tissue constitutes an *injury* to that tissue in the most exact sense and definition of the term. As a result of tissue injury, brain *dysfunction* becomes apparent. The term, brain dysfunction, implies and connotes a description of the organism. It is a characterization of the organism. Brain dysfunction is the result of brain injury. As a result, ". . . in the absence of critical brain tissue capable of normal function, there will be disturbances in the biological integrity of the child" (Cohn, 1964).

This writer has consciously not utilized the term, minimal, in describing the brain-injured child. Cohn ably discusses this point and sets forth three basic criticisms of this word. In addition, however, to Cohn's important concepts, this writer feels that the word, minimal, as applied to brain injury is meaningless. The term has apparently been employed by some in an effort to differentiate between cerebral palsy children with motor problems and those whose neurological insult results in severe learning problems and in ego deficit although in no gross motor manifestations. In this connection Cohn's concept of an *ensemble of signs* (Cohn, 1964) is helpful in conceptualizing the brain-injured child. There is nothing minimal about the impact of tissue injury of whatsoever nature or extent on the child or on his attempts to deal with it from the point of view of learning, ego development, and total personality integrity. The professions will do well to rule this term out of their thinking and writing and to face the issue fully as it is.

It is not to be implied in applying the term, brain-injured, to these children that in every instance present-day diagnostic procedures will be able unequivocally to define the injury and its nature or extent. Psychology, neurology, and electroencephalography, in particular, are too gross in their method and instrumentation as yet to be able to define accurately every child's problem as might be hoped. As a matter of fact, because proof of neurological deficit and injury is sometimes required by state or local educational systems before financial reimbursement can be made or before admission to educational services can be effected, many children are not served. (See also Chapter 4.) This is a tragic situation and one which should not be tolerated. However, the inability of the diagnostician to be specific and to obtain proof-positive is not to say that no injury to tissue exists. It is hypothesized that emotional disturbances, for example, may produce chemical imbalances which under appropriate developmental circumstances produce injury in neurological tissue. It has been stated, right or wrong, that the great majority of reading problems is the result of neurological insult. It is doubtful, if this is true, that specific injury could be presently isolated in even a significant minority of the cases, yet injury may well be present. It is hypothesized then, that tissue damage will be present in these children—gross or fine, specific or diffuse—and that this damage is inherent in the creation of a long series of characteristics by which the brain-injured child can be identified. It is hypothesized that if diagnostic procedures were available to permit accuracy and unequivocal statement, children possessing the characteristics discussed in this volume would be demonstrated to have tissue damage or injury and thus accurately be called brain-injured. Until that time and with these considerations in mind, this writer chooses to use the term, brain injury, as the one which most satisfactorily permits communication between professionals.

The Definition

There is another problem, however, upon which agreement must be reached. It is that of definition. Here, too, if we are honest and forthright, there is confusion. The confusion in definition is more complex because value systems and theoretical dynamics are involved. This situation is apparent in Chapter 2, for therein Gallagher in his psychoeducational definition of the brain-injured child approaches the problem from the point of view of developmental imbalances and symptomatology. He utilizes a behavioristic frame of reference which is important and significant. At the same time Rappaport and others in the book point up a system of characteristics of brain-injured children based on etiology and define them in terms of ego-psychology concepts. Neither is fully complete. In juxtaposition they provide a fuller understanding of the brain-injured child. On the one hand there is a description of the child and on the other an understanding of the dynamic impact of the tissue damage which the child has experienced. The two positions are not opposite to one another, nor indeed are they argumentative. They supplement one another and complement each other to the end that a full understanding of the brain-injured child is possible.

It is interesting in reading the several papers of this volume to note that many of the authors have attempted their own definition of the brain-injured child. At times this has been done from a neurological point of view. Again another has brought to bear a psychoanalytic orientation. Still another sees the child in terms of a specific psychodiagnostic frame of reference as, for example, Gallagher and the Illinois Test of Psycholinguistic Abilities. This is a conceptual point of view which comes from an instrument which has been designed versus a concept which is based upon inherent characteristics of children. Both are needed; both are valid in the total understanding of the brain-injured child.

It is doubtful to this writer that the profession of education can be content with just an educational definition. The brain-injured child by reason of the many dimensions which he exemplifies must be understood in a multivariate perspective. Educators will perform a disservice to the child if they view the child only from the point of view of educational adjustment. Similarly, the brain-injured child is more than a neurological problem to the neurologist; he is more than a psychological problem to the psychologist. An interdisciplinary definition is essential, and such a definition must have universal acceptance to the professions which are involved in the brain-injured child's habilitation.

In attempting to bring clarity to the problem, Task Force One, previously mentioned, speaks of these children as being of "near average, average, or above average general intelligence with learning and/or certain behaviorial abnormalities ranging from mild to severe, which are associated with subtle deviant function of the central nervous system. These may be characterized by various combinations of deficits in perception, conceptualization, language, memory, and control of attention, impulse, or motor function." This writer would agree with this statement except to point out that there are brain-injured children of less than average intelligence who are excluded by this definition. Historically this entire problem, in education, originated in the area of mental retardation, and the retarded brain-injured child should not now be excluded from professional considerations. The definition likewise does not include quite enough.

The eighteen members of the Seminar together with the observers were not oblivious to the issue of definition. They viewed the problem as significant and certainly as a basic one in the preparation of teachers of brain-injured children. From an initial definition which was presented to the Seminar by Gallagher, this group sought a basis for an inclusive educational definition. It was apparent in the development of these statements that the group was forced to move from one strictly conceived in terms of education dimensions to one which, while encompassing education, broadened to an interdisciplinary point of view and incorporated ego-psychology concepts. The Seminar participants stated that "definitions may be developed for a variety of purposes. The specific purpose of the present one is to provide an educationally oriented approach to the identification and remediation of special learning problems that result from organic insufficiencies in the developmental process." Against this preamble the definitions suggested by Gallagher and by Rappaport may be considered.

Gallagher in Chapter 2 states that from an educational point of view brain-injured children may be considered children with developmental imbalances. He states, "Children with Developmental Imbalances are those who reveal a developmental disparity in psychological processes related to education of such a degree (often four years or more) as to require the instructional programming of developmental tasks appropriate to the nature and level of the deviant developmental process." Rappaport in approaching the problem states for the Seminar, "Children with Developmental Insufficiencies are those who reveal notable deficiencies in some of the primary skills prerequisite to academic achievement and who erect response patterns which, although aimed at protecting them from awareness of those deficiencies, interfere with their academic and interpersonal growth. They require multidisciplinary assistance to the educator and interdisciplinary habilitative programming appropriate to the nature and level of the deviant developmental processes." He goes on further to state that "the many biological factors which affect nervous system function and might cause developmental insufficiencies have not as yet all been identified, nor is there as yet adequate understanding of the role of such factors in the child's total life adjustment."

The two statements contain many essentially common ideas. There is also variance, as the reader will quickly note. Gallagher speaks of developmental imbalances; Rappaport, of developmental insufficiencies. It is appropriate in conceiving an educational definition to think of imbalances, for it is the imbalances with which the educator must deal. These imbalances, however, are the result of neurological, psychological, indeed biological insufficiencies which have been experienced by the organism at some point in its prenatal or postnatal life. In conceptualizing a definition of the brain-injured child, the concept of insufficiency undoubtedly has a more universal applicability. Rappaport, viewing the matter from breadth rather than from the perspective of education alone, as Gallagher had been asked to do, incorporates ego-psychology concepts into his statement in saying that these children "erect response patterns . . . aimed at protecting them from awareness of . . . deficiencies," and which "interfere further with their academic and interpersonal growth." While an education definition can stand without this factor, an inclusive definition of the brain-injured child cannot overlook the highly personalized and uniquely dynamic nature of the ego deficit and the struggle which goes on as the child attempts to understand his phenomenal self and to expand the self of which he is cognizant simultaneously in the face of the threat which society presents to him and in the face of barriers which society establishes to protect itself from him. The dynamics of this confrontation of two determined protagonists affect every aspect of the child's life including all aspects of school achievement and adjustment. Educators who are concerned for brain-injured children must extend their notion of responsibility and must be aware of the dynamics which have just been suggested. To the degree that educators can expand from their traditional area of responsibility and encompass the ego factors of the brain-injured child into the daily school programming, they will be approaching the goal of meeting the total needs of the child.

The Rappaport definition brings to the reader's attention still another issue which all too often is overlooked in schools and in a definition which is specific only to education, namely, the fact that these children *require* multidisciplinary assistance in conquering their deficiencies and insufficiencies. As the definition states, "multidisciplinary assistance to the educator and interdisciplinary habilitative programming" through the teachers is required "appropriate to the nature and level of the deviant developmental processes." Schools rarely are able to demonstrate effective interdisciplinary action. Although such action is considered desirable, there is little precedent for such an approach. Lack of knowledge of the true function of interdisciplinary action almost always dooms these attempts to failure. It is appropriate that this issue has been raised in definition as it is again by Knoblock in Chapter 19. One of the essential competencies of educators—teacher, principal, general administrator —who work with brain-injured children is a realistic understanding and experience in an interdisciplinary structure. Without this, the "programming of developmental tasks appropriate to the nature and level of deviant developmental process," as Gallagher states, will be met with frustration, discouragement, and ultimate failure for the child and his family.

It appears immaterial to this writer whether the definition of brain-injured children be conceived from the point of view of one profession or the other. It is important that several essential elements be included in whatsoever definition is formulated. These elements are basically included in the two definitions which have here been briefly examined. Any definition of brain-injured children must recognize (1) etiology which neither of the above do fully. This will be disputed, not in fact, but because there is not general agreement as to etiology. Clements in the Task Force One report points out the hurdles to agreement on this and other matters, stating that difficulties in resolving a concept of brain injury "gyrate around our incomplete knowledge of the human organism and our communication failures." This writer is assuming that brain-injured children are just that, i.e., children who, as previously stated, have suffered a diagnosable or undiagnosable central nervous system tissue damage. As such this must be included in any definition of imbalance or insufficiency.

Other essentials of definition must include (2) the concept of developmental imbalances due to developmental insufficiencies, (3) the universally observed struggle which the child has in protecting, aligning, and expanding his ego concept, and (4) the statement that, in almost complete contradistinction to normal children, brain-injured children are defined by the fact that their growth into socially acceptable beings is predicated upon interdisciplinary programming and attack.

SELECTED REFERENCES

There follows below a selected list of references which may give direction to the general educator who is attempting to become knowledgeable regarding brain-injured children. This list is extremely limited and in no way is to be considered inclusive. Reading is suggested, however, from a sufficient number of sources and points of view to provide an excellent background to further planning regarding teacher education.

Abercrombie, M. L. J. "Marianne Frostig Developmental Test of Visual Perception," *Perceptual and motor skills,* Monograph Supplement 3-V18, 1964, 583–594.

Arden House Conference. *Ten million and one: Neurological disability as a national problem.* New York: Paul B. Hoeber, 1957.

Bateman, Barbara. "Learning disabilities—yesterday, today, and tomorrow," *Exceptional Children,* Dec. 1964, 31, 167–177.

Bender, Lauretta. *Psychopathology of children with organic brain disorders.* Springfield, Ill.: Charles C Thomas, 1956.

———. *A visual motor Gestalt test and its clinical use,* Research Monograph No. 3. New York: American Orthopsychiatric Association, 1938.

Birch, H. G. (ed.). *Brain damage in children: The biological and social aspects.* Baltimore: Williams & Wilkins, 1964.

Bryant, N. D. "Characteristics of dyslexia and their remedial implication," *Exceptional Children,* Dec. 1964, 31, 195–199.

Cohn, R. "The neurological study of children with learning disabilities," *Exceptional Children,* Dec. 1964, 31, 179–185.

Cruickshank, W. M., Bentzen, Frances A., Ratzeburg, F. H., and Tannhauser, Mirian T. *A teaching method for brain-injured and hyperactive children.* Syracuse: Syracuse University Press, 1961.

Gallagher, J. J. *The tutoring of brain-injured mentally retarded children.* Springfield, Ill.: Charles C Thomas, 1960.

Gesell, A., and Amatruda, Catherine S. *Developmental diagnosis: Normal and abnormal child development.* New York: Paul B. Hoeber, 1941.

Getman, G. N., and Kane, E. R. The physiology of readiness. Minneapolis: Programs to Accelerate School Success, 1964.

Haeussermann, Else. *Developmental potential of preschool children. An evaluation of intellectual, sensory, and emotional functioning.* New York: Grune & Stratton, 1958.

Halstead, W. C. *Brain and intelligence.* Chicago: University of Chicago Press, 1947.

Hellmuth, J. (ed.). *Learning disorders. Vol. I.* Seattle: Special Child Publications, 1965.

Hewett, F. M. "A hierarchy of educational tasks for children with learning disorders," *Exceptional Children,* Dec. 1964, 31, 207–214.

AN INTRODUCTORY OVERVIEW   19

Hoch, P. H., and Zubin, J. (eds.). Psychopathology of communication. New York:
Grune & Stratton, 1958.

Kephart, N. C. "Perceptual-motor aspects of learning disabilities," *Exceptional
Children,* Dec. 1964, 31, 201–206.

——. *The slow learner in the classroom.* Columbus, Ohio: Charles E. Merrill,
1960.

Lewis, R. S., Strauss, A. A., and Lehtinen, Laura E. *The other child.* 2nd ed.; New
York: Grune & Stratton, 1960.

Radler, D. H., and Kephart, N. C. *Success through play.* New York: Harper &
Row, 1960.

Rappaport, S. R. (ed.). *Childhood aphasia and brain damage: A definition.* Narberth, Pa.: Livingston, 1964.

——. (ed.). *Childhood aphasia and brain damage. Vol. II: Differential diagnosis.* Narberth, Pa.: Livingston, 1965.

Rioch, D. McK., and Weinstein, E. A. Disorders of communication. Baltimore:
Williams & Wilkins, 1964.

Strauss, A. A., and Kephart, N. C. *Psychopathology and education of the brain-
injured child. Vol. II: Progress in theory and clinic.* New York: Grune &
Stratton, 1955.

Strauss, A. A., and Lehtinen, Laura E. *Psychopathology and education of the
brain-injured child. Vol. I.* New York: Grune & Stratton, 1947.

Taylor, Edith M. *Psychological appraisal of children with cerebral defects.* Cambridge, Mass.: Harvard University Press, 1961.

Tyson, M. C. "Benton battery of right-left discrimination," in *Perceptual and
motor skills,* Monograph Supplement 3-V18, 1964, 602–608.

Chapter 2

Children with Developmental Imbalances: A Psychoeducational Definition

JAMES J. GALLAGHER, Ed.D.

EDITORIAL NOTE.—The reader is referred to the latter pages of Chapter 1 for a discussion of the place of Dr. Gallagher's definition in the total issue of children with brain injury. In this chapter the author seeks to describe the brain-injured child from the point of view of symptomatology in an educational frame of reference.

DR. JAMES J. GALLAGHER, Associate Director of the Institute for Research on Exceptional Children, University of Illinois, Urbana, Illinois, received his B.S. degree in Psychology from the University of Pittsburgh in 1948. He obtained his M.S. degree in 1950 and Ph.D. degree in 1951 from Pennsylvania State University. Prior to coming to the University of Illinois in 1954, he served as Director of Psychological Services for the Dayton Hospital for Disturbed Children in Ohio and Assistant Director of the Psychological Clinic at Michigan State University.

Among his books and monographs are: *A Comparison of Brain-Injured and Non-Brain-Injured Mentally Retarded Children on Several Psychological Variables; The Tutoring of Brain-Injured, Mentally Retarded Children; Teaching Gifted Children;* and *The Productive Thinking of Gifted Children.*

Chapter 2

Children with Developmental Imbalances:
A Psychoeducational Definition

JAMES J. GALLAGHER, Ed.D.

The purpose of this paper is to provide a definition of a distinctive group of children who have shown the need for special educational treatment. This will be done by revealing the deficiency in existing definitions, presenting the need for an educational orientation, providing an alternative definition, and showing some of the implications of the new definition for educational practice and teacher training.

Is it really true that "a rose by any other name would smell as sweet"? Of course not. One can quickly think of a number of labels which, if applied, would cause you to turn from this fragrant flower with dismay and disgust. It is because labels and definitions are so important, determining in many instances the direction of our thought and action, or inaction, that the task of presenting some ideas on the definition of these troublesome and troubled children is such a challenging one.

Of what use can a definition be? Surely a precise and clean-cut definition is not the first, but the last, result of exploration in a given field of knowledge. A clear definition is the ultimate sign of triumph in the battle against ignorance. But, if the battle has not yet been won, how can the act of defining be used to further the pursuit? The problem is analogous to the person with binoculars staring out to sea. He can perceive, fuzzily, a craft of some sort, and his binoculars will help him to discern the object to be observed. Furthermore, if he can turn the right dials, he can bring it into even sharper focus. If a definition is to be of some use, it must sharpen the image of those children to be observed and help distinguish them from others who have different problems.

THE PROBLEM WITH STRUCTURAL DEFECT DEFINITIONS

The historical term, brain-injured children, has certain graphic value. Each of us can picture a collection of children in memory that were dis-

23

tinctively different. For many reasons this term does not seem adequate to present purposes. Yet, no paper discussing "brain-injured children" is really complete that does not pay homage to Alfred Strauss and his many collaborators, Lehtinen, Werner, Kephart, *et al.* The sustained interest of these pioneers in brain-injured children helped to shift the focus of interest from the impact of neurological damage upon the adult organism to the very different problem of the effect of damage to the still maturing organism.

The definition presented in the Strauss and Lehtinen volume is of interest both historically and as something upon which to build:

> A brain injured child is a child who before, during, or after birth has received an injury to, or suffered an infection of, the brain. As a result of such organic impairment, defects of the neuromotor system *may* be present or absent; however such a child *may* show disturbances in perception, thinking, and emotional behavior, either separately or in combination. These disturbances can be demonstrated by specific tests. These disturbances prevent or impede a normal learning process (1947, p. 4).

Note the conditional statement; *may* suggests that *some* (how many?) brain-injured children may not have these characteristics. A second major reservation in the use of this definition is that it often was not the neurological evidence that determined the diagnosis of brain injury but the supposed behavioral results that defined it, so that the definition became wondrously circular.

The easy fluctuation from a discussion of neurological cause to behavioral result that has characterized this field can be shown in Table 1, which lists terms which are often considered synonymous despite their clearly different connotations.

TABLE 1
SAMPLE TERMINOLOGY FOR "THESE CHILDREN"

Referring to Etiology or Neurological Damage	Referring to Behavioral Components
Exogenous	Hyperkinetic
Brain-Injured	Perceptually Handicapped
Cerebral Dysfunction	Learning Disorders
Cerebral Dysynchronization	Aphasoid
Cerebral Agenesis	Conceptually Labile

The leap from neurological insult to educational problem can be made effectively only under two assumptions.

1. The nature and extent of injury is directly related to the nature and extent of behavioral problems.

However, Cohn (1964) has pointed out that minimal neurological signs do not necessarily mean minimal cortical injury. He presented case histories where numerous neurological signs added up to relatively limited neurological damage or, conversely, where hardly any signs at all accompanied massive neurological destruction.

2. The set of all children who have neurological injuries and the set of all children who have perceptual problems (or other behavioral signs) are identical.

The weight of developmental evidence suggests that the more likely model to consider is that these two sets overlap as follows:

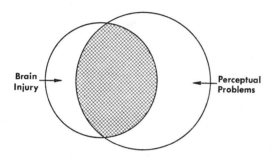

Thus, while it is possible to have brain injury accompanied by perceptual problems, it is also possible to have brain injury unaccompanied by perceptual problems or to show perceptual difficulties in the absence of brain injury.

One interesting paradox among many is that the term, brain-injured child, is often reserved for children for whom the label cannot be proved or validated. If contention *can* be proved, the label becomes more specific, such as cerebral palsy, hydrocephaly, epilepsy, and so forth. It is only when the label cannot be validated that one is reduced to a presumption of neurological insult through observation of certain behavioral characteristics. There is no practical or useful way to substantiate such presumption at the present time.

In many clinical teams the following situation may seem familiar. A child who is "different" is referred. He is having trouble in school, and his hyperkinetic behavior and lack of attention have been noted and remarked upon. He is set upon by the clinical team, each member of which conducts his own examination and then compares notes with the others. The neurologist, surveying glumly his own ambiguous findings, brightens considerably when he sees the psychologist's report which suggests possible minimal brain damage.

In the case conference that inevitably concludes such investigations, the neurologist presents his findings on the child as suggesting minimal brain injury. The psychologist, who secretly wonders about the efficiency of his own instruments, is glad to have the confirming evidence of the neurologist to support his own tentative judgment. So each specialist goes away fortified by the notion that their judgment has been strengthened by evidence from other disciplines.

Stevens and Birch (1957) have summarized the defects of the use of the term, brain-injured, with regard to children as follows:

1. The term is an etiological concept and does not appropriately describe the symptom complex.

2. The term is associated with other conditions some of which have no relation to the symptom complex commonly referred to as "brain injured."

3. The term does not help in the development of a sound therapeutic approach.

4. The term is not suited for use as descriptive and it results in oversimplification.

However, inadequate definitions usually owe their existence to the absence of more effective ones. If the old is to be discarded, a new definition must be formulated that can be utilized more effectively and is more faithful to what is known about these children.

EDUCATIONAL RELEVANCE

Even if there were less significant problems with the neurological term, brain injury, than have been noted above, there is a real question as to whether a definition that satisfied the purposes of another profession or discipline would fit the educational needs of those concerned with the problem. The many possible descriptions of these children under discussion must be viewed with the recognition that, for different purposes, different definitions might serve as "best."

It is not unreasonable to assume that intensive study of these children could result in greater knowledge of cortical functioning or could produce more sophisticated theories of how the human being can process incoming information in such a way that one says he is "paying attention." But that is not the present purpose; we must deal with the educational problems that remain after the injury, from whatever source, has occurred. Strauss and Kephart (1955) stated clearly that

. . . when we deal with brain injury we are dealing with the aftermath of an accident to the organism . . . we need to consider not the organism itself but the developmental process which is taking place.

Such a statement serves to place the proper focus on the situation, particularly for educators. Some eight years ago, the writer stated the issue from the standpoint of the special educator, and the words remain appropriate today:

> Does the educator not gain more information from the fact that a child is perceptually disturbed than from the fact that he is brain injured? Brain injury is the proper province of the neurologist; but the perceptual distortions, disinhibition and problems of association that sometimes occur in some brain injured children are the problems of the educator and the psychologist. It would seem reasonable to expect the educator to make his own educational diagnosis of each child's perceptual development, personality skills, or language development, and make his plans accordingly whether or not a diagnosis of brain injury had been medically determined (1957, p. 69).

The educator is interested in function rather than structure. Bender (1959) has made a plea for the neurologist to pay attention to *function impairment* as the key to proper diagnosis and remediation, and there would seem to be little doubt that it is the *function impairment* that one must deal with whether as neurologists, psychologists, or educators.

In clinical practice or research it has been the disturbance in function that has taken precedence over the disturbance in structure. Witness the experiment by Cruickshank *et al.* (1961) that studied the results of special educational intervention on brain-injured and hyperactive children. Many of the children in the study showed no definitive neurological damage but were included in the study on the ground, quite properly, that they showed similar disturbance in function.

A final caution—the definition should not result in a paralyzing reduction of professional anxiety. The tranquillizing effect on a profession of the application of some distinguished label and accompanying description such as schizophrenia, infantile autism, or minimal brain injury is too well known to require extended comment. These terms describe extraordinarily vague entities, explain nothing, and lead to no clear prescription as to what should be done. They provide only a false sense of order and knowledge. The relief that is obvious at a case conference once one of these labels is convincingly pinned on the child is evidence that all tend to seek certainty and security, sometimes at the expense of broadening professional wisdom.

PSYCHOEDUCATIONAL DEFINITION

The problem facing the person who wishes to describe these children behaviorally is that there are always an impressive number of exceptions to every behavioral generalization that one would wish to make: Some are perceptually disturbed; some are hyperkinetic; some show attention difficulties, and so forth. In order for a definition to encompass the range of children's behavior manifested by this group one must abandon the approach of searching for a particular characteristic. One way out of this dilemma is to focus on a definition of ability patterns rather than of specific abilities.

> *Children with Developmental Imbalances[1] are those who reveal a developmental disparity in psychological processes related to education of such a degree (often four years or more) as to require the instructional programming of developmental tasks appropriate to the nature and level of the deviant developmental process.*

There appear to be many biological factors affecting nervous system function that may cause such developmental disparities, although such etiology need not be assumed in every instance. Appropriate treatment of any associated medical difficulties should be a part of any total remedial program.

This present definition parts company with many that have previously been attempted for these unusual children. The emphasis here is on behavior and patterns of development, with fewer assumptions made about the neurological etiology. This change is not due to any predisposition on the part of the writer to doubt neurological etiology of many of these cases. It is instead a presumption that a definition based upon developmental patterns has greater educational promise by focusing emphasis on psychological development and appropriate remedial practices.

The gulf between present knowledge of neurology and the theories of human behavior is immense. Such terms as cerebral dysynchronization, cerebral agenesis, or minimal brain injury sound full of scientific acumen to the uninitiated. Instead, they are confessions of the most dismal ignorance. In summary, they say that we think *something* is wrong *somewhere* in the central nervous system. But—(1) we don't know what caused the damage, (2) we are not sure where the damage is (nor in many cases can we prove that there has been damage), (3) we don't know how to repair the damage that has taken place, (4)

---

[1] The writer profited materially from the discussions held in the conference regarding definition, but this definition is his responsibility alone.

we can't predict what the behavioral consequences of such damage will be. (In fact, it is often the behavioral symptoms that call attention to the central nervous system dysfunction rather than the other way around.)

To the teacher who must face a group of difficult children Monday morning, such a label or such an orientation can provide scant comfort. While the long-range goal of the behavior and biological sciences is to bridge this gap between them, another generation will probably have to pass before this laudable goal can be approached. For the foreseeable future, the educational programs must be based on theories of human development and behavior. This is not necessarily a pessimistic statement for these children. Impressive contributions to the knowledge of human behavior have been made by such pioneers as Piaget, Freud, Skinner, Montessori, and others who have referred infrequently, if at all, to basic neurology. It is for these reasons that the writer suggests that, while all children with developmental imbalances should receive the best and most complete medical diagnosis and care, the basic orientation of the definition should recognize and confront the essentially educational and psychological nature of the problem facing the educator.

It is the disparity in developmental patterns of those abilities important to school learning that bother people and call for special attention and education. Although a child's general language development might appear at a six-year level, his perceptual-motor skills might be at a two- or three-year level. Or his motor functions might be developing in a reasonable fashion for a seven-year-old, but the child is substantially without effective language. It is as if one sees a child who is six feet tall weighing only eighty-five pounds. The developmental disparity impresses itself on the observer.

The key characteristic that identifies this child to the observer is the substantial *difference* between the worst and the best of his developing intelligences, or the substantial intraindividual differences noted within the child. The children with large developmental imbalances can be counted on to cause considerable difficulties in any educational program which is based on the assumption that a child's developmental processes will be within rather narrow limits. If his perceptual development is at a certain level, his social and attentional performance on that level are taken for granted. If his language is that of a six-year level, he is expected to "behave" according to that standard.

While the school-age, mentally retarded child shows developmental disparities of these skills with chronological age, the disparity usually exists across all of his abilities. There is not usually substantial intraindividual variation in their intellectual skills. This does not mean that a child could not be mentally retarded or emotionally disturbed *and* show developmental imbalances as well.

MEASUREMENT AND OPERATIONAL DEFINITIONS

A definition, in order to be valid and useful and not a semantic shadow, must be tied to the appropriate measuring instruments, since it is these instruments that establish the practical boundaries of any definition. No matter how esoteric or how abstract the semantic description, the practitioner must fall back upon the information provided by the tools available for the task. Thus "intelligence" becomes the I.Q. test results; "personality" becomes a Rorschach profile; and "neurological integrity," an E.E.G. pattern.

An explicit distinction should be made between classification and diagnostic measuring devices. Classification instruments allow educators to place children in various learning environments, such as a special class, or in the hands of a remedial teacher or counselor. Diagnostic instruments, on the other hand, give direction to the person responsible for the remedial work by identifying the injured area and determining the degree of difficulty.

Much of the measuring instruments used historically with these children have been classification tools—thus, the I.Q. score, the achievement grade point score, or the percentile ranking on a personality questionnaire. They are not diagnostic in the sense that they do not tell what to do with the individual in order to help solve his particular problem.

For this purpose a different type of test is needed that reveals the individual's strengths and weaknesses in his own development. This information can be used by the remedial person to plan a treatment program. In the case of the children with strong developmental imbalances, the tests or battery of tests such as proposed by Frostig, Wepman, Kirk and McCarthy, *et al.* seek not a general statement of mental development, but probe for special areas of weakness in the complex of abilities of the individual child.

A legitimate question may be raised as to what constitutes developmental balance? Is it a flat, even profile of skills so that all appear at the same age level? We lack accumulated evidence as to how much diversity in pattern represents normal limits. It would seem safe to say that a deviation of four years or more between the best and worst skill is beyond that normal limit.

Figure 1 shows the obtained profile of a student based on his performance on the Illinois Test of Psycholinguistic Abilities (ITPA). The great disparity of five years between his most and least advanced abilities establishes this youngster as one with significant developmental imbalance. The information provided by this patterning of abilities is much more important than his single mental age score or language age score. While his Binet mental level is listed as between five and six years, his internal variation from three to eight years is the more important educationally diagnostic information. It not only establishes the fact of developmental imbalance, but it locates the areas of specific disability. (In this instance, Mike shows specific weakness in the Sequential Tests in the model and remedial work would be centered on this disability.)

FIGURE 1. ITPA PROFILE

MIKE					REPRESENTATIONAL LEVEL						AUTOMATIC-SEQUENTIAL LEVEL		
					DECODING		ASSOCIATION		ENCODING		AUTOMATIC	SEQUENTIAL	
					1	2	3	4	5	6	7	8	9
Binet M.A. Verbal	M.A. Verbal	M.A. Perfor.	Other Tests Peabody	Ages	Auditory	Visual	Auditory Vocal	Visual Motor	Vocal	Motor	Auditory Vocal	Auditory Vocal	Visual Motor
				9-0									
				8-6									
				8-0									
				7-6									
				7-0									
				6-6									
				6-0									
				5-6									
				5-0									
				4-6									
				4-0									
				3-6									
				3-0									
				2-6									
				2-0									

One may infer that some neurological trauma has been a part of the etiology of such an imbalance in this child, but such inference does not advance the central issue of educational remediation. This does not mean that one should ignore the important ancillary contribution that might be made by medical specialists. Recent advances in drug therapy, for example, have suggested that agents are available that can influence the attentional mechanism and, hence, provide an important stabilizing effect on children with problems in this dimension. Who knows what lies ahead regarding ribonucleic acid (RNA) and the improvement of memory?

IMPLICATIONS FOR TEACHERS

If a definition is to be useful, it should also provide some possible implications for teacher preparation in this area. The emphasis in the definition on the idiosyncratic nature of each child's problem, the move from the description of global intellectual ability to specific abilities, and the change from a medical to an educational focus carry strong implications for teachers.

1. *Diagnostic methods*. While it is unreasonable to assume teachers would be accomplished psychodiagnosticians, it is not unreasonable to ask them to be aware of the areas or dimensions of development in which the child is to be evaluated and to have at their fingertips informal methods of diagnosis that will enable them to obtain some rough pattern of the youngsters' abilities and disabilities.

2. *Remedial procedures*. The teacher of these children should have in mind various remedial exercises and methods designed to meet specific deficiencies and, further, should be able to sequence these exercises in developmental order. This means a much greater emphasis in the training program for teachers on the developmental processes and less concern with group data on development.

3. *Educational program*. The implication of this definition is that the educational environment in which such work needs to be done must allow for necessary individual attention and tutoring. This, in turn, means a substantially different and, hopefully, an imaginative approach in educational planning that does not blindly follow a pattern that may have been successfully used with other groups of exceptional children but which may not fit the peculiar needs of these youngsters.

Ordinarily a definition is supposed to extract those characteristics that these individuals have in common and that establish their membership in a class. Thus, mentally retarded children all have in common a slower rate of mental development than the average child. But what do the children with developmental imbalances have in common? *They have, in common, that they are all different—not only different from average children but different from one another.* This fact has great implications for teacher training and for the orientation of teachers to these children.

The similarity of one mentally retarded child to another has led to the special class program so widely used in our public schools. However, the reflex action of starting classes for "brain-injured" children in the same pattern overlooks the idiosyncratic nature that is the basis for the definition of these children. Obviously a much greater emphasis on individual planning, diagnosis, and remediation is one of the foundation blocks around which the educational environment should be constructed.

Above all, this educational definition should alert the educator to the fact that he has the major responsibility, as the educational specialist, for the nature of remedial program. It is his responsibility to see that the child receives proper treatment of auxiliary problems such as speech difficulties or special medical problems by referrals to specialists in these areas who are best qualified to handle them. The nature of the training program for the child is his chief responsibility, and it is the goal of a professional preparation program to see that he is ready to fulfill that responsibility.

It is the belief of the writer that the definition of these children in terms of developmental imbalances provides the context within which a more effective educational and remedial program can go forth. The intensive work now being done in this area promises that a more precise definition of these children can be presented a half decade from now.

SELECTED REFERENCES

Bender, Lauretta. *Psychopathology of children with organic brain disorder*. Springfield, Ill.: Charles C Thomas, 1959.

Birch, H. G. (ed.). *Brain damage in children*. Baltimore: Williams & Wilkins, 1964.

Cohn, R. "The neurological study of children with learning disabilities," *Exceptional Children*, 1964, 31, 179–186.

Cruickshank, W. M., Bentzen, Frances, Ratzeburg, F. H., and Tannhauser, Mirian. *A teaching method for brain-injured and hyperactive children*. Syracuse: Syracuse University Press, 1961.

Gallagher, J. J. "A comparison of brain-injured and non-brain-injured mentally retarded children on several psychological variables," *Monograph of the Society for Research in Child Development*, Serial No. 65, 1957, 22, 2.

————. *The tutoring of brain-injured mentally retarded children: An experimental study*. Springfield, Ill.: Charles C Thomas, 1960.

Kephart, N. C. *The slow learner in the classroom*. Columbus, Ohio: Charles E. Merrill, 1960.

Kirk, S. A., and McCarthy, J. J. "The Illinois Test of Psycholinguistic Abilities— an approach to differential diagnosis", *American Journal of Mental Deficiency*, 1961, 66, 399–412.

Stevens, G. A., and Birch, J. W. "A proposal for classification of the terminology used to describe brain-injured children," *Exceptional Children*, 1957, 23, 346–349.

Strauss, A. A., and Kephart, N. C. *Psychopathology and education of the brain injured child: Vol. II*. New York: Grune & Stratton, 1955.

Strauss, A. A., and Lehtinen, Laura. *Psychopathology and education of the brain injured child*. New York: Grune & Stratton, 1947.

Wortis, J. "A note on the concept of the 'brain injured' child," *American Journal of Mental Deficiency*, 1956, 61, 204–206.

Comment

Editorial note.—As commented upon in Chapter 1, Dr. Sheldon Rappaport responded to Dr. Gallagher's comments with a lengthy discussion based in large measure on ego-psychology concepts. The positions which the two psychologists take, as noted in Chapter 1, are not completely opposite one from the other. While viewing the brain-injured child from different points of view, the two statements were felt by the Seminar participants to complement each other in large measure. Together the two positions form a significant concept in understanding and in defining the brain-injured child.

Dr. Rappaport (See Chapter 3 for biographical data regarding this participant): Dr. Gallagher's comments call to mind what Dr. Sam Clements set forth in April of 1965 ("Minimal Brain Dysfunction in Children: Terminology and Identification") as a result of work sponsored jointly by the National Institute of Neurological Diseases and Blindness and the National Society for Crippled Children and Adults. It would be worthwhile to consider these two views on the definition of brain-injured children, particularly Dr. Gallagher's, first from the standpoint of a conceptual frame of reference and, secondly, from the day-to-day functional or operational standpoint.

At the outset of his paper, Dr. Gallagher stated that if a definition is to be of some use, it must sharpen the image of those children to be observed and help distinguish them from others who have different problems. No one would question the worthiness of that goal. As Dr. Gallagher continued to investigate the different aspects of definition, he indicated that Strauss and Lehtinen observed twenty years ago that brain-injured children *may* have certain neurologically caused symptoms, that too frequently the term, brain-injured, is applied because clinicians do not know more clearly what else to call the child, that even if a neurological cause were established it would not "advance the central issue of educational remediation," and that these children have in common only that they are all different.

In his paper, Dr. Clements cited Strauss and Lehtinen as having refocused on the neglected area of individual differences among and within children. After cautioning that to look at the whole child equal weight must be given both to organic and to environmental factors, and after indicating that the symptom complex can be quite different depending on whether one is dealing with a minimal or subclinical problem or with a severe one, such as cerebral palsy, and after stating the difference in viewpoint between the purist and the pragmatist, *and* after listing the different labels used by those who stress the organic aspect of the condition as opposed to those who emphasize one component or the consequence of the condition, Dr. Clements classified the commonly encountered symptoms according to where they appear in the different aspects of the clinical examination. Then he stated that although that approach leads to the obvious conclusion that the disability has a protean nature, certain symptoms do cluster into recognizable clinical entities, such as the hyperkinetic syndrome. Dr. Clements concluded that the final objective of diagnosis is to indicate the cause of the exhibited learning and behavior deviations and, in turn, to point the way for their amelioration. He pleaded that we not treat simply for the sake of treatment, but first know for what we are treating. And he indicated that these children are the concern and responsibility of everyone; their difficulties and their treatment are the province of no particular discipline, but certain aspects of such a child are more pertinent to specific fields.

It seems that all are in agreement concerning the goal of definition. It further seems that one becomes aware of symptom clusters or commonalities only as one finds a conceptual framework which makes that possible. For example, Dr. Clements' concept that the symptomatology of these children is on a continuum enabled him to go beyond the conclusion that the only commonality is that these children are all different. It enabled him to recognize that a "subclinical" group has a different symptom cluster than a "severe" group.

Apparently, what is needed is a conceptual model which will allow us to bridge the gap between the organic and the environmental, between the subclinical and the severe, between the purist and the pragmatist, between organicity and its everyday consequences, and between structural and functional impairment. Such a conceptual model is not easily found. This I know, because I spent ten years looking for it. Perhaps what I did find, taken largely from the realm of ego psychology, will prove to have so many inadequacies that it will be discarded for a better conceptual model, but it may serve at least as a stepping-stone to formulate a conceptual model for the present purposes.

In the development of interest in brain-injured children from a conceptual standpoint, amelioration of the learning problems of these children was pioneered by Strauss and his associates. They attempted to identify the learning disabilities characteristic of the brain-injured child and to make suggestions concerning educational approaches which would help him to learn despite those disabilities. It was concluded that the basis for the learning and behavioral problems lay in organically caused perceptual handicaps. The characteristic symptoms of disinhibition, hyperactivity, and distractibility were regarded as manifestations of "abnormal responsiveness to environmental stimuli" and, therefore, as reactions beyond cortical control. Hence, there came the recommendation to structure the environment and the teaching materials used with these children in such a way as to reduce their abnormal responsiveness to environmental stimuli. The object of the environmental regulation was to educate the child in the proper utilization of his perceptual processes so as to bring them under conscious cortical control, thereby alleviating the characteristic symptoms of disinhibition, hyperactivity, and distractibility. The thesis was held that as the child developed his perceptual-motor processes, he would not need the externally regulated environment and materials as much as previously.

Both in identifying the characteristics of the brain-injured child and in advocating particular educational techniques, the conceptual framework used by Strauss and his colleagues was a neuropathological one. This placed emphasis on the damaged brain tissue and, therefore, led to the prognostic impression that such children could make only limited progress. Strauss shared with such leading clinicians as Gesell (Gesell and Amatruda, 1941, p. 239) the conclusion: In all these cases we are dealing with an extremely complicated interaction of developmental potentialities and dynamic forces, even though the original motor injury was mild, the damages in the personality sphere may be considerable and more or less permanent." Perhaps that is why Strauss addressed his efforts solely to the perceptual handicap.

When Dr. Cruickshank undertook the monumental job of investigating Strauss' basic tenets, he followed in the latter's footsteps by viewing the hyperactive brain-injured child's difficulties as stemming primarily from an organic perceptual-motor disorder. Confining his conceptual model to the neuropathological frame of reference led him to state: "In terms of educational efficiency, the psychopathology inherent in the child cannot be removed. This is true due to the fact that the psychological problems are inherent in damaged tissue somewhere in the vital areas of the central nervous system, or due to the fact that they are functional manifestations of a complex emotional problem which in itself is physical, and which only can be modified at too slow a rate to insure satisfactory educational and social growth." (Cruickshank et al., 1961, p. 14). In keeping with this conceptual framework, Dr. Cruickshank hypothesized four elements as essential to a good teaching environment for these children: (1) reduced environmental stimuli, (2) reduced space, (3) a structured school program and life plan, and (4) an increase in the stimulus value of the teaching materials which are constructed to cope with the specific characteristics of the disability under consideration. Those factors were designed to provide the children with a classroom as devoid of stimuli as possible in which each child worked in a cubicle approximately three feet square, in an educational program completely teacher-directed, so that there would be little opportunity for choice or conflict or failure on the part of the child.

Since then, the brain-injured child has been viewed from the conceptual framework of the effect of brain damage on the child's ego development and, therefore, total life adjustment (Rappaport, 1961, 1964, 1965). In the 1961 paper the following conceptual model was presented: (1) Behavioral and learning disturbances of brain-injured children are not due solely to damaged brain tissue per se and, therefore, are not necessarily irreversible; (2) but they are due to a considerable degree to the disturbance which that damage causes in the epigenesis of the ego; (3) the deviant ego maturation in turn fosters a disturbed parent-child relationship which in its turn further interferes with proper ego development; and (4) the disturbance both in ego development and in the parent-child relationship can be alleviated by a proper treatment program.

In the conclusion of the paper was the plea: "Perhaps the time is nearing when those who have been concerned with the brain-damaged child will enlarge their scope sufficiently to view him from the framework of ego development. . . ." Strauss and Kephart emphasized the importance not only of considering all the possible effects of brain injury on the total organism but also considering the effect of the injury "upon the development which is in process and the effect upon the organism which will eventually result from the deviation of this development." They trace the brain-damaged child's disturbances to dysfunctions of such basic processes as perception, language, and concept formation. What they are discussing is the epigenesis of the nervous system and its effect on the organism's later activities. Perhaps it is not a giant step from the epigenesis of the nervous system to Erikson's concepts of the epigenesis of the ego, so that the damaged cognitive processes which they discuss could be viewed as the ego's primary apparatuses of autonomy. To combine their work, together with that of Hebb, Piaget, Richter, Gottschalk, and others, into the conceptual matrix of ego psychology would not only enhance our knowledge of the cognitive and behavioral distortions of the brain-damaged child, but would also further our knowledge of cognitive and behavioral structures in general.

In the 1964 volume appeared the following: "The constellation of response patterns that identifies brain-damaged children does not have a single etiology. It does not, for example, arise only in cases where there was maternal flooding or dehydration during the first trimester of pregnancy, or in cases of Cesarean section because of cephalocaudal disproportion, or in cases of prolonged labor, anoxia, kernicterus, encephalitis, or coeliac disease. It may be found in cases having any or none of these etiologies. Moreover, the constellation is not associated with any specific neurological signs, but any of a wide gamut may accompany it. The common denominator in brain-damaged children appears to be that when insult occurs to the brain—that most vital organ, both phylogenetically and ontogenetically—the integrity of the organism is interfered with, and this in turn is reflected in some type of disruption of the development of the child's ego. Hence, the constellation of reactional characteristics of brain-injured children represents different facets of insufficiency or disturbance in ego development.

"The ego, of course, is the central directing force of the mind. It is to the mind what the executive branch of government is to the country. A child is not born with an ego, only with the potentiality for developing one.

"Because ego development is first of all contingent upon the fetal development of the central nervous system and its extrauterine maturation, any neurological insult which the child experiences must interfere to some extent with his ego development. Only when born with his central nervous system intact does the child have the inborn capacities that develop, through growth, experience, and learning, to become the primary apparatuses of the ego. These include such important basic skills as motility, perception, concept formation, and language. Unlike the average child, the brain-damaged child is not born with these intact ego apparatuses which serve as the primary guarantees of the organism's adaptation to its environment.

"The lack of intactness of these primary ego apparatuses in turn distorts the response pattern of mother to child, thus interfering with his first stage, the mutuality phase, of ego development. The perinatally brain-damaged child presents an altered stimulus to the mother, so that she responds differently than she would to a normal offspring, who would be a wished-for extension of herself. Her altered response pattern may manifest itself in not stimulating the child adequately, in rejecting or in overprotecting him, thereby robbing him of opportunities for growth. In each case, the altered maternal response combines with the deficient primary ego apparatuses to interfere with the child's developing a sense of being 'one who can.'

"Particularly when motility is inadequate, the child is deprived of the pure pleasure of functioning and of being able to master new functions, interfering with the natural development of an early sense of self-esteem. Inadequacy of the motor apparatus is also a roadblock to the development of other ego functions. It interferes with exploration of environment and differentiation between self and the external world. Inadequacy of fine visual-motor coordination also deprives the child of added information about the environment by which to test reality and to widen his scope of interests and pleasures. Thus, the inadequate motor apparatus interferes with the development of the ego functions of mastery, integration, reality testing, and impulse control.

"In addition to the primary, secondary apparatuses of the ego also develop. These are entirely learned and include defense mechanisms such as repression, reaction formation, et cetera. Without intactness of both the primary and secondary apparatuses, the ego has difficulty in maintaining its relative autonomy, that is, an adaptive balance in response to instinctual drives from within and from the world around it.

"Because to varying degrees all brain-damaged children find difficulty in achieving mastery over themselves and successful accomplishment in the external environment, the resultant narcissistic wounding produces in them a strong and pervasive sense of inadequacy. This is particularly true of the child who has experienced seizures, because seizures cause an overwhelming sense of loss of control, helplessness, and catastrophic terror. In general, the defective self-concept contributes greatly to the non-adaptive behavioral responses so characteristic of the brain damaged child.

"Thus, whether a child suffers from perinatal brain damage or from an active intracranial pathology, the damage interferes with one or more phases of ego function, and manifests itself through ego insufficiency or disturbance. Of course, when there is active intracranial pathology, medicinal or surgical intervention is necessary, but to effect complete rehabilitation, the child must nevertheless be aided to build a well-functioning ego.

"In our experience (based both on clinical observations and ongoing research) brain-damaged children of at least normal intellectual potential, on whom there are positive neurological findings, show in varying degrees and combinations the following response patterns:

I. Inadequate impulse control or regulation
    A. Hyperactivity
    B. Hyperdistractibility
    C. Disinhibition
    D. Impulsivity
    E. Perseveration
    F. Lability of affect
    G. Motor dysfunctions

   II. Inadequate integrative functions
      A. Perceptual difficulties
      B. Conceptual difficulties
  III. Defective self-concept and narcissistic hypersensitivity
      A. Low frustration tolerance
      B. Flight from challenge
      C. Overcompensation
      D. Control and manipulation of others
      E. Negativism or power struggle

"We therefore define the Brain Damage Syndrome as a combination of response patterns reflecting the ego dysfunctions of inadequate impulse control or regulation, inadequate integrative functions, and defective self-concept and narcissistic sensitivity. Manifestations of these patterns are found neurologically, psychologically, clinically, and educationally."

In the 1965 symposium, Dr. Mitchell Dratman expanded the concept: "To set up the proper theoretical and practical frameworks, we should not emphasize the *brain* disorder, because the component of brain damage may not be verifiable or may be quite silent, whereas the clinical disorder clamors for recognition. Thus, we should focus on the constellation of behavioral symptoms, or the 'organic ego syndrome.' Such behavior is characterized by a rigidity which is at first unyielding and over which the child has little control. In this context we may also speak of an *organic-neurotic* ego or an *organic-psychotic* ego, referring to a child having either neurotic or psychotic components as well as brain damage. Such an approach permits us to consider the child as a whole, while concentrating on that part of him affected by internal processes, organic or not; namely his personality. In this approach theoretical demands are satisfied because our dynamic model remains intact, allowing us to see more of the process by which the child manages to stay human despite gross deviations in his primary ego. Practical considerations are satisfied also, because we cannot yet treat the organic damage itself, even when it is known to exist, but only that part which is left.

"Differential diagnosis should not be made by exclusion. When no organic cause can be found by history and laboratory tests, let us not say, 'Ergo the child is neurotic or psychotic.' When organic damage *is* found, let us not say the distractibility, hyperactivity, or any of the other symptoms are necessarily the result of misfiring of neurones, or lack of control of lower centers by higher ones, or higher ones by lower ones. Instead let us begin to say that *the symptom is in service of the ego,* helping the child to maintain some form of integration. . . . The major emphasis of this symposium is on the ego which results from functional derangement of the organ of mental life, the brain. Clinical experience suggests that that ego defends the rest of the personality from awareness of its defects by distractibility, hyperactivity, impulsivity, perseveration, and lability of affect. Even perceptual and conceptual difficulties can be used secondarily as defense against awareness of perceptual or conceptual deficits. . . . Therefore, I believe that the best way of understanding this disease process is through the dynamics of the interaction of organic effect on the child's ego. . . . By using this holistic concept we do not have to be hampered in the treatment of such a child because there is little we can do for the damage itself. The rest of the child can be handled, and he has a better chance for help, if we can conceive of his symptoms as part of the ego process of integration."

The conceptual model described above provides an opportunity to examine the interaction between the organic defect and the child's resultant self. It enables us to conceptualize and categorize the symptoms which have been apparent since Strauss' early work and which appear not only in the classroom but in every phase of the child's life. It further enables us to understand the child's responses so that we are able to devise appropriate programs to help him overcome those aberrant reactions, whether they appear in the classroom, at the dinner table, or wherever. It also enables us to see a commonality between a child who has a mild, subclinical perinatal damage and one who has a severe, intracranial pathology which necessitates a hemispherectomy. And it provides the matrix for planning treatment programs which can and have habilitated both such children.

The "organic ego" concept clearly points to a multidiscipline team approach which views the problem from the standpoint of interactional patterns of the total child, while being vigilant of those based on his intraindividual needs, those arising from his effect on his family and their needs, and those stemming from his and his family's response to the needs and expectations of society. Since education is an essential aspect of the child's treatment, the educator must be an integral member of that team. At the same time, this conceptual model necessitates that everyone dealing with the child view him neurologically as well as developmentally and educationally. This prevents the possibility of assuming that a child is perinatally damaged, never looking at him neurologically again, and finding that the child dies of an ongoing intracranial pathology whose symptoms were not different from a perinatal damage.

Such a conceptual framework also enables the clinician, including the school psychologist, to transcend the immediacy of his measuring instruments, so that he does not accept intelligence as being nothing

more than an I.Q., or personality as nothing more than a Rorschach profile, or neurological integrity as nothing more than an E.E.G. pattern.
Instead, it insists on investigating which factors are responsible for a
child not functioning at his grade level and for his not achieving one
academic grade per year. It also insists on the clinician determining if
those factors can be overcome, and if so, how. It means that all situations
in which the child is involved, including the classroom, will be opportunities for diagnostic observation which continuously supply data to the
treatment team; data they need in order to identify the ego insufficiencies
resulting from brain damage and to facilitate the transition of those
insufficiencies into skills. To accomplish that, at one time the neurosurgeon might lead the team, at another, the psychotherapist or the
educator. Regardless of who leads, the goal always is to build intact and
functioning ego skills. All members of the team—which includes, among
others, the educator, the pediatric neurologist, the psychotherapist, the
parent counselor, the parents, and the visual-motor specialist—are intent
upon the goal of aiding the child to develop those skills which he lacks
because of neurological impairment to the development of his ego.

For those who believe that it is unrealistic to instrument such a team
approach in public education, one should at least be cognizant of the
possibility that the team approach would substantially reduce the total
amount of time required for these children to spend in special education
classes and, of equal importance, to sustain the gains made in such classes
after returning to regular class. Then undoubtedly it would be less ex-
pensive to use the multidisciplinary team in public education and thereby
to enhance the opportunity for these children to go on to regular class
and to become self-sustaining citizens than not to use it and bear the
expense of special classes which do not habilitate the youngsters and
prepare them only for being lifelong expenses to society.

In our work thus far we have encountered a mean stay of three years
per child. We estimate the cost of the team approach in public education
to be $1,372.50 per child per year in addition to expenses regularly
encountered in special education classes. When one considers that in
1962 the average cost per institutionalized patient in this country was
$1,998.24 a year, and that if not properly helped many of these children
are institutionalized for decades or for life, the expenditure of an additional $4,117.50 to save a child and his family is a good investment.

I firmly believe that a present obligation is to decide not only what
to label these children, but also what broad habilitation plan will be
employed with them, so that attention can be focused on specifically
what the teachers will do with them. If not, we can hardly answer the
question of what we should train teachers for.

REFERENCES

Cruickshank, W. M., Bentzen, Frances A., Ratzeburg, F. H., and Tannhauser, Mirian T. *A teaching method for brain-injured and hyperactive children.* Syracuse: Syracuse University Press, 1961.

Gesell, A., and Amatruda, C. S. *Developmental diagnosis.* New York: Paul B. Hoeber, 1941.

Rappaport, S. R. "Behavior disorder and ego development in a brain-injured child," *Psychoanalytic Study of the Child,* 1961, 16, 423–450.

————. (ed.). *Childhood aphasia and brain damage: A definition.* Narberth, Pa.: Livingston, 1964.

————. (ed.). *Childhood aphasia and brain damage, Vol. II. Differential Diagnosis.* Narberth, Pa.: Livingston, 1965.

Chapter 3

Personality Factors Teachers Need for Relationship Structure

SHELDON R. RAPPAPORT, Ph.D.

EDITORIAL NOTE.—This paper is based in part on the keynote presentation at The Pathway School's third annual Institute, Philadelphia, April 9, 1965. The paper was so well received and presented then and was such a significant addition to educational planning for brain-injured children that Dr. Rappaport was asked to redevelop his concept for inclusion in this series of papers. Personality factors in teachers are not necessarily a competency in the same sense as other papers will consider them, but personality is certainly a significant factor in making it possible for the teacher to utilize and apply his educational competencies effectively. The concept of "relationship structure" suggested by Rappaport is significant and fundamental to the acquisition and employment of all competencies needed by a teacher of brain-injured children.

DR. SHELDON R. RAPPAPORT received his undergraduate education at Temple University, Philadelphia. The Ph.D. was awarded by Washington University, St. Louis, in 1950.

Dr. Rappaport is founder and Executive Director of the Pathway School for brain-injured children in Jeffersonville, Pennsylvania. Prior to the founding of Pathway, Dr. Rappaport was engaged in the private practice of clinical psychology. His chief areas of endeavor were in the diagnosis and treatment of the neurologically impaired child. Since 1963, he has been actively engaged in research on the staffs of Eastern Pennsylvania Psychiatric Institute and Jefferson Medical College.

He is a diplomate in clinical psychology, appears in *Who's Who in the East* and *American Men of Science*, and is editor of two recent publications: *Childhood Aphasia and Brain Damage: A Definition. Vol. I* and *Childhood Aphasia and Brain Damage: Differential Diagnosis. Vol. II.*

Chapter 3

Personality Factors Teachers Need
for Relationship Structure

SHELDON R. RAPPAPORT, Ph.D.

Teachers of brain-injured children have been made aware of the importance of environmental structure, educational program structure, and the structure of teaching materials. There is still another structure which gives evidence of being of major importance to this work—*relationship structure*, which means the ability of the adult (parent or teacher or therapist or otherwise) to understand the child sufficiently well at any given moment, through his verbal and nonverbal communications, to relate in a way which aids the child's development of impulse control and other ego functions.

EFFECTS OF NEUROLOGICAL IMPAIRMENT ON DEVELOPMENT

To understand the role of relationship structure, one must consider, first of all, how neurological impairment affects the child's total development. This can be done by tracing its effect on certain crucial aspects of the hyperkinetic brain-injured child's development, in contrast to normal growth.

No child is born with awareness of others, impulse control, frustration tolerance, or ability to mediate between biological drives on the one hand and environmental demands on the other. Such higher ego functions are *developed* as an outgrowth of more basic ego functions, such as motor control, perception, attention span, and communication, which also emerge through development. Simply by virtue of being born with an intact central nervous system, a child has the inherent opportunity to develop all such ego functions in the usual course of growing up.

First, with cephalocaudal neural maturation, he has the opportunity for deriving satisfaction from control of his gross motor discharges. He wants and needs the gratification to be able to move on to higher levels of development. To an observer, the infant seems compelled to exercise the same movements over and over again. Even in such a rudimentary attempt to gain mastery over one aspect of himself, he is developing a basic part of his ego.

With further neural maturation, cortical inhibition takes place, allowing him the opportunity for volitional practice. That, in turn, provides him with greater opportunity for mastery and the resultant gratification of self-esteem. The first few years of life—in which a child learns such sensori-motor skills as to walk, talk, perceive, feed himself, and be toilet trained—provide literally hundreds of daily opportunities for being pleased with himself, for the budding of a positive identity which later will bloom into the conviction of "I am one who can!"

While that goes on *within* the child, his strivings are appealing and prideful to his mother and stimulate her normal maternal responses so as to provide him also with an *external* source of gratification. This, in turn, gives the child the approval, encouragement, and stimulation he needs to achieve even greater mastery and self-esteem.

As a result, from both the child's inner feelings about his accomplishments and the environment's approval of him, his feeling of self-worth is nurtured. If his parents are not too encumbered by neurosis and his environment is reasonably wholesome, his primal feeling about his experiences in this world will be positive. From that matrix he can establish healthy identifications with his parents and other key figures in his life, and he can interact successfully with other people and with the environment, so that the higher, or secondary, ego functions (such as frustration tolerance and consideration for others) become established and then strengthened.

In marked contrast is the child who is not born with an intact central nervous system. Primary ego functions, such as motility and perception, can develop only with the maturation of the central nervous system. Secondary ego functions, while developing from the child's interaction with his environment, are rooted in and prerequire those primary functions so that they may develop adequately. Hence, lack of neurological intactness itself robs this child of the inherent opportunity to develop ego functions in the usual course of growing up. His attempts at mastery result not in success, but in frustration; not in self-esteem, but in self-derision; not in a sense of "I am one who can," but in a sense of "I am one who can *not*."

His lack of intactness also robs him of the ability to stimulate his mother's normal maternal responses. Instead of pride and love, he provokes in her anxiety and frustration. For example, a mother expects to find gratification in feeding her infant. When he cannot suck and when each feeding is a harassment of alternate screaming and falling asleep, she obviously reacts to him differently than she would to another child. Conversely, his experience in being fed is very different from that of another child. He does not feel the world to be secure and calm and benign in its giving.

The feelings of frustration and inadequacy within himself and the feelings of tension and rejection he gets from the environment form the nonverbal matrix in which he will mold his basic concepts of himself and the outside world. Within himself he is frustrated because his whole biology commands him to try, to do, to master, and he either cannot or, at best, achieves only arduously and then without facility. At the same time, mother reacts, at best, in an unstimulating fashion, if not in an actively rejecting, or defensively oversmothering way. Thus, his introduction to this world is not a pleasant one. It is one which fosters feelings of frustration and rejection.

When he does belatedly achieve a skill, such as motility, he tends to use it continuously, as if to make up for lost time and to inundate himself with gratification previously unattainable. Such a surge of activity usually is met by heightened dismay, anxiety, and resentment on the mother's part. The power struggle which ensues may last a lifetime. For example, on the one hand, the child is delighted that at last he has achieved motility, and as a substitute for mastery he practices it continuously and in double time. Up at 5:00 a.m., he arouses everyone else by 5:05, has thoroughly mixed the sugar and flour and pots and pans on the kitchen floor by 5:15, is gleefully tramping on them by 5:18, and moves on to conquer such new horizons as living-room drapes by 5:20. On the other hand, not understanding his motives, his mother is convinced that his sole purpose in life is to torment her and deprive her of the last vestige of sanity.

Often, in desperation, she then feels driven to beat her child into submission, to lock him in his room, or otherwise to make him capitulate to her will. In that way she tries to preserve some semblance of self-respect; for, after all, a three-year-old simply cannot terrorize a grown woman. In turn, the child is only beginning to have some rudiment of positive identity; to pride himself in being a lamp-knocker-over, or a drapery-climber, or a sugar-spiller, or one who beats all others getting up in the morning. These things he now *can* do. These are triumphs he wants to share with his mother. These he regards as first steps to her love and affection. But she does not "read" his intentions, and so she does not praise him for his long-awaited and hard-won skills. She comes with stern thou-shalt-nots, and he feels his budding identity to be in mortal danger. If a child has no identity, he has no life; and so he often will fight harder to preserve his identity than life itself (Erikson, 1950, p. 212).

This youngster—who had lived in a deprived world because his lack of neurological intactness robbed him of the means to mastery—in his first experience with what *he* regards as success, meets only with derision and obstruction. Therefore, he must fight back. He must do something which will give him some recognition, which will enable him in some way to be somebody who can. And because she cannot live with him, the mother must try to subjugate him.

Through the years this interaction spirals with ever increasing velocity, viciousness, and futility. In so doing, it continuously reinforces the child's conceptual model that he is alone in an enemy land whose purpose is to torment him by constantly hurting his pride, if not to extinguish his identity altogether. That conceptual model is further reinforced because his congenital skill deficiencies continually make him "odd man out," creating bitter jealousy of the success he sees other children achieve and of the admiration and affection adults lavish on them.

THE TEACHER'S EXPECTATIONS

If one is to teach this child when he is of school age, one must remember that the experiences which have comprised his microcosm were very different from those of the average child and have fashioned for him an ego very different from theirs. To be of genuine help to him, one must be aware of his concept of his inner and outer worlds, because it will pervade and dominate every contact the teacher has with him. This writer would counsel the teacher: Expect him to regard you as an enemy; enemies are all he has known. Expect to have to prove yourself to him; his life experience gives him no reason to trust others. Expect him to test you in all different ways to see whether you will grow angry and reject him and further hurt his pride; no one has passed his tests yet. Expect it to take a long time for him to trust you and to stop contesting with you; his psychic life is at stake. Expect him to need you to control his impulses, no matter how much he protests he does not; as yet he has not had the opportunity to develop such ego functions. In brief, expect him to react to you with all the habitual attitudes and patterns of defense he has devised over the years.

Therefore, expect to be an ego bank which provides him the wherewithal for genuine achievements and a sense of mastery still unknown to him. Expect to be an ego bank which provides the opportunity to have others respond to him with approbation, not opprobrium. Expect to be an ego bank which provides limitless love in the form of facing with him his difficulties, in the form of helping him to understand why he does those irksome things, and in the form of letting him know that you will help him constantly until he is able to respond in a fashion pleasing both to himself and to others. Expect to be an ego bank with patience; it will take the child months or years to be able to perform volitionally what you expect of him.

If one really hopes to habilitate this child, one must remember that the ego has an extrauterine epigenesis just as the fetus has an intrauterine one. It must evolve through an orderly progression of stages of growth precisely as the fetus must. Neither is capable of hurrying through those stages in kaleidoscopic fashion simply because one wishes it. Unless the teacher dedicates his talents, time, techniques, and material to the promotion of those stages of growth, this child cannot achieve true maturity or ego autonomy. He cannot achieve these by himself. By school age the deviation is too much for normal development to overcome, for if that were not so, he would not even have come to the special teacher's attention. His skill deficiencies, his supersensitive and vulnerable pride, his painful experiences with others, and his means of defending himself against these are so entrenched that his ego cannot proceed for long without being enslaved by demands either from his inner or outer world. Then his patterns of response continue to be nonadaptive, and often become increasingly antisocial.

If the intent is not simply to give his mother a respite, but to enable him to become a self-supporting and self-respecting adult, it is the teacher's responsibility to begin the relationship with him where he is at that time, not where one may wish him to be. It is the teacher's responsibility to communicate that he understands what the child is struggling with now, and has been for years; to convey that he is neither fearful of nor rejects the child for the habitual response patterns he has been practicing for most of his life; and to let the child know that the teacher does not expect him to give up those defensive patterns until he can replace them with the genuine success he will be helped to achieve. It is also the teacher's responsibility to cope with his deviant reactions, because he cannot do so for himself, until he can replace them with truly gratifying ways of relating; to know that because the child is unable to handle either his inner drives or the demands and stimulations of the outside world, the teacher must provide for him a total-life structure which will enable him to cope with both successfully; and to realize that the core of that total-life structure is the teacher's ability to relate with him in a fashion which says, "I am here to *help* you, not to hurt you or to have a contest of wills with you; to help you recognize your problems and limitations and suffering so that you can overcome them and begin to use effectively and joyously the assets I know you have."

When the teacher's *relationship* communicates that, the child will begin to recognize that the teacher *can* feel good about him and wants him to feel good about himself. He will begin to perceive a difference between this, which the teacher represents, and the hurt which the world has always meant to him. If that difference persists long enough and is evident in enough persons who are important to him, he will have a sufficiently consistent basis for comparison to be able to discriminate between his present world and that of his past, so as to form the realization that the whole world is not the way he had previously conceptualized it.

If the relationship does not communicate that to him, one cannot teach him, help him to build skills, aid him to achieve more adaptive behavior, nor, in time, even coexist with him.

In fifteen years of working with these children, this writer has not seen *one* who did not emerge victorious in a battle with an adult who did not understand him. First of all, fear and anger neurologically and psychologically militate against learning, as well as any other taking-in process. Secondly, his ultimate weapon is "You can't *make* me learn." From infancy, when he first had a bottle jammed into his mouth with the fervent hope that he would go to sleep and stop bothering everybody, he has practiced refusing to take anything others offered him except under his own terms. Then certainly *you* cannot force him to learn in the classroom.

When properly structured, relationships form the nucleus from which all other structuring emanates; the child eventually identifies with the teacher, internalizing the teacher's goals and expectations for him. *Then* he wants to please and is motivated to accept help in learning those skills which he should have acquired as a normal part of his ego's epigenesis. Whatever his skill deficiencies, relationship structure provides both him and the teacher the *opportunity* to develop in him skills which otherwise would remain only nascent.

THE TEACHER'S ATTRIBUTES

Before one embarks on the frontier of teaching brain-injured children, however, one must make sure he is the right person for the job. This can be of telling significance in the lives of many children and their families, and it can also determine one's own success and happiness. Personal dedication and knowledge of classroom subjects do not alone qualify one. It is mandatory that he also have personality qualities which will enable him to be of genuine and lasting help to these particular children.

First, one must have *true* self-respect. This does not mean cocksureness, especially as manifested by what Adlai Stevenson called "the twin sins" of ignorance and arrogance, nor does it mean the defensive conviction that the way something has always been done is the only way to do it. Conversely, it means that one is not afraid to try new techniques or new materials on an experimental basis, with careful observation, for a circumscribed period of time. Nor does it mean refusing to try something new until it has been demonstrated and shown to be infallible. Equally, it does not mean the erudite phrases and postures of a knowing façade which proves paper thin whenever the question, "why," is asked.

True self-respect does mean that one is willing to use what one already knows while carefully evaluating its effectiveness and making whatever changes observations and creativity dictate. It means a willingness to admit, with proof, that a hypothesis or technique was inadequate or inappropriate, and it means a desire to learn or to create a more effective way of accomplishing the goal. The person with true self-respect can accept his own mistakes as steps to learning, without needing to pass the blame in order to maintain the delusion of perfection. It means, too, that one is not "sugar-sweet" when facing colleagues or pupils only to decimate them behind their backs. It means that one does not regard "grinding others under your heel" as the sole means of ascending to power and self-importance.

One should not need to be a jealous mother-father-playmate-therapist-teacher to each child in the class. One can find gratification in the role of teacher while sharing both responsibility and accolades for a child's progress with other members of the habilitation team, which includes the parents.

Secondly, one must have the maturity to realize that the school, the class, and the progress of the children cannot proceed according to one's vagaries. Brain-injured children do not develop permanent skills by means of conventional teaching methods. Neither do they achieve well-integrated skills when the teacher has no specific frame of reference in which to work, but instead dabbles in various educational philosophies and whims. To become a teacher of brain-injured children takes great self-discipline even for an experienced teacher of normal children—first to learn thoroughly the principles underlying the classroom program, and then to prepare thoughtfully the individualized lesson plans and materials needed for each day. Although the teacher does need the diversion of recreational and social activities, and a well-rounded life, he cannot race the children for the door each afternoon. Also, no explanation should be required as to why it is untenable to arrive late even a few mornings a week. Similarly, maturity enables one to have sufficient respect for others not to keep parents waiting twenty minutes for their appointed conference. It also enables one to be prompt for appointments with other team members and to utilize those times effectively. Team conferences should be used both to learn more about the children in the class and to impart information which would aid others to help them, rather than for diversionary tactics or for being stiffly silent to prevent others from interfering with your teaching or from "picking your brain."

Maturity allows one to feel comfortable with regulations—recognizing that the organization which imposes the rules affords the advantages which would not otherwise be available and in exchange for which the individual gladly gives up some autonomy. With maturity comes pleasure from performing, rather than merely pretending, the cooperation, coordination, and communication which are essential to a well-functioning team.

If an individual possesses the attributes of true self-respect and maturity, it is likely that he also has the other traits prerequisite to proficiency in relationship and the other structures intrinsic to teaching brain-injured children. However, for the sake of completeness, below are given other necessary personality characteristics.

Sufficient sensitivity is needed to understand why a child reacts as he does. At the same time, one needs a good enough sense of one's own identity to maintain objectivity in the role of a helping person with him. One cannot help him by falling into the same patterns of overprotection or rejection as did his parents.

A well-integrated identity also enables the individual to be comfortable with a child's volatile hostility, his sudden dejection, or his outburst of tears when expectations are set forth to him. For a long time he may feel the defensive need to fight against what the teacher knows to be best for him. Compassion for his distress does not, however, interfere with continuing to maintain, quietly and firmly, those expectations which are best for his future welfare.

To be of steadfast help to him in the face of his defensive behavior, which is at the least unpleasant and trying, the teacher needs an abundance of frustration tolerance. This does not mean that the teacher's own anger is so intolerable to him that he must defensively banish it from consciousness. It means, instead, that he is strong enough to tolerate being frustrated and abused even when he knows his goals and motives are acmic. It means that in the face of great stress his own emotions or defenses do not render him unable to do the necessary job.

Frustration tolerance allows one, despite one's own strong and uncomfortable feelings, to maintain the relationship structure the child needs. When angry with his behavior one may even say, "Okay, so you managed to make me angry with you. It doesn't make you twenty feet tall, and it doesn't help you to read like other ten-year-olds do. When you let me help you with it, you'll see you can do this page. You don't have to act up because you're scared of it." In the ten seconds it took to clarify each of the positions, relationship structure was used to help achieve the immediate goal of that particular lesson. And, that goal could not have been facilitated by hitting, shaking, or yelling at the child.

The personality attributes of true self-respect, maturity, proper sensitivity, well-integrated identity, and abundant frustration tolerance empower the teacher to be the ego bank brain-injured children must draw upon to build their own permanent and integrated ego skills. If an individual does not have the attributes essential to that bank, he should not seek to teach these children, because the venture will fail. On the other hand, if he possesses a well-established ego bank, he should invest in brain-injured children; the dividends will be great. He will enable children whose pasts were the nadir of defeat and defensive hatred to see their futures as bright with the promise of success and acceptance.

SELECTED REFERENCES

Erikson, E. *Childhood and society*. New York: Norton, 1950.
Rappaport, S. R. "Behavior and ego development in a brain-injured child," *Psychoanalytic Study of the Child*, 1961, 16, 423–450.
———. (ed.). *Childhood aphasia and brain damage. A definition*. Narberth, Pa.: Livingston, 1964.
———. (ed.). *Childhood aphasia and brain damage. Vol. II. Differential diagnosis*. Narberth, Pa.: Livingston, 1965.
———. (ed.). *Childhood aphasia and brain damage. Vol. III. Habilitation*. Narberth, Pa.: Livingston, 1966.

Chapter 4

The Child, the Teacher, and the Physician
HERBERT J. GROSSMAN, M.D.

EDITORIAL NOTE.—Following the Seminar, Dr. Grossman was asked to prepare a statement which in summary form would indicate from a medical point of view certain elements which involve commonalities of point of view of both medical and educational specialists. While this book is concerned primarily with educational competencies, there is a point at which medicine and education must come together in a harmony of ideas. Dr. Grossman points out that the "medical diagnosis is not synonymous with an educational diagnosis." It is essential, however, that the teacher have sufficient background in pediatric neurology and in pediatrics generally so as to be able to understand the medical diagnosis and to convert appropriate information therein into an educational plan. Similarly, the physician must sufficiently understand the educational programming so as to understand its method, goals, and potentials for the solution of a child's problems. The materials presented in this chapter and in the preceding three chapters form a background of general information regarding brain-injured children on which specific competencies must be developed from the concepts included in the remaining chapters of the book.

DR. HERBERT J. GROSSMAN is the Director of the Illinois State Pediatric Institute and Professor of Pediatrics at the University of Illinois College of Medicine, Chicago, Illinois. He is head of the pediatric-neurology service at the University of Illinois Research and Educational Hospitals and consultant in neurology at Presbyterian–St. Luke's Hospital in Chicago.

A graduate of the University of Illinois College of Medicine, Dr. Grossman completed his pediatric training at the University of Illinois Hospitals. He taught at the University of Illinois College of Medicine in the Departments of Pediatrics, Neurology and Psychiatry. He had a residency in neurology at the U.C.L.A. Medical Center in Los Angeles, California, and he was on the faculty of the U.C.L.A. School of Medicine in the Departments of Pediatrics and Medicine (the Division of Neurology). He has taught post-graduate courses at Illinois Teachers' College, Chicago, North, and is the author of numerous articles which have appeared in professional publications.

Chapter 4

The Child, the Teacher, and the Physician
HERBERT J. GROSSMAN, M.D.

Everything seen or heard or felt is transmitted to the brain by the complicated network of nerves. In the brain these impressions are sorted with astronomic speed and efficiency, interpreted, and messages sent out through other nerves to direct the individual's response. This system of intake, integration, and output enables the individual to function in the infinite number of ways that he does. Damage to any part of this system may impair function. Clinical neurology is the medical approach to understanding this complex human nervous system. This encompasses all problems relating to the nervous system from those involving the peripheral nerves and muscles to impairment of the brain.

In the last two decades professional people have learned a great deal about the relationship of brain function to learning and behavior. Some of this work in the area of psychopharmacology is discussed elsewhere in this book. Much of the information which has been gained relates to the clinical problems encountered by the physician. More and more, individuals who deal with learning and behavior disorders are trying to gain a better understanding of these problems by learning more about nervous system function. As a result of this interest, increasing numbers of children are being referred to the physician for the purpose of determining the state of function of the nervous system from a medical standpoint.

It should be emphasized that there is still not as much information in this area as is needed. Unfortunately, there are few well-conceived, well-designed longitudinal studies that provide sufficient data to allow a clear understanding of the findings or of the problems they attempt to explain. There is need for collaborative research concerning the learning process and behavioral patterns. Hopefully, this kind of teamwork in research will provide information helpful in understanding the complexities of these problems.

59

REFERRAL TO THE PHYSICIAN

Physicians are often surprised to have a parent bring a child with a note from a school official suggesting that the child be given a "neurological examination and an E.E.G." Often these referrals contain little or no information which would aid the physician in understanding the child's difficulty in school. Other referrals include reams of material that relate to any and all problems ever encountered with a particular child. Needless to say, it will be a most unusual person who would assume the task of wading through this mass of information. Even when he does, he is often disappointed because there is little information of current value. When a physician receives a referral from the school, he frequently has no idea how the information from the medical examination will relate to the better understanding of the child's problems by the school staff. He is aware that school personnel sometimes hope for a medical answer to the child's problems; he knows that his medical findings cannot lead to a "solution" of such complex difficulties.

Evaluation of a child's functioning and potential requires the help of people in a variety of disciplines. Certainly the parents and the teacher must contribute their knowledge of a particular child, but in addition, information is needed from the school psychologist, the principal, and the nurse. Sometimes the physical education teacher or the art and music instructors can also help in understanding this child. One of the major difficulties in the evaluation of children with learning and/or behavior problems is often a lack of communication between representatives of the various disciplines. Unfortunately, the child and his family are often caught in the middle of professional confusion, sometimes apathy, or rivalry. Although all professions have a great deal to learn, establishing effective means of communication between the various disciplines would accomplish a major break-through in efforts to help these children.

The writer has found that one of the most effective means of referral is for a representative of the school to telephone the physician (with the parents' permission) and informally discuss the problem. This preliminary exploration will often indicate what steps, if any, need to be taken to evaluate the child from a medical point of view. The physician will learn what is the major concern of school personnel and, most importantly, the physician will have a chance to hear the teacher's firsthand observations of the child. He will also have a much better idea of what kind of information may aid the school staff in understanding the youngster and his problems.

The physician's findings should be interpreted within the framework of the school setting and in terms of problems that have meaning in the school. It is tempting for the staff of the school to hope that medical information will be helpful in resolving a child's learning and/or behavioral difficulties. The fact is that medical information can, at best, help the teacher understand more fully the complexities of a child's problems. It is of little educational consequence insofar as classroom teachers are concerned to know that cranial nerves are, or are not, functioning properly and whether the electroencephalogram is normal or abnormal.

CLINICAL NEUROLOGICAL EXAMINATION

History

The physician relies on the medical history to provide specific information as well as clues to the cause of a given disability. For this reason detailed information regarding the family history (with genetic implications), the mother's pregnancy, birth and neonatal period are extremely important. Occurrence of illnesses, injuries, or infections are also carefully documented. The relationship of difficulties in any of these areas to clinical problems has been well established. (On the other hand, history of such difficulty does not indicate that a specific disorder will always result.)

Patient's General Physical State

The patient's general state of health is obviously important. During this examination there is a reassessment of function of the special senses such as vision and hearing with appropriate referral for consultation where indicated. Certain conditions (such as congenital malformations or alterations in body structure) that may provide a clue to accompanying disturbance of the nervous system are also reevaluated.

The Neurological Examination

The neurological examination in itself is a rather complex task. Complete examination requires not only competence on the part of the examiner but awareness of the problem and ability to cooperate on the part of the patient. Many of the more subtle and refined aspects of the neurological examination can be done only with cooperative patients. In some of the complicated aspects of sensory and motor function and coordination, young children cannot give the cooperation necessary to allow the physician to make adequate assessment.

The developmental course of a given youngster is important in the over-all assessment of his neurological function. Many of the tasks have to be evaluated in regard to the expectations for a given chronological age. Obviously, certain abilities to function increase with chronological age, and what may be perfectly normal at one age may be abnormal for another. For this reason, the concept of developmental neurology is most critical in the assessment of children. Indeed, professional people who have not had much training or experience in dealing with children may be at a disadvantage in rendering these assessments.

In the neurological examination, the physician tries to assess the function of the nervous system by utilizing diverse methods. Examination of the cranial nerves gives information relating to vision, eye movements, pupillary function, sensation about the face and head, the muscles of facial expression and muscles of mastication, taste, hearing, and vestibular function (equilibrium), swallowing, and the ability to speak.

The next area is the examination of the complex components that control motor function. These range from high centers in the brain to the muscle itself. Pathology in any of these areas may cause some disturbance. In general, the physician can assess motor function with far greater accuracy than some other parts of the nervous system. One can usually establish whether a given disturbance of motor function is due to some impairment of muscle, peripheral nerve, or the anterior horn cells in the spinal cord. One can also determine whether such disturbance occurred as a result of an alteration of function of the long tracts of the spinal cord and brain—the so-called pyramidal system. Other areas of the nervous system that control movements and coordination (particularly the basal ganglia and cerebellum) can also be identified with some accuracy.

There are a number of reflexes which are elicited during a neurological examination. Some are important as they relate to motor function, but none of the reflexes has any specific correlation to learning and/or behavior.

Examination of the sensory nerves requires the most cooperation on the part of the patient. It is very difficult for young children to cooperate sufficiently to give meaningful information. This is particularly true of some of the more complex aspects of cortical sensory function that have to do with perception, finger agnosia, and double tactile stimulation.

Other aspects of the neurological examination include assessment of autonomic nervous system function, gait, coordination, communication, and behavior. The ability of youngsters to read, copy geometric designs, draw figures, and other such tasks must be carefully assessed. Although the physician may try to screen for these functions, it should be recognized that an accurate assessment should be completed by a qualified psychological examiner. Advances in the field of neuropsychology which have contributed greatly to our understanding of these problems are discussed elsewhere in this book.

The physician does make an over-all estimate of the patient's mental state including intelligence, cooperation, and behavior. This evaluation is not made with the help of any carefully standardized tests or charts. Rather, it is the physician's clinical impression based upon his training and his experience.

Evaluation of the nervous system can be rather well defined in certain instances (such as disturbances of motor function). In other situations, specific signs may be difficult to assess. The physician often talks of "soft" neurological signs. These signs usually reflect mild coordination difficulties, minimal tremors, choreo-athetosis, gross awkwardness, exaggerated deep tendon reflexes, and/or pathological reflexes. Such signs are often minimal and, in themselves, do not reflect any profound disturbance of motor function. They cannot be specifically correlated with learning or behavior problems. Actually, there is no syndrome, no aggregate of neurological signs, that can be correlated with any specific learning and/or behavior disorder. Indeed, many youngsters with profound aberrations of motor function do well in school, in their studies and in their interpersonal relationships. Conversely, some children with considerable difficulties in learning and behavior may present few findings in the neurological examination.

Specialized Diagnostic Procedures

From time to time findings on clinical examination indicate the need for further laboratory investigation. Studies such as X-rays of the skull, angiograms (special X-ray techniques using injections of radio-opaque dyes in blood vessels of the brain), pneumoencephalograms or ventriculograms (air in the ventricular system) are rarely indicated. Specific biochemical studies—examination of the spinal fluid, radioisotope studies, and chromosome analysis—may sometimes be needed. These studies are not done specifically because of learning and/or behavioral difficulties. It is important to emphasize that most of these studies are indicated only when certain clinical findings are present.

The most common laboratory procedure used in evaluating youngsters with learning and/or behavior difficulties is the electroencephalogram (E.E.G.). Probably no laboratory procedure has had so much use —and overuse—in the assessment of nervous system function. The electroencephalogram, when properly used, can contribute a great deal to the understanding of clinical disorders of the human nervous system. This is particularly true in seizure disorders (epilepsy). However, many people seem to think that the electroencephalogram can give all the answers to all problems. The question of diagnosing brain damage from an abnormal electroencephalogram is often posed. Actually, all that is being measured on the electroencephalogram is the electrical activity of the human brain. Abnormalities in these recordings mean little unless they are correlated with specific clinical problems. Attempts have been made to correlate electroencephalographic deviations with abnormal learning and/or behavior, but there are many problems in this application. Many studies have been done, but it would appear that each investigator has approached the phenomenon somewhat differently and there is no consensus of opinion. Thus far, there does not appear to be any specific electroencephalographic abnormality that correlates with a specific aberration in learning and/or behavior.

In this discussion of the neurological examination, it is important to remember that a *medical diagnosis is not synonymous with an educational diagnosis*. It follows, then, that medical management may have a limited relationship with educational planning. However, the medical diagnosis, with the physician's recommendations for medical management, can contribute considerably to the school staff's understanding of this child, his problems, and his potential.

BRAIN INJURY

The term, brain injury (or brain damage), means different things to different people, and this problem of terminology is basic to the goal of better interdisciplinary understanding. Furthermore, in dealing with children and their parents, professional persons must be sensitive to the fact that terms commonly used in professional communication can be very disturbing to the unsophisticated lay person. Parents can be extremely upset by the term, brain damage. Physicians would seem to be more conservative in their use of the term than other disciplines. When the physician talks of brain damage, he is usually referring to some organic change related to specific etiological factors which is reflected in disturbance of motor, sensory, or mental function. Fully aware of the great number of factors that can affect learning and behavior, he is somewhat reluctant to use the term, brain injury, without substantive data.

There is no single common denominator that characterizes all children with learning and/or behavioral difficulties. As a result, as Cruickshank states in Chapter 1, a vast number of terms come into common usage which reflect the varied, and varying, symptomatology. The terms, perceptual handicap, mixed dominance, brain damage, mental retardation, organic syndrome, and neuro-physiological dysynchrony, are but a few of the terms commonly used. To add to the confusion, these terms are often used in sequence or even interchangeably. These phrases are all descriptive of the symptomatology; they do not reflect an understanding of the specific etiology in an individual case. Parents, and subsequently the child, are most often the victims of this lack of clarity.

Another criticism of the term, brain damage, is that it seems to indicate a static condition, an irremediable situation. It is important to recognize that even in cases where there are identifiable organic components, the child will continue to grow. With this growth, development of the brain will also occur, and many of the clinical problems that one encounters will change, very often for the better. Proper handling of these children from the educational, social, and emotional aspects can add to the further resolution of these difficulties. Poor management, or lack of coordinated assistance, can often lead to further deterioration.

Despite the multiplicity of symptomatology, certain clusters of clinical manifestations have emerged which seem to delineate problems with more similarities than differences. These clusters, or syndromes, seem to have an identifiable organic component.

Primary Reading Disabilities

Children with so-called primary reading disabilities seem to show a greater incidence of crossed laterality, difficulty in differentiating right from left, and other "soft" neurological signs.

Hyperkinetic Behavioral Syndrome

These youngsters have rather characteristic patterns of marked hyperactivity and explosive, unpredictable behavior which seem to be unrelated to specific social or emotional etiological factors. The neurological examination and electroencephalogram may provide supportive evidence of an organic problem. (This does not mean that organic pathology is present in every child with these behavior patterns, however.)

Mild Choreiform Syndrome

These children have minimal abnormal involuntary movements, particularly of the small muscles of the hands. They may, or may not, present evidence of difficulties in school.

Cerebral Palsy

This is a rather nebulous term still in common usage. Some of the youngsters who have well-identified neurological findings such as mild spasticity, choreo-athetosis, and other disturbances of motor function are often categorized as having cerebral palsy.

The Clumsy Child

This is another category of children where the outstanding feature is their clumsiness. This can be of such a degree that it leads to great personal disability, interferes with education, and leads sometimes to a mistaken diagnosis of mental retardation. Although these children show clumsiness in dressing, feeding, walking, writing, drawing, and copying, they usually do not have a demonstrable defect in the pyramidal, extra-pyramidal, or cerebellar pathways which control volitional motor activity.

There are other clinical syndromes with obvious neurological signs where the medical history seems to indicate brain damage of a specific etiology. Examples might be youngsters with hemi-paresis or athetosis. It is of interest that children with these syndromes do not necessarily have any associated learning or behavior difficulties. Another example of brain damage with a specific etiology might be mental retardation caused by encephalitis or birth injury.

SUMMARY

How can the teacher apply the foregoing information? It is important to restate the fact that learning problems in children should be interpreted and assessed within the operational framework of the school. The neurological data provided by the physician would at best serve to provide a better understanding of the child's total problems. In an occasional situation, administration of psychopharmacological agents may be indicated, but they are only an adjunct to the total plan of management. The physician should not be expected to provide an educational diagnosis and/or a plan of management. He is not trained or qualified to provide this information. He can, however, materially aid in providing a greater depth of understanding of the complexities which have contributed to a given child's learning difficulty.

SELECTED REFERENCES

Apgar, V., Girdany, B., McIntosh, R., and Taylor, H. C. "Neonatal anoxia," *Pediatrics*, 1955, 15, 653.

Birch, Herbert G. (ed.). *Brain damage in children: The biological and social aspects*. Baltimore: Williams & Wilkins, 1964.

Cohn, Robert. "Delayed acquisition of reading and writing abilities in children: A neurological study," *Archives of Neurology*, 1961, 4, 153–164.

Critchley, M. *Developmental dyslexia*. Springfield, Ill.: Charles C Thomas, 1964.

Crothers, B., and Paine, R. *The natural history of cerebral palsy*. Cambridge, Mass.: Harvard University Press, 1959.

Gallagher, James J. "A comparison of brain injured and non-brain injured mentally retarded children on several psychological variables, *Monograph of the Society for Research in Child Development*, Serial No. 65, 1957, 22, 2.

Glaser, G. (ed.). *EEG and behavior.* New York: Basic Books, 1953 (particularly Chap. XIII by C. Henry).

Money, John (ed.). *Reading disability: Progress and research needs in dyslexia.* Baltimore: Johns Hopkins Press, 1962.

Rabinovitch, Ralph. "Reading and learning disabilities," Chap. 43 in *American handbook of psychiatry,* Silvano Arieti (ed.). Vol. I. New York: Basic Books, 1959.

Sugar, Oscar. "Congenital aphasia: An anatomical and physiological approach," *Journal of Speech and Hearing Disorders,* 1952, 17, 301.

Teuber, Hans L., and Rudel, R. G. "Behavior after cerebral lesions in children and adults," *Developmental Medicine and Child Neurology,* 1962, 4, 3.

Walton, J. N., Ellis, E., and Court, S. D. M. "Clumsy children: A study of developmental apraxia and agnosia," *Brain,* 1962, 85, 603.

PART II
EDUCATIONAL COMPETENCIES

Chapter 5

The Needs of Teachers in the General Area of Elementary Education
MIRIAN T. TANNHAUSER

EDITORIAL NOTE.—The teacher of brain-injured children is first and foremost a teacher. As such he must have all of the skills and competencies and understanding of good teachers and must understand the developmental processes related to growth and development and achievement of normal children. Mrs. Tannhauser has prepared a basic statement concerned with what the teacher of brain-injured children must take from elementary education. In the face of the competencies demanded of teachers of brain-injured children as discussed in this book, the elementary education competencies will (1) in large measure be preservice emphases or (2) be presented in rigorously different ways at the graduate level concomitantly with specialized competencies.

MIRIAN T. TANNHAUSER, Supervisor of Instruction, Special Education, Montgomery County Public Schools, Rockville, Maryland, is an outstanding educator in the general area of education of handicapped children. In 1952 she organized classes for brain-injured children in the Montgomery County public schools; in 1956–58 collaborated with Syracuse University in a research project which is reported in the book, *A Teaching Method for Hyperactive and Brain-injured Children* by Cruickshank, Bentzen, Ratzburg, and Tannhauser. In 1963–65 Mrs. Tannhauser served as a consultant in special education to Peru through the auspices of the Fulbright Commission and assisted in organizing programs for brain-injured children there.

Mrs. Tannhauser received her B.S. degree in elementary education from Georgia Teachers College, Collegeboro, in 1939, her M.A. in special education at Teachers College, Columbia University in 1943 and continued advanced graduate studies in special education at Teachers College in 1962.

Chapter 5

The Needs of Teachers in the General Area
of Elementary Education

MIRIAN T. TANNHAUSER

INTRODUCTION

The establishment of standards for teacher preparation, the identification of teacher competencies, the development of teacher education programs, and the evaluation of the persisting needs of teachers have concerned millions of professionals, scores of national organizations, hundreds of teacher training institutions, teachers themselves, and outspoken members of the general public, throughout the history of education. Thousands of books, magazines, articles, newscasts, and public speeches have dealt with the values, trends, and problems as they have been appraised by each succeeding generation in all countries of the world. An historian over a span of time may conceivably bring together significant elements from the past. A detailed research study could review the field of current literature and opinions. In dealing with the needs of teachers in the general area of elementary education for the purposes of this paper, however, definite limits must be imposed.

The scope of this paper, therefore, will be limited to a discussion of the needs of teachers in the general area of elementary education, as seen from the points of view of the goals of education to be achieved, certification requirements, requirements of teacher training institutions, standards set by national accrediting organizations, the analysis of good teaching practices, and educational research. A few select references will serve to demonstrate these areas of concern. The references used are in no sense inclusive, nor do they represent all points of view. They are included because they represent what seems to be a general trend in current thinking. In conclusion, criteria, evolved through experience, will be applied in a suggested recipe for the selection of elementary teachers for further specialized training.

71

GOALS OF EDUCATION—TEACHER REQUIREMENTS

School systems, in general, attempt to identify those competencies which will enable teachers to fulfill the avowed goals of education of the system. Among the goals of education of the many school systems in the United States, there are many common elements. These common elements reflect the leadership work of national organizations and the basic democratic principles which the educators in our society endorse.

Two of the best known definitions of the purposes or goals of education were formulated by educators in 1918 and 1938. The first definition, proposed by the Commission on the Reorganization of Secondary Education, established seven cardinal objectives of education to include health, command of fundamental processes, worthy home membership, vocational competency, effective citizenship, worthy use of leisure, and ethical character. The second definition, established by the Educational Policies Commission in 1938, developed objectives under the headings of self-realization, human relationships, economic efficiency, and civic responsibility.

In discussing what democracy demands of the schools, Russell M. Cooper identified in 1956 the following goals in his text, *Teacher Education for a Free People:*

1. The schools must help children achieve the traditional fundamentals of reading, writing, and arithmetic while yet meeting the new imperatives.
2. Society demands that schools help pupils achieve a basis for democratic citizenship.
3. The school must help the child achieve maturity in personal adjustment.
4. The school must continue to reflect and enrich the aesthetic values of our culture.
5. Society expects the schools to foster occupational readiness among their pupils.

The Educational Policies Commission of the National Education Association, in *The Central Purpose of American Education* (1961), explained the goals of education in relation to the development of rational powers. These powers, which involve the processes of recalling and imagining, classifying and generalizing, comparing and evaluating, analyzing and synthesizing, deducting and inferring, are discussed as the essence of the ability to think. Rational processes make intelligent choices possible. Through the process of rational thought, a person becomes aware of the basis of choice in his values and of the circumstances of choice in his environment. Rational powers are broadly applicable in life. They provide a basis for the development of competency in all areas with which the school has traditionally been concerned.

If teachers are to assume a responsible role in the fulfillment of the goals of education which they endorse, then it would seem that: (1) Teachers must be products of the culture which the school values; (2) teachers must exemplify those values inherent in the goals of education to be achieved, and (3) teachers must be able to guide and inspire students in the development of the rational powers needed to perpetuate the esteemed values of society.

CERTIFICATION REQUIREMENTS

Turning from a philosophical to a concrete attempt to determine the needs of elementary teachers in general, one must examine certification requirements. Certification requirements, established by each state but reciprocal among many, represent an attempt to measure and record the competencies of teachers. The measurement is both quantitative and qualitative. It records both academic achievement in specified course work and experience in supervised professional activity.

Certification requirements for school personnel in the United States have been published biennially since 1951. The latest manual was published in 1964 by the National Education Association, through the cooperative efforts of the National Commission on Teacher Education and Professional Standards and the National Association of State Directors of Teacher Education and Certification.

In 1964, one state, California, required five years of preparation for beginning elementary teachers, the fifth year being completed within the first five years of employment. Forty-five states required the bachelor's degree; five states required two but less than three years of college work; and one state required less than two years. Nine states mandated the completion of a fifth year for secondary school teachers, thus indicating a trend in requirements which in time will probably be expected also of elementary teachers.

Another important trend is the effort to overhaul and improve the "approved-program" approach in which a specific number of course credits will be required in specified subject areas. This approach is now in use in forty states.

A third trend among the states is toward the strengthening of the academic preparation of teachers in the areas of general education requirements. In some states this is done by increasing the academic requirements in general, while reducing the course credits required in professional education courses. In other states the trend is toward requiring concentration in one field for an academic major and a minor in education.

Still another significant trend is toward the use of the National Teachers Examinations as a qualifying hurdle, imposed in addition to the completion of the approved teacher education program for certification or as a supplement to accreditation.

There has been an increase in the trend toward state acceptance of the certification standards proposed by the National Council for Accreditation of Teacher Education and reciprocity of certification among states. In 1963 and 1964, however, NCATE was subjected to vehement attacks.

James B. Conant recommended in 1963 that NCATE be relegated to an advisory role only in accrediting. He proposed that NCATE serve as an advisory body to the teacher education institutions. These institutions, he felt, should assume the authority and responsibility for setting and maintaining specifications for certification. Teacher education institutions would in time, he believed, establish their reputation for producing good teachers. Those who failed should be denied the right to continue to function as teacher training institutions. Conant proposed a bachelor's degree with an academic major plus practice teaching as a minimum requirement for certification. A majority of the articles on certification appearing in professional journals since the publication of Conant's book have been reactions to his proposals.

Certification in Education by Lucien B. Kinney (1964) is a thoughtful consideration and analysis of state teacher certification philosophy and practice. James D. Koerner, in *The Miseducation of American Teachers* (1963), was highly critical of current practices.

If the needs of teachers in the general area of elementary education are determined, measured, and recorded through a process of certification requirements, then it would seem that teachers must have at least a bachelor's degree, hopefully an academic major, and certainly practice teaching.

REQUIREMENTS OF TEACHER TRAINING INSTITUTIONS

While teacher training institutions are cognizant of state certification requirements and attempt to provide for them, most institutions exercise independence in determining the nature of the content to be included within their required program of teacher education.

Betty J. Humphry reported in December 1963 on "A Survey of Professional Education Offerings in NCATE-Accredited Institutions." She examined the Summary of Requirements in Teacher Education Curricula of the National Council for Accreditation of Teacher Education

(1958–62), reviewed course offerings in college catalogues, and sent questionnaires to 363 teacher training institutions, 248 of which responded. The purpose of the survey was to determine the current professional education courses required, in common, of both prospective elementary and secondary teachers. She discussed her findings in relation to the professional education requirements related to psychology courses and to the professional education courses in societal foundations of education requirements. These findings as shown in her article are presented in Tables 2 and 3.

Variations were found in course requirements among the institutions. While 141 institutions required a course in educational psychology, others also required courses in human growth and development. Still other institutions required either one or the other.

A tabulation of the textbooks listed for the various courses related to psychology and human development indicated similarities in content of courses having different titles.

Variations in required courses dealing with societal foundations of education (including introduction, principles, history, philosophy, social foundations, and so forth) existed both in number, variety, and content of courses required. Again, the lists of texts used indicated similarity of content in courses of different titles.

At least two hundred different course titles were used to describe courses relating to psychological and societal foundation courses. In some cases, course descriptions clearly indicated the content; while in others, the descriptions were left to be too vague for classification. In general, however, it was felt that while there were many variations in the course titles, there was more agreement concerning the basic content taught than seemed readily apparent.

James Koerner made a two-year study of teacher training institutions and published his findings in 1963. Through an analysis of transcripts of credits of a sampling of teachers who were graduated in 1960 and 1961 from thirty-two teacher training institutions, Koerner shows what these teacher training institutions included on their programs of teacher education. For purposes of his analysis, he grouped the institutions in three categories. Group I institutions were liberal arts colleges, especially those confined to undergraduate work; Group II were universities, usually with separate schools or colleges of education; and Group III were teachers colleges and so-called multipurpose colleges that were formerly teachers colleges and still train teachers as their primary function. Table 4, reproduced from Koerner's book, *The Miseducation of American Teachers,* shows a tabulation of his findings for elementary teachers.

TABLE 2

PROFESSIONAL EDUCATION COURSES IN PSYCHOLOGY REQUIRED IN COMMON
OF PROSPECTIVE ELEMENTARY AND SECONDARY TEACHERS
AT 248 INSTITUTIONS

Course Titles	Number of Institutions Requiring Course	Number of Institutions Using One or More Basic Texts Listed for Educ. Psych. Courses
Educational Psychology	141	141
(Human Development II)*		
Human Growth and Development ..	47	10
General Psychology	33	2
Human Development	29	3
(Psychology of)		
Psychology of Learning	10	9
Child Psychology	7	
(Development)		
Mental Hygiene	7	
Adolescent Psychology	6	
Psychology of Childhood and		
Adolescence	6	
The Learning Process	6	4
Introduction to Psychology	6	2
Child Growth and Development ...	3	1
(Develop. of Child and Youth)		
Development Psychology	4	1
The Learner	4	
(Pupil)		
Development and Learning	2	2
Psychology for Teachers	2	1
Learning and the Learner	2	2
Psychology of Adjustment	3	1
Education of Exceptional Children ..	1	
Psych. and Soc. Found. of Educ.	1	1
Tests and Measurements	27	11
Measurement and Evaluation	16	12
Evaluation	11	9
(of Learning)		
(of Education)		
Evaluation and Guidance	6	1
Guidance	4	

* Parenthetical notations indicate alternate titles.

TABLE 3
PROFESSIONAL EDUCATION COURSES IN "SOCIETAL" FOUNDATIONS OF EDUCATION
REQUIRED IN COMMON OF PROSPECTIVE ELEMENTARY AND SECONDARY
TEACHERS AT 248 INSTITUTIONS

Course Titles	Number of Institutions Requiring Course	Number of Institutions Using One or More Basic Texts Listed for Intro. to Ed. Courses
Introduction to Education	75	75
(Professional Ed.)*		
(Teaching)		
(Teacher and the School)		
Philosophy of Education	29	
School in American Society	20	16
(Life)		
(Community)		
History and Philosophy of Education	19	
Foundations of Education	18	8
History of Education	11	
American Education	13	11
(Public)		
School and Society	11	4
Professional Orientation	9	7
(Planning a Career in Teaching)		3
Principles of Education	6	3
Orientation to Education	9	
(Teaching)		
Development of Educational Thought	6	1
Social Foundations of Education	6	1
Teacher in School and Community ..	6	
Foundations of American Education	7	1
Soc. and Philosoph. Found. of Educ.	4	
Educational Sociology	3	
History of American Education	2	
Contemporary Educational Thought	2	1
Social and Histor. Found. of Educ. ..	1	
Comparative Education	1	

* Parenthetical notations indicate alternate titles.

TABLE 4

Academic Profile, Drawn from the Transcripts of Credit, for 435 Recent Graduates of Elementary Teacher Training Programs	Group I Liberal Arts Colleges	Group II Universities	Group III Teachers Colleges
1. Mean semester hours devoted to professional education	36.7	49.6	55.0
2. Mean semester hours devoted to academic education	84.0	72.1	67.4
3. Percentage of total program devoted to professional education	30.4%	40.8%	44.9%
4. Percentage of total program devoted to academic education	69.6%	59.2%	55.1%
5. Percentage of time devoted to professional education in an assumed 120-semester-hour program	30.6%	41.0%	45.8%
6. Percentage of time devoted to academic education in an assumed 120-semester-hour program	70.0%	60.3%	55.1%
7. Composite grade point average in professional education	3.00	2.97	2.84
8. Composite grade point average in academic education	2.57	2.50	2.54
9. Mean semester hours devoted to practice teaching	6	8	10
10. Mean semester hours devoted to methods of teaching	8	12	12
11. Mean semester hours devoted to field of English	13	13	11
12. Mean semester hours devoted to field of mathematics	2	1	3
13. Mean semester hours devoted to field of science	11	8	11
14. Mean semester hours devoted to field of foreign languages	7	5	1
15. Percentage of transcripts showing no advanced work in any academic field(s)	9%	42%	67%
16. Percentage of transcripts showing 1–6 semester hours of advanced work in any academic subject(s)	27%	25%	20%
17. Percentage of transcripts showing 7–12 semester hours of advanced work in any academic subject(s)	41%	15%	12%
18. Percentage of transcripts showing over 12 semester hours of advanced work in any academic subject(s)	23%	18%	1%

James M. Hanlon (1965) discussed five major forces influencing teacher education today and pointed up the direction toward which he believes teacher education is moving. These five major forces are: (1) the drive toward professionalism; (2) accreditation; (3) state certification requirements and local pay scales; (4) research in education and related fields; and (5) experimental programs in teacher education.

These forces or trends lead Hanlon to believe that teacher education is moving toward the following developments:

1. *A pre-education program* similar in concept to pre-medicine, of four to five years duration, which will include: (a) a broad liberal arts background; (b) scholarly study of one subject field; (c) thorough grounding in the social and behavioral sciences; and (d) a basic sequence in the historical, philosophical, psychological, and sociological foundations of education.

2. *An internship program* of two to three years of teaching under the supervision of the intern's college, pursued while attending lectures and seminars designed cooperatively by his school and his college which include such areas as diagnostic and remedial techniques, test construction, and an exposure to possible areas for further specialization such as guidance, supervision, or administration. (Hanlon proposes that at the end of the internship program the student teacher should pass a state-administered examination to secure a license to teach.)

3. *Expanded professional studies for specialists* (leading to Ed.S., Ed.D., or Ph.D. degrees) demanding high intellectual output, outstanding skill, definite levels of professional ethics, and dedication, and culminating in field experience and/or internship experience in the area of specialization.

4. *A program of continuing education* to provide educators at any level with the up-to-date knowledge and skill which their job requires.

5. *Closer cooperation between schools and teacher training institutions.* If Hanlon's assumptions concerning trends in teacher education are correct, then it would seem that:

1. Teacher training institutions will require a broad academic major, courses in educational foundations, and courses in social and behavioral sciences as prerequisites for work in the practical aspects of teaching.

2. Courses in methods and techniques of teaching, in curriculum development, in the use of instructional materials, diagnostic and remedial techniques, and the evaluation of instruction will be offered as a part of an extended period of internship training and practice teaching.

3. Teacher training institutions will need to develop long-range programs of continuing education.

4. The total requirements and offerings of teacher training institutions will have to be developed in cooperation with school systems. Each must assume certain responsibilities in a cooperative program.

5. Overlapping content, confusion in course titles and content, and discrepancies in course requirements should be corrected by teacher training institutions if they are to assume a major role in determining and meeting the needs of teachers in the general area of elementary education.

REQUIREMENTS OF NATIONAL ACCREDITING ORGANIZATIONS

Future developments in teacher education institutions are closely allied with the work of the various national organizations concerned with the accreditation of teacher training institutions.

The National Commission on Teacher Education and Professional Standards, The American Association of Colleges for Teacher Education, and The National Council for Accreditation of Teacher Education —in cooperation with various regional accrediting associations and appropriate state departments of education—take an active interest in standards of teacher education. Each organization in separate publications and, in some instances, through joint reports deals with the needs of teachers in the general area of elementary education and ways by which these needs may best be met. Recent interest has been focused on professionalism of teaching and standards for accreditation of institutions who are to assume an expanding role of responsibility in the preparation and, hopefully, the certification of professional teachers.

THE ANALYSIS OF GOOD TEACHING

Equally interested in teachers' needs, competencies, and preparation, but approaching the problem from a different focus of concern, is a large group of educators who are involved in the recruitment, employment, retention, and professional advancement of teachers in the operation of schools. This group of educators and those professors in institutions who share their concerns have been involved in many studies which have attempted to identify the elements involved in good teaching, in the hope that these elements may be identified and developed in a larger percentage of the teaching staff.

One way, then, to judge the needs of teachers in the general area of elementary education is through the process of observing and analyzing good teaching in action.

Russell M. Cooper (see Cottrell, 1956) suggested the following qualities as those which are significant in effective teaching:

1. *The good teacher motivates students to want to learn.* The enthusiasm of his own personality, the fixing of concrete goals for achievement, the ready recognition of success, and encouragement despite failures—all give new zest to the child's activities.

2. *The good teacher will relate new material to the child's past experience and present purposes.*

3. *The good teacher makes appropriate adjustments to meet individual needs and differences of pupils.* The teacher is enthusiastic, imaginative, and insightful in sensing and responding to the feelings of pupils. He is skillful in the use of instruments, procedures, and resource personnel in acquiring an understanding of the individual needs and differences of pupils. He has the professional knowledge, skill, and aptitude for adapting teaching methods to the special needs of pupils.

4. *The good teacher will make sure that each pupil is actively involved in classroom activities.* Each will learn how to lead and how to follow. Each will become so committed to the enterprise at hand that he feels a personal stake in the success or failure of the classroom assignment.

5. *A good teacher helps the child to combine direct experience with generalization.* Without concrete experience, generalizations tend to be sheer verbalisms that are soon forgotten. Without generalization, concrete experiences are unrelated incidents devoid of meaning.

6. *The good teacher cooperates readily with the total staff in fostering broad educational values and solving school problems.*

The work of William M. Alexander (1959) called attention to the "marks of a good teacher" by examining the results the teachers achieve. He said,

In my own experience, the following stand out as the results (also the "symptoms") of effective teaching:

1. High achievement of pupils, especially in relation to their ability.

2. Liking for the class, subject, activities, and the teacher.

3. Eager participation in all classroom activities, including prompt completion of assignments.

4. Close attention of pupils to the activities of the classroom.

5. High interest and understanding of pupils regarding what is being done.

6. Harmonious interpersonal relations among pupils and with the teacher.

Phillip W. Jackson is currently conducting a study among a group of elementary teachers selected as outstanding to determine how they judge their own success and what gives them the greatest sense of satisfaction as teachers. Jackson explained that when principals were asked to identify their most outstanding teacher, they were able to do so without hesitation. Sixty-eight teachers designated as outstanding on all counts, out of a teacher population of two to three thousand, participated in the study. While the processing of data was not completed when Jackson gave his report in September 1965, he felt that a significant pattern of responses was developing. The teachers did not judge their success on the basis of objective evidence of achievement of students but rather on their observation of student behavior. As a group, they felt that standardized tests were not particularly helpful either in measuring progress or in indicating instructional needs. Instead, they judged the effectiveness of their work by the reactions of their students. The expression of students' eyes, their involvement, the things they said, the ideas and materials they shared, their changing attitudes, awakening interest, ability to put new ideas to work, coming alive, snapping out of it, the dawn of light—these were the student behaviors which assured teachers that they were succeeding.

Teachers gained greatest satisfaction from the feelings they experienced in teaching. Helping children develop, teaching them new things, watching them overcome problems and develop new interests and skills, having students who have succeeded in life come back to see them— these were the things which made the teachers feel good about their work.

Jackson questioned many of the ways in which teachers are supposedly helped by college professors and school administrators. Implied was the idea that the needs of teachers, as seen by teachers, are not necessarily the same needs as those which have been identified by professors and administrators.

RESEARCH

Researchers in recent years have studied many aspects of the teaching-learning situation. Much evidence seems to indicate that the personalities of the teachers and the learners are real determinants, not just basic variables, of the effectiveness of teachers. Personalities and their interaction affect the outcome of instruction more than the content being taught or professional preparation of the teachers.

Louis M. Heil, in reporting on studies of personality variables (1964), indicated that these variables in the classroom can be discussed in relation to three general types of teachers: those who might be described either as self-controlling, as self-accepting, or as self-effacing. The self-controlling type teacher is most comfortable in a highly structured and ordered atmosphere, where immediate goals and limits are set. The self-accepting teacher is a creative person who values originality and prefers to work in a stimulating, imaginative, unstructured situation. The self-effacing teacher is generally apprehensive, fearful, vague, uncertain, and lacking in imagination. He needs to work in an environment in which specific directions are given on all minor details. The implication of Heil's report is that teacher education programs, job assignments, and group assignments must be individualized for teachers in recognition of these important personality differences.

Projects in which the effectiveness of teachers has been measured in relation to ways of teaching, believed to be associated with teacher personality, have shown that the effectiveness of one approach as compared with another depends also on the personality structure of the students involved.

Studies of the relation of teacher preparation to teacher effectiveness seem to indicate that professional versus academic preparation of teachers is not the significant factor in predicting their success.

In addition to a multitude of current research studies related to teaching efficiency, there has also been a great deal of research in education which has implications for what the elementary teacher of the future should be able to do.

Donald D. Bushnell (see Editors of Education U.S.A., 1964) points out, for example, that teachers in 1970 will need to be skillful in selecting, organizing, and programming information; in monitoring machines; in referring students to appropriate instructional materials, and in supervising independent study projects. The teacher will be using and teaching research techniques, the application of logic in decision-making, information theories, and computer language systems.

If the needs of elementary teachers in general are to be judged in light of the research cited, one would assume that a mature, social-service-motivated, well-adjusted teacher who enjoys working with students and gains satisfaction from their enthusiastic responsive participation will succeed as a teacher, if he has mastered the skills needed to help the right students manipulate the right machines and can keep the students intellectually and emotionally alive while they are engaged in a push-button process of education.

STATEMENT OF THE PROBLEM

Everyone recognizes and appreciates good teaching. The best teacher in the school can be identified by the principal or supervisor without hesitation. Little children love and adore a good teacher and cry when they must miss a day from school. Older students are stimulated, inspired, and work hard when they have a good teacher. Parents beam with pride and glow with satisfaction when their children have good teachers. Communities honor and respect good teachers. Professional leaders in all walks of life speak with reverence and gratitude about some teacher who had a positive influence on their lives and in some ways influenced their professional choice.

No one has a problem in determining who the good teachers are. There are two problems, however, which to date have not been solved. The body of this paper has dealt with, but has not solved, these two problems. The evidence which this paper has brought to bear on these problems will be accepted by some people and rejected by others— because the divergence of opinion is a part of these problems.

1. What are the significant elements of good teaching?
2. How are these elements developed?

SELECTING TEACHERS OF BRAIN-INJURED CHILDREN

If the purpose of considering the needs of teachers in the general area of elementary education is to establish a foundation upon which specialized preparation may be built to develop special education teachers to teach brain-injured children, then the purpose can be achieved and the problem solved quite simply. The recipe offered has been evolved and tested through many years of experience.

1. Identify those teachers from kindergarten through third grade whom everyone agrees are outstanding teachers.

2. Watch them work with children—in formal planned visits, in informal drop-in observations, and in marginal day-to-day contacts.

3. Select from these those who really enjoy teaching. Don't ask them; just watch and see. Are they facing each day with enthusiasm, as an adventure in learning? Do they have a sense of humor which the children enjoy? Do the children share with them their own feelings, confide in them, and seek their help when it is needed? Does each child feel that he is an important part in the total scheme of things? Does he feel safe and free to learn by trial and error? Is learning fun—fun which the children and the teacher share?

4. From the outstanding primary teachers who enjoy teaching, select those in whose classrooms the following conditions prevail: (a) the children all understand what they are doing and why; (b) all children feel reasonably sure that they will succeed at the task assigned; (c) the children know what instructional aids, materials, and resources are

available and can use them correctly and independently without interrupting the teacher or class; (d) possible behavior problems are anticipated and prevented by redirecting a situation which could lead to trouble; (e) children move individually and as groups from one activity to another without confusion or loss of purpose; (f) the interests and efforts of the children are invested in the achievement of a task rather than in pleasing the teacher; (g) the teacher sometimes makes a mistake; and when she does, the children call it to her attention and help her to rectify the situation with the same good humor and tolerance which they enjoy when they are found in error; and (h) children with special problems know what their problems are and know that the teacher and class understand and are willing to help; and even though they still sometimes "goof," they feel certain that they are improving.

5. From those teachers who survive steps 1–4, select those who: (a) are secure in their dealings with principals, supervisors, psychologists, medical consultants, and parents; (b) are interested in and willing to try new ways of dealing with old problems; (c) are enthusiastic about experimentation and (d) are highly motivated to work with children who have special problems.

Teachers who meet those requirements can be guaranteed of success when they have received adequate specialized training, provided that during the initial phase of their adjustment to meeting new requirements they: (1) maintain good health; (2) have no major family crisis; and (3) do not feel pressured to take courses to meet certification requirements in an area not directly related to their new assignment.

SUMMARY

In summary, the determination of the needs of teachers in the general area of elementary education is a complex matter involving the consideration of many people and many organizations. This problem has been dealt with herein in relation to social values, goals of education, certification, teacher training programs, the analysis of good teaching, and thorough extensive educational research. Everyone knows when a teacher is good, but what the elements of good teaching are and how these elements can best be developed is an area in which consensus has not been reached.

When one must examine the needs of teachers in the general area of elementary education in order to establish a foundation upon which a program of specialized training can be planned, in order to develop teachers for brain-injured children, one turns in the final analysis to a pragmatic approach. One begins with those teachers easily identified as being outstanding and selects from this group persons who demonstrate the qualities and achievements which have been found to be important elements among those teachers who for many years have had remarkable success in teaching brain-injured children.

SELECTED REFERENCES

Alexander, William M. *Are you a good teacher?* New York: Rinehart, 1959.

American Association of Colleges for Teacher Education. *Revised standards and policies for accrediting colleges for teacher education.* National Education Association (N.E.A.), 1201 Sixteenth St., N.W., Washington, D.C. 20036, 1961.

Conant, James B. *The education of American teachers.* New York: McGraw-Hill, 1963.

Cottrell, Donald P. (ed.). *Teacher education for a free people.* New York: The American Association of Colleges for Teacher Education, 1956.

Cyphert, Frederick R., and Spaights, Ernest. *An analysis and projection of research in teacher education.* Columbus: Ohio State University Research Foundation, 1964.

Editors of Education U.S.A. *The shape of education for 1964. A handbook on current educational affairs.* Vol. IV. National School Public Relations Association in cooperation with Division of Press, Radio and Television Relations, N.E.A., 1964.

Educational Policies Commission, N.E.A. *The central purpose of American education.* 1962.

Hanlon, James M. "Changes in teacher education: Influences, directions, implications," *The Journal of Teacher Education,* 1965, 16, 25–28.

Heil, Louis M. "Personality variables: An important determinant in effective elementary school instruction," *Theory in practice.* Vol. III. Columbus: Bureau of Educational Research and Service, Ohio State University, 1964.

Humphry, Betty J. "A survey of professional education offerings in NCATE-accredited institutions," *The Journal of Teacher Education,* 1963, 14, 406–410.

Jackson, Phillip W. "Focus on good teaching." Reported in meeting of Montgomery County, Maryland, Administrative Staff, Sept. 1965.

Kinney, Lucien B. "Assignment and the teaching credential," *California Teachers Association Journal,* May 1960, 11–13.

Koerner, James D. *The miseducation of American teachers.* Boston: Houghton Mifflin, 1963.

National Commission on Teacher Education and Professional Standards. *New horizons for the teaching profession.* N.E.A., 1961.

National Commission on Teacher Education and Professional Standards and National Association of State Directors of Teacher Education and Certification. *Certification requirements for school personnel of the United States.* N.E.A., 1964.

National Council for Accreditation of Teacher Education. *Standards for accreditation of teacher education.* NCATE, 1750 Pennsylvania Avenue, N.W., Washington, D.C. 20006, 1960; Reprint 1964.

Chapter 6

The Needs of Teachers for Specialized Information on Reading
MARIANNE FROSTIG, Ph.D.

EDITORIAL NOTE.—It is not possible to divorce reading and the teaching of reading for brain-injured children from competencies needed by teachers in the areas of perception, handedness, visuomotor training, cognition, and others. It is artificial to consider it separately, and yet, since there is a recognized body of knowledge in the area of reading, it is appropriate that specialized competencies for teachers in meeting these needs of brain-injured children be recognized and discussed as such. Dr. Frostig's broad background of experience and her significant contribution in the area of diagnosis of perceptual problems which are basic to abstract learning as in reading make it particularly appropriate that she be asked to prepare this paper.

Research basic to this paper has been supported in part by the Rosenberg Foundation.

Dr. Marianne Frostig is currently Director of the Marianne Frostig Center for Educational Therapy in Los Angeles, California. Dr. Frostig holds the B.A. degree from the New School for Social Research, the M.A. degree from the Claremont Graduate School, and the Ph.D. degree in educational psychology from the University of Southern California. Her professional experience includes positions in the areas of social work and school psychology, as well as university teaching. Dr. Frostig has made significant contributions in the areas of evaluation and education of children with visual perceptual disabilities. Her major publications include *A Developmental Test of Visual Perception for Evaluating Normal and Neurologically Handicapped Children, The Frostig Program for the Development of Visual Perception,* and *The Marianne Frostig Developmental Test of Visual Perception.*

Chapter 6

The Needs of Teachers for Specialized Information on Reading

MARIANNE FROSTIG, Ph.D.

INTRODUCTION

Many methods proposed for the teaching of reading advocate an approach to be used with all children, because it is hoped that the same ingredients will always lead to the same results. In contrast, this paper advocates a prescriptive approach, based on an understanding of the symptomatology of each child. It is suggested that the term "educational therapy" be used for this approach, because it implies the application of specific, highly developed skills to ameliorate defects caused by illness or developmental abnormality. It does not imply that the "educational therapist" wants to step into the shoes of the physician.

It has been demonstrated that the teacher in special education needs highly developed diagnostic and remedial skills. Where reading is concerned, these must be aimed not only at improving the reading process per se, but also at improving the underlying basic abilities which are necessary for the reading process to proceed smoothly. Fortunately, such methods have recently become available: for example, training in auditory perception suggested by Myklebust (1963), the language methods developed by Kirk and his group (1940), and the visual-perceptual materials which have been developed (Frostig and Horne, 1964). Hart in Australia, Lloyd Dunn and James Smith of Peabody College (1965) and the staff of the writer's center in Los Angeles have also developed methods for teaching language based on the Illinois Test of Psycholinguistic Abilities (1961). Training in higher thought processes has been promoted by Aurelia Levi of Albert Einstein University (1965) and by E. A. Peel (1960) in England. Both of these workers are strongly influenced by Piaget's theories (1952, 1954, 1959), and Jerome Bruner's work (1962) is also of great significance in this respect.

89

90   THE TEACHER OF BRAIN-INJURED CHILDREN

Many of the contributors in this volume have mentioned their concern with training other skills involved in reading. The application of these basic skills to the process of reading is suggested in this paper. The training of these is essential. However, it should be noted that clinical experience suggests that beginning reading can often be introduced before the initial reading readiness training is completed. This is especially significant for the treatment of older children for whom time saved is of the greatest importance within the limits set by a slow step-by-step progress designed to insure continued success and to overcome the characteristic sense of hopelessness. Remedial methods will vary according to age level as well as disturbed functions. These basic rules should be kept in mind during the discussion of specific difficulties.

GENERAL STATEMENT

Teachers are more concerned with the reading progress of their charges than they are with any other phase of school progress because they recognize that reading is necessary in all aspects of life. Even in the age of television and radio, reading is still the primary means of gaining and disseminating information. Various activities such as finding a telephone number or the correct streetcar or bus, receiving a note from a friend, following the recipe in a cookbook or the instructions for a household appliance, or obtaining a license to drive a car are all contingent upon the ability to read.

Reading, however, is a complicated process. Many skills are involved in gleaning meaning from the printed page. The words have to be recognized, their forms associated with sound patterns, and the sound patterns in turn associated with meaning. This chain of associations depends on correct visual and auditory perception, language, memory, and thought. If there is one weak link in the chain of associations, the process of reading will be distorted or interrupted. It is important for the teacher to realize that optimum remediation depends on careful diagnostic exploration, because remediation has to vary according to the disturbance. No single teaching method can be the correct approach for all children.

DEVELOPMENTAL CONCEPTS IMPORTANT FOR UNDERSTANDING THE READING PROCESS

A short survey of the range of reading difficulties is one of the requisites in the education of teachers of children with learning difficulties. The survey should not only include a discussion of the abilities which are necessary for reading to proceed smoothly; it should also embody an overview of the development of psychological functions from infancy through adolescence. Such a survey will make the concept of "readiness" a clear and useful one. The teacher will learn that readiness is not only dependent upon maturational development, but can also be promoted by good teaching practices. The teacher is the key professional person responsible for the promotion of a child's readiness.

There are distinct phases in a child's development which characterize certain age levels and which can be regarded as the usual, as well as the optimal, age ranges for the maximum development of specific major psychological functions. These phases are not sharply delineated, but overlap each other.

The first is the sensori-motor phase. During the first two years of life movement and the reception of stimuli become fused into a single act. Visuomotor skills and eye movements, which are the basis of later perceptual development, are established at this time. It is now recognized that sensori-motor training will, therefore, have to be included in readiness training. Unfortunately, this aspect of training, which had been neglected for a long time, has been made a fetish by some workers and equated with complete readiness training. The teacher should understand its importance—so well explained by current developmental theories such as those of Piaget (1954), Werner (1957), and Gesell (1947), and by age-old practice as in Itard (1962), Froebel (1900), and Montessori (1965)—but also recognize its limitations. Good sensory-motor development does not guarantee smooth progress during later developmental phases; extremely inhibited sensori-motor development may be followed by the normal development of language and higher thought processes, as in some children with cerebral palsy.

During the period from approximately two to four years of age, language is the major developmental task. This includes the growth of those auditory-perceptual skills which are involved in speech. The teacher will therefore be concerned with auditory-perceptual skills, language, and speech development as part of the readiness program.

The maximum development of visual perceptual abilities occurs during the period from approximately four to seven and a half years of age. This is the period during which children are expected to learn to read, but lagging visual-perceptual skills are a frequent deterrent to successful reading at this time.

Higher thought processes develop predominantly after the age of about seven and a half and become increasingly important. While a lag in perceptual skills is most handicapping in beginning reading, deficits in such abilities as concept formation or thinking in logical sequences are frequently the cause of later reading failure. Reading readiness training after about six and a half or seven years of age should therefore emphasize the development of higher thought processes (Braun, 1963). The following outline of the skills necessary in reading, and of the methods used in their promotion, is based upon this developmental point of view.

Sensori-Motor Skills

Lags in motor development are frequently observed in children with reading difficulties. These children are often clumsy and have difficulties with recognition of direction. They frequently show poor eye-hand coordination and regressive eye movements in reading. To help the child with these aspects of sensori-motor development, a multiplicity of methods has to be employed (Kephart, 1960; Montessori, 1965; Radler and Kephart, 1960). Exercises for the development of body image, concept, and schema* (Frostig, 1964, pp. 19–45) and a general program of physical education (Frostig, 1964; Mosston, 1965) are of great importance for these children, as are manipulatory and play activities, such as copying patterns and designs and reproducing them from memory either with beads, pegs, forms, or with pencil and paper.

Despite claims to the contrary, the writer's own research, as well as that of others (Ayres, 1965; Reitan) has shown but a slight correlation between mixed dominance or sinistrality and reading disturbances. Nevertheless, established hand preference is important for awareness of direction and left-to-right progression. To promote hand preference, a variety of exercises may be used (Frostig, Lefever, and Whittlesey, 1964; Kephart, 1960, 1963). The use of a weighted armband has been especially helpful.

Sensori-motor skills may be evaluated by the Kephart Scale (1960, 1963), the Winter Haven Exercises (Sutphin, 1964), the Cureton Motor Fitness Test (1942), the Kraus-Weber Test (1963), and others. A new standardized scale by Kephart is in the offing.

Observation or testing of eye movements is also necessary, for smooth eye movements are important for reading (Abercrombie, 1960). Exercises to promote them are included in the writer's earlier publications (1964, pp. 68–71) and in Kephart's books (1960, 1963; Radler and Kephart, 1960).

Visual and Auditory Perceptual Skills Involved in the Reading Process

Numerous studies have explored the correlation of beginning reading with visual-perceptual skills, and the findings are generally in agree-

---

* The term, anti-gravity, has been used by optometrists and by Kephart to denote this concept.

ment. There is no such precise agreement in regard to the degree of importance of auditory-perceptual skills. Visual perception is always involved in reading; blind children cannot use ordinary reading materials. Auditorily handicapped children can compensate for their defect, as is proven by the fact that deaf children can learn to read. It is difficult to measure correlation where one factor is an ability for which other skills can compensate to a high degree.

In regard to visual skills, M. C. Potter (1949) found a correlation of .53 between reading grades and scores on the perceptual discrimination subtests of the Lee-Clark Reading Readiness Test. Other studies since that time have shown correlations between .4 and .5. The correlation between perceptual quotient (P.Q.) as measured by the Frostig Developmental Test of Visual Perception and teacher ratings of reading achievement in the first grade was found to be .44 (1964, p. 495). These are all medium high correlations. One can therefore conclude that visual-perceptual ability plays an important role in the acquisition of reading, but that other skills are also involved.

Visual and auditory perceptions have certain common characteristics. They are the sense channels which convey the most information about the outside world. They occur as single static experiences or in sequences. They are usually integrated with the information from other sense channels, and they are important aids in communication.

For the purpose of education, the differentiation between static and sequential perception seems to the writer as important as differentiations between the sense modalities. In this paper, therefore, visual- and auditory-perceptual abilities will be discussed together, but divided into four different groups. The first group comprises static visual perception and memory for single statically perceived visual perceptions (a written number, a letter, or a short word). The second group comprises auditory perceptual abilities and memory for single statically perceived auditory stimuli (sounds and words). The third and fourth groups comprise, respectively, the auditory-perceptual and the visual-perceptual skills which are necessary to recognize and to remember sequences.

To repeat, there is a very important differentiation between the various auditory and visual perceptual skills involved in the static perception of symbols and of those involved in the recognition and reproduction of sequences of symbols. Research up to now has shown that there is little correlation between these various abilities, especially between sequential and static perceptual abilities in a given modality, and even less between those of different modalities. However, even within each group, there seem to be distinct abilities. For instance, the ability to remember a sequence depends not only on the modality involved, but on factors such as the length of the sequence, the speed of presentation, and the time elapsed since it was shown. The ability to perceive a shape has a very low correlation with the ability to perceive its direction, or the ability to differentiate it from its ground, although these abilities are all subsumed under static visual perception. Therefore, testing and remediation of perceptual disabilities need to be specific.

Difficulties with perception of auditory and visual sequences may cause distortion of the meaning of sequentially presented material. Such disturbances are not limited to reading. A child could have difficulty in understanding the sequence of movies, comic strips, or sentences in stories; or, he could be unable to perceive the sequences involved in music, despite excellent discrimination of single sounds. The perception of sequences has to be explored in all major sense modalities, in addition to the perception of single stimuli.

Static visual perception.—Words are composed of letters, and letters are complicated shapes. The perception of both form and direction is required to recognize letters. Failure to differentiate between "b" and "d" may indicate difficulty in perceiving the directions of letters. Difficulty with form perception may result in failure to differentiate between letters of the same direction but similar shape, such as between "n" and "r," or "n" and "m." Children with difficulty in form perception may also have difficulty with matching letters and words when written in different print types.

Inadequacy of figure-ground perception may lead to failure in the analysis of longer words when letter groups and syllables need to become successively the "figure." A child with figure-ground perceptual problems may be unable to "find" a word in a dictionary, or a page number in a table of contents, to answer a question referring to a particular sentence on a page, or to find the relevant numbers in word problems in arithmetic. The child with difficulties in figure-ground perception is, therefore, frequently handicapped in his study skills.

Visual sequences.—Difficulties with the perception of visual sequences may result from inadequacy in figure-ground perception, as well as from inadequacy in the perception of spatial relationships. These abilities show a medium to nonsignificant product-moment correlation with each other (.37 at kindergarten age level to .01 at third-grade level) for public school children generally, but a much higher correlation with each other for children with learning difficulties (.48). Both abilities involve perception of relationships within the entire visual field. Figure-ground perception divides the field into two parts—the prominent (figure) and the unobtrusive (ground)—while in spatial relationships the various parts of the field are given equal attention or weight. Grossly incorrect eye movements may be one of the causes, or the main cause, of difficulty in figure-ground perception or in spatial relationships in certain children.

The sequential characteristics of perception are much more important in the perception of spatial relationships than in figure-ground perception. When the perception of spatial relationships is disturbed, letters may be interchanged. For example, "Nora" may become "Aron," "around" may be read as "adroun" or "aroma." Words may also be interchanged in phrases or sentences. Children with difficulties in any kind of space perception may have difficulties in spelling. If they learn to spell by purely auditory methods, then they may remember a letter sequence and write it down correctly, but may be unable then to read the word.

In summary, several visual-perceptual abilities are involved in reading: form perception, figure-ground perception, perception of position in space, and perception of spatial relationships, as well as specific abilities necessary for following and remembering sequences. Fortunately, treatment of these difficulties, if systematically applied, is usually successful with children below eight years of age.

It is important to realize that there is not a one-to-one relationship between perceptual inadequacy and reading difficulty. Many children who are deficient in a basic psychological ability or who are not able to learn through one sense modality are able to compensate for their handicap. However, frequently the expenditure of energy and the stress involved in learning a task in the presence of disability leads to anxiety, anger, despair, and even to behavioral deviations. Studies have shown (Maslow, Frostig, and Whittlesey, 1964) a highly significant correlation between teacher ratings of classroom adjustment and scores on the Frostig Test at kindergarten and first-grade levels.

For younger children a graded perceptual training program which differentiates among various specific abilities has been developed (Frostig, 1964). Specific methods and exercises suited to the interest and age level of older children will have to be designed. The subject matter of art, geography, anatomy, geometry, astronomy, and space travel could be adapted for this purpose.

The teacher should know that the following techniques are available for diagnosis of the visual-perceptual abilities involved in the reading process: the Marianne Frostig Developmental Test of Visual Perception (Frostig, Lefever, and Whittlesey, 1964), the visual-motor sequencing subtest of the Illinois Test of Psycholinguistic Abilities (Kirk and McCarthy, 1961), observation of reading errors, and careful observation of eye movements.

Auditory perceptual skills.—The second sense channel involved in reading is the auditory one. Auditory perception develops slowly. Even in infancy the baby must master some auditory-perceptual skills as he listens to sounds and later imitates his first words. But the recognition of single letter sounds in the context of the word requires highly developed sequential auditory skills and evolves during the fifth to seventh years of life. For many children in the primary grades it is still a difficult task which needs patient training.

The difficulty in making a distinction between static and sequential perceptions is greater in regard to hearing than in regard to vision, because visual perception constitutes a spatial sequence, and auditory perception constitutes a temporal one. However, auditory perceptions resemble visual perceptions because they can be perceived as wholes.

Clarification of the role of auditory perceptual abilities in reading may be facilitated by drawing parallels between auditory- and visual-perceptual skills. The static auditory discrimination of speech sounds corresponds to the visual discrimination of letter forms; the ability to blend sounds or the ability to perceive the sound pattern of a word as a whole corresponds to the ability to perceive the form of a word as a whole; the perception of sequences of sounds in words corresponds to the perception of the sequence of letters in words, letter groups, or syllables. Thus, the child with difficulties in auditory perception may not be able to differentiate between sounds, to blend them into words, or to perceive the order in which sounds occur.

The analysis of sounds in the context of a word is primarily needed in spelling; the synthesis of sounds is needed in reading. Both abilities are frequently disturbed in children with neurological handicaps, who may have difficulty in perceiving single sounds, sequences, or both.

Methods for evaluating the auditory perception involved in reading include the Wepman Test of Auditory Discrimination (Wepman, 1948), the digit-span subtest of the Wechsler Intelligence Scale for Children (Wechsler, 1949), the auditory vocal sequencing subtest of the Illinois Test of Psycholinguistic Abilities (Kirk and McCarthy, 1961), word-span and sentence-span tests, and tests of the ability to follow verbal directions.

Without such formal evaluation of basic auditory and visual perceptual abilities it is frequently impossible to determine the reasons for difficulty in reading. Observation and analysis of actual reading errors is also most helpful.

If no auditory- or visual-perceptual disabilities are manifested, then the cause of the reading difficulty may lie in the child's inability to associate visual or auditory perceptions, or to associate meaning with words.

Difficulty with association between the auditory and visual sense modalities.—When a child reads silently, associations have to be formed between simultaneously perceived auditory and visual stimuli. Without fusion of the auditory and the visual percept, reading becomes haphazard. The order of letters or the order of sounds will be changed so that they do not correspond to each other. A child with these difficulties may try to skip the sound sequence in the association chain (visual percept–sound sequence–meaning) and refer directly to the meaning. He may read "look" instead of "see," "big" instead of "tall," "fast" instead of "rapid." Or, he may read words which are completely different from what is printed because he refers only to the shape of the word and may read ⌐dig⌐ instead of ⌐boy⌐ or ⌐hay⌐.

Strauss and Kephart (1955) have postulated that the basis of the associational difficulties in reading is the inability to translate the spatial sequences of the printed symbols into the temporal sequences of the auditorily perceived words. This difficulty is not restricted to reading. Gooddy (1963) has pointed out that children with this difficulty often show various signs of brain dysfunction.

Readiness and remedial programs for these children should include exercises in cross-modality associations. Many of the exercises are the same as those used in training auditory perception, such as following directions (auditory-motor associations), describing a picture (visual-vocal association), and finding a specific object in a picture the teacher describes (auditory-visual associations) (Frostig, 1965).

Difficulties in Higher Thought Processes

Sensori-motor, perceptual, and language abilities develop during preschool and the beginning school years. It has therefore been customary to include training in perception and in language in the readiness programs in kindergarten and first grade, although this has often not been done in a sufficiently systematic way. Higher thought processes, however, develop only after the age of approximately seven or seven and a half years (Piaget, 1952, 1954, 1959) and become more and more important for reading. Any of these abilities may be disturbed, causing reading to remain at a low level and requiring appropriate remedial training.

Under the phrase, higher thought processes, or, higher cognitive processes, are subsumed all those mental processes which lead to cognition (awareness and understanding) of the environment and of ourselves, but which are not limited to the recognition of the immediately present stimuli. Such processes include memory (which in turn includes immediate and delayed recall of single stimuli and immediate and delayed recall of sequences), classification and concept formation, recognition of relationships, thinking sequentially, generalization, drawing conclusions, translation of one mode of representation of an idea into another mode (i.e., using symbols), hypothesizing and devising strategies to prove hypotheses, and many other abilities. Since not all these processes are basic to early reading, discussion will be limited to those higher cognitive functions which are necessary for the young reader.

Difficulties with higher thought processes interfere with the child's comprehension and memory of what he reads. He may not be able to keep the thought long enough in mind to remember the beginning of a story when he reads the end; he may have difficulties in understanding words and phrases because he lacks the concepts they denote; or he may have difficulties in imagery and be unable to grasp any but concrete and present events.

Memory defects in children may be specifically related to reading. Or, a child with memory defects may have difficulties with comprehending what he reads because he suffers from a general lack of retrievable information on which to build new experiences.

Repetition is one of the most frequently used methods to help a child remember. Memory can be trained not only by repetition, but also by using imagery. This training is an essential part of the entire educational process. Difficulties in recalling previous events are often caused by difficulties in picturing them in the mind. Remedial exercises can be used to help the child recapitulate previous kinesthetic, visual, or auditory experiences, as well as experiences which include all these elements. Preliminary research with a small sample (fifty-five) of children with learning difficulties (mean age, seven years, 4 months; age range five years, three months through eight years, eleven months) showed that the motor-encoding subtest of the ITPA showed the second highest correlation of all ITPA subtests with the WISC and also was one of the most depressed subtests in this sample. The motor-encoding subtest requires a minimum of motor skills, but necessitates utilization of specific information, visualization, and expressive abilities.

Concept formation, recognition and manipulation of relationships (including abstraction and generalization), manipulating symbols, and keeping one or more ideas in mind while exploring variables are all necessary to form reasoned judgments and to think logically. All these abilities are involved in learning to read critically, and they play an increasing role as the child grows older. Teachers should be acquainted with the training methods devised by Aurelia Levi (1965) and Jerome Bruner (1962).

Because the ITPA evaluates conceptual functions, language programs developed from this test include training in higher thought processes (Dunn and Smith, 1965; Frostig, 1965; Hart).

Association of symbols with meaning.—Some children who seem to have fairly high intelligence and who have no difficulties with association between the auditory and the visual sense modalities can master the *mechanics* of reading with ease and fluency. However, although they understand spoken language, they do not understand the content of what they read. This difficulty is sometimes overlooked because these children read with good intonation. Listening to them, one can erroneously suppose that they grasp the meaning of what they are reading. If these children can understand what is read to them, but are unable to understand what they read by themselves, then their problem does not lie in a general difficulty in language decoding, but with establishing a connection between visual symbols and meanings. Specific reading methods which will be discussed later are helpful. Training in visualization should be included in the program for these children.

ETIOLOGY

Myklebust (1963) has stated that the causes for learning difficulties in children may be threefold, namely, sensory deprivation, emotional disturbances, and deficits in the central nervous system.

The main content of this paper is concerned with those reading failures which occur because of deficits in the central nervous system, be it because of disease, accident, or congenital and developmental factors. However, a few words should be said about emotional disturbances as a cause of reading disturbances, because emotional disturbances are also factors in many cases of specific dyslexia.

Emotional disturbance can be caused by such factors as the child's difficulties in the home environment, traumatic experiences, or emotional deprivation. They may also occur as a consequence of and not a cause of a child's reading failure. Gallagher (1962) stated that many children develop anxiety reactions because of their inability to read. The child's self-concept is disturbed by his failure, and the reactions of parents and teachers reinforce his feeling of despair and loneliness.

Ingram and others (1965) have stated that even night terrors, aggressive behavior, temper tantrums, severe withdrawal, lack of trust and severe depression, as well as attitudinal changes which later affect all learning in an adverse manner, may be the result rather than the cause of learning difficulties.

In other cases children may be initially emotionally disturbed and may then become more upset as they fail in school subjects. Then, the primary emotional disturbance and the secondary ones caused by school failure becoming intertwined.

Emotional disturbances are very frequent among brain-damaged children. A person teaching such children must be aware of the importance of so structuring the classroom environment and directing her relationship with the children and their relationships among themselves that both emotional health and school achievement improve.

Reading is strongly influenced by the emotional status of the child, be he brain-damaged or not. The amelioration of emotional problems may be the key to resolving a child's reading difficulties, regardless of etiological classification, because emotional disturbances interrupt the physiological processes necessary for smooth reading and prevent a child from learning. It is the teacher who is most frequently the only one who can act as a therapeutic agent in the child's life, for professional psychotherapy could hardly be available for more than a fraction of the vast number of poor readers.

Deficits in the central nervous system which may cause reading difficulties can be divided into two main subgroups: (1) those caused by disease, accident, or brain damage and (2) those which are thought to be the results of a developmental disturbance or a constitutional difficulty. Developmental lags are often regarded as physiological deviations and not as constituting brain damage or pathology. The differentiating feature is considered to be the child's total behavior. The child with minor brain injury will show behavior disorders, uncontrolled movements, clumsiness, and hyperactivity, while the child with constitutional dyslexia may seem well behaved, well controlled, and without learning difficulties in those school subjects which do not require reading or spelling. British researchers concerned with reading difficulties, such as Critchley (1964), Vernon (1957), and Bannatyne (1965), attempt to make a sharp differentiation between these two kinds of reading disturbances. Word blindness, or specific dyslexia, is supposed to be of constitutional origin. In this country opinions differ in this regard. Wepman et al. (1960), Lauretta Bender (1956), Katrina de Hirsch (1952), and others, differentiate between learning difficulties caused by brain pathology and those caused by developmental lag; others, such as Myklebust (1963), are of the opinion that such strict division cannot be made. If the latter is correct, then the concept of constitutional dyslexia or specific word blindness serves no purpose.

The writer's own experience does not indicate that specific reading disturbance is very specific. When a variety of auditory- and visual-perceptual abilities, sensori-motor skills, language functions, and higher thought processes are carefully examined, then the dyslexic is frequently found to have multiple handicaps. In classroom teaching it is certainly not necessary to differentiate between a specific reading disability and minimal brain damage, as treatment depends on the specific symptoms. Nevertheless, teachers need to be acquainted with the concept of specific dyslexia, as it frequently appears in the literature.

Specific Techniques in Remedial Reading

When the multiplicity of psychological processes which enter into the reading process are contemplated, one does not wonder that so many children have trouble in reading, but is rather astonished that so many can read after all. Fortunately, although the multiplicity of abilities entering into the reading process causes frequent difficulties, it also affords a multiplicity of levers to help the child who cannot read. One ability or method of attack can compensate or substitute for another. For instance, we know that reading is a visual process; nevertheless, the blind can learn to read by tactile methods. We realize that auditory processes are involved in reading, but the deaf can read the same material as the hearing child. The aphasic who cannot make sense of sound patterns can learn to grasp the meaning of words and sentences through methods which help him to make the word symbol more concrete. But for each of these handicaps special methods have to be devised so that optimum reading skills can be acquired.

The remedial methods which can be used to advantage can be divided roughly into two groups: those which attempt to strengthen the lagging abilities and those which substitute intact functions for the lagging ones. The division is not always a sharp one. For instance, kinesthetic methods are helpful because they substitute the kinesthetic mode of perception for the visual one, but they can also improve and strengthen visual perception. A technique which is a crutch and used for compensation may at the same time train the defective ability. For example, the use of a marker or a trailing pencil compensates for defective eye movements in reading, while at the same time promoting smoother eye movements.

There are, of course, a multitude of remedial methods, which it is impossible to describe or enumerate in this paper. However, a few basic considerations will be mentioned.

No area of development—sensori-motor, language, perception, higher intellectual functions, emotional and social adjustment—should be neglected. It is also necessary for the teacher to be aware of what part of these areas is affected. For example, difficulties in visual perception and in auditory perception both need consideration. Auditory-perceptual difficulties can be ameliorated by specific or by functional teaching of phonics. (The writer's bias favors functional teaching.) An extended period of readiness training may be necessary before the child can learn phonics or can learn to read by any phonic methods. Such readiness training has been outlined herein. Phonics are also helpful for those children who have difficulties with the visual analysis and synthesis of words—the auditory skills (auding) help to compensate for the difficulties in visual perception. In any case, the purpose of phonics is to help the child recognize the correspondence between the phoneme and the grapheme (between the auditory stimulus and the printed symbol). Phonics and so-called linguistics readers can be used for training; phonic workbooks may be of help if not used mechanically.

The teacher should recognize that the majority of remedial reading methods use the phonic approach because the essence of the reading process is the establishment of correspondence between the visual stimuli (letters and words) and the auditory stimuli (the sounds of letters and words). The teacher should, therefore, be cognizant of such methods of approach as the Initial Teaching Alphabet (Downing, 1964) and the Gillingham method (1946).

The disadvantage of phonic methods is that they may be stultifying and discouragingly difficult for children whose auditory perception is inadequate. With such children, a visual approach (the whole-word method) or a kinesthetic approach (Fernald, 1943) may have to be used extensively while auditory perception is developed simultaneously. Whether or not specific kinesthetic methods are used, the integration of reading, writing, and spelling is helpful for all children, and especially helpful in the acquisition of phonics.

While kinesthetic methods form a bridge between temporal sequences (hearing) and spatial sequences (seeing), they are not the only methods which can be used to help facilitate the association between the printed letter or the word and its sound. Such association depends also in part on the presentation of the letter or word. If implied movement is a component of the visual stimulus, or if actual movement occurs with it, association is made easier for many children. If the letter "R" is presented in the shape of a man running or if a child is told to jump as he reads the word "jump," learning will be facilitated. Another method for promoting word-sound association is the simultaneous presentation of auditory and visual stimuli by means of a tape recorder. This method is essential for some children.

The kinesthetic methods discussed before employ another sense modality in addition to the visual and auditory ones. However, there are cases in which one sense modality has to be completely eliminated and another substituted, if learning to read is to be accomplished. Methods in which a child learns a word by writing it while blindfolded have been described in a paper on corrective reading (Frostig, 1965).

Some children can establish associations between the printed word, its sound pattern, and its meaning quite easily, but cannot establish a stable memory trace. Children with this difficulty need a great deal of overlearning. Methods utilizing overlearning have also been discussed in the afore-mentioned paper (Frostig, 1965).

Whenever there is any difficulty in the recognition of previously learned words, repetition is the best method to promote learning. Repetition, however, should not be automatic, too frequent, or boring. Because the difficulty could be caused by a problem in constancy of perception, repetition should never be exactly the same but should use slight variations of form or context. The language program based on the ITPA (Frostig, 1965) also includes remedial exercises for memory functions.

Imagery is necesary for the comprehension of what is read by the child or what is read or said to him, and exercises in imagery have been found to be most helpful and most necessary.

As has already been discussed, the training of higher thought processes is also important, and in this respect the teacher should be especially aware of the work of Bruner and of Levi.

SUMMARY

This paper has outlined the need for special methods for teaching reading based on the symptomatology of each child. Etiology was discussed because it is most important that the teacher understand the role of etiology. It was not considered in depth, however, for the postulate basic to this paper is that diagnosis and evaluation of the symptoms, and not etiological findings, must be the foundation of any remedial teaching.

Many functions are involved in the act of reading. They should be explored in the testing situation. For the purpose of training, however, a clear-cut separation of these functions is not always possible, nor should such a separation be attempted, because one training procedure may train many abilities simultaneously. This is not only a necessity but also an advantage.

The following areas of reading should be considered and developed whenever they are found to be disturbed:

1. Sensori-motor skills.

2. Visual-perceptual skills, both static and sequential, including the ability to perceive forms, to discriminate between figure and ground, and to recognize position in space and spatial relationships. Especially important is the perception of and memory for sequences.

3. In regard to auditory skills, training should be given in the dis-

crimination of sounds (especially speech sounds), blending sounds, differentiating sounds both in isolation and in the context of words, and in the perception of and memory for auditory sequences.

4. The association between auditory and visual stimuli is sometimes disturbed in children who show no evidence of deficits in either auditory- or visual-perceptual skills alone. The teacher should know what methods can be used to help a child associate these two sense channels.

5. Higher thought processes enter increasingly into the reading process as the child grows older. A child should learn to keep a thought in mind, to manipulate ideas, and to develop all those mental abilities which lead to comprehension and judgment of what the child reads, such as concept formation, manipulation of relationships, translation of symbols, and other higher cognitive functions.

6. Finally, some children have some specific difficulties with the association of symbols with meaning. Techniques are continuously being developed and refined in order to ameliorate this difficulty.

One aspect of the teaching of reading, which is immensely important, has been intentionally omitted because of space considerations, namely, helping children who cannot read because of emotional disturbances. It should at least be stated, however, that the teaching of reading to any child should always take into consideration his emotional needs and difficulties.

Clinical experience indicates that children with deficits in visual or auditory perception or in language skills, or even with a general lag in intellectual development, can most frequently learn to read, and even learn to do so relatively effortlessly, if the proper specific methods are used.

SELECTED REFERENCES

Abercrombie, M. L. J. "Perception and eye movements: Some speculation on disorders in cerebral palsy," *Cerebral Palsy Bulletin,* 1960, 2(3), 142–148.

Ayres, Jean. "Patterns of perceptual-motor dysfunction in children: Factor analytic study," *Perceptual and Motor Skills,* 1965, 20, 335–368.

Bannatyne, Alex. "Research needs in dyslexia," *Word Blind Committee Bulletin,* 1965, 1, 5–10.

Bender, L. *Psychopathology of children with organic brain disorders.* Springfield, Ill.: Charles C Thomas, 1956.

Braun, Jean S. "Relation between concept formation ability and reading achievement at three developmental levels," *Child Development,* 1963, 34(3), 675–682.

Bruner, J. S., Goodnow, J. J., and Austin, G. A. *A study of thinking.* New York: Science Edition, 1962.

Critchley, M. *Developmental dyslexia.* London: Heinemann, 1964.

Cureton, Thomas. "18-item motor fitness test," *Physical fitness workbook.* Champaign: University of Illinois, 1942.

de Hirsch, Katrina. "Specific dyslexia of strephosymbolia," *Folia Phoniatrica,* 1952, 4(4).

Downing, J. "The prevention of communication disorders by the use of a simplified alphabet," *Developmental and Child Neurology,* 1964, 6, 113–124.

Dunn, L., and Smith, J. O. *Peabody language development kit.* Minneapolis: American Guidance Service, 1965.

Fernald, Grace M. *Remedial techniques in basic school subjects.* New York: McGraw-Hill, 1943.

Froebel, F. *The education of man.* New York: Appleton, 1900.

Frostig, M. "Corrective reading in the classroom," *The Reading Teacher,* 1965, 18(7), 573–580.

———. "Language program based on the Illinois Test of Psycholinguistic Abilities," Research draft, available from the author, Los Angeles, Calif.

Frostig, M., and Horne, D. *The Frostig program for the development of visual perception.* Chicago: Follett, 1964.

Frostig, M., Lefever, D. W., and Whittlesey, J. R. B. *The Marrianne Frostig developmental test of visual perception.* Palo Alto, Calif.: Consulting Psychologist Press, 1964.

Gallagher, J. R. In *Word blindness or specific developmental dyslexia.* A. W. Franklin (ed.). London, 1962.

Gesell, A., and Amatruda, C. S. *Developmental diagnosis.* New York: Paul B. Hoeber, 1947.

Gillingham, A. *Remedial training of children with specific disability in reading, spelling and penmanship.* Distributed by the author, 1946.

Goldstein, K. *Language and language disturbances.* New York: Grune & Stratton, 1948.

Gooddy, W. Directional features of reading and writing. *Proceedings of the Royal Society of Medicine, Section on Neurology,* 1963, 56, 206–209.

Hart, N. S. W. "Experimental language development programme, based on Osgood's language theory and ITPA profiles," mimeograph, available from the author, Department of Education, University of Queensland, Australia.

Ingram, T. T. S. "The dyslexic child," *Word Blind Committee Bulletin,* 1965, 1(4), 1–5.

Itard, Jean M. G. *The wild boy of Aveyron.* New York: Appleton-Century-Crofts, 1932.

Kephart, N. C. *The slow learner in the classroom.* Columbus, Ohio: Charles E. Merrill, 1960.

———. *The brain injured child in the classroom.* Chicago: The National Society for Crippled Children and Adults, Inc., 1963.

Kirk, S. A. *Teaching reading to slow-learning children.* Cambridge, Mass.: Houghton-Mifflin, 1940.

Kirk, S. A., and McCarthy, J. P. *Illinois Test of Psycholinguistic Abilities.* Urbana: University of Illinois Press, 1961.

Kraus, H. "Kraus-Weber tests for minimum muscular fitness," in *Therapeutic exercises.* Springfield, Ill.: Charles C Thomas, 1963.

Levi, Aurelia. "Treatment of a disorder of perception and concept formation in a case of school failure," *Journal of Consulting Psychology,* 1965, 29(4), 289–295.

Maslow, P., Frostig, M., Lefever, D. W., and Whittlesey, J. R. P. "The Marianne Frostig developmental test of visual perception, 1963 standardization," *Perceptual and Motor Skills,* Monograph supplement, 1964, 19(2).

Montessori, Maria. Dr. *Montessori's own handbook.* New York: Shocken Books, 1965.

Mosston, Muska. *Developmental movement.* Columbus, Ohio: Merrill Books, 1965.

Myklebust, Helmer. "Neurological learning disorders in children," in *Conference on children with minimal brain impairment.* Urbana, Ill.: Easter Seal Research Foundation, 1963.

Peel, E. A. *The pupil's thinking.* London: Oldbourne, 1960.

Piaget, J. *The construction of reality in the child.* M. Cook (trans.). New York: Basic Books, 1954.

———. *Judgment and reasoning in the child.* M. Warden (trans.). Paterson, N.J.: Littlefield, Adams & Co., 1959.

———. *The origins of intelligence in children.* M. Cook (trans.). New York: International Universities Press, 1952.

Potter, M. C. *Perception of symbol orientation and early reading success.* New York: Columbia University Teachers College, Bureau of Publications, 1949.

Radler, D. H., and Kephart, N. C. *Success through play.* New York: Harper, 1960.

Reitan, R. "A research program on the psychological effects of brain lesions in human beings," in *International review of research in mental retardation.* N. R. Ellis (ed.). New York: Academic Press.

Strauss, A. A., and Kephart, N. C. *Psychopathology and education of the brain injured child. Vol. II. Progress in theory and clinic.* New York: Grune & Stratton, 1955.

Sutphin, Florence E. *A perceptual testing and training handbook for first grade teachers.* Winter Haven, Fla.: Winter Haven Lions Research Foundation, 1964, pp. 15–16.

Vernon, M. D. *Backwardness in reading: The study of its nature and origin.* New York: Cambridge University Press, 1957.

Wechsler, D. *Wechsler Intelligence Scale for Children.* New York: The Psychological Corporation, 1949.

Wepman, J. M. *Wepman test of auditory discrimination.* Chicago: Language Research Associates, 1958.

Wepman, J. M., Jones, L. V., Bock, R. D., and Van Pelt, D. "Studies in aphasia: Background and theoretical formulations," *Journal of Speech and Hearing Disorders,* 1960, 25(4).

Werner, H. *Comparative psychology of mental development.* New York: International Universities Press, 1957.

Comment

FROSTIG: The teacher of reading has not only to know specific methods which improve the reading process per se, but also those methods which improve underlying abilities basic to difficulties which the child has that have to be improved before the child can gain in reading.

When we find that the child has difficulties in language or with the language program, we work with perceptual programs. We work with programs of higher phonic dysfunctions, although we do not necessarily postpone the reading, which is very often integrated from the beginning.

We suggest application of basic skills to the *process* of reading and combine readiness training with beginning reading so that time is saved when possible.

Slow step-by-step progress and continued success is necessary to overcome the sense of hopelessness in the older child. This is true with all children, but there has to be continued success, especially, with older children.

The methods must vary not only with disturbed functions but also with the child's age level, because the interests of the child change. It is important for the teacher to realize that optimum remediation depends on careful diagnostic exploration because remediation may have to vary according to the disturbance, and therefore, no one single method will be the correct approach for all children.

Teaching is always based on a diagnostic survey of the child's disabilities. A short survey of the range of reading difficulties is one of the necessary prerequisites for the education of teachers of children with learning difficulties. This survey should not only include a discussion of the abilities which are necessary for the reading process to proceed smoothly, but it should be an overview of the development of psychological functions from infancy through adolescence. Such a survey will make the concept of readiness not only a maturational concept, but it can be the basis of the teaching practices. The teacher is the key professional person responsible for its promotion. The teacher in the classroom is not always able to make a diagnosis, but he obtains the outline of the child's difficulties and then develops a teacher evaluation sheet which is the reworking of what he is getting from the psychologist. He must then work with the psychologist and with the educational therapist.

The developmental steps which we consider are the sensori-motor phases. We must try to help the teacher understand their importance, which is well explained by developmental theory—Piaget and Gesell, for example, who from very different sides arrived at the same conclusions. Even age-old practices all point in the same direction, but we also want the teacher to understand the limitations. We want him to know that good sensori-motor development does not guarantee smooth progress during later developmental stages. Despite extremely inhibited sensori-motor development, language and higher thought processes may develop normally, as in some children with cerebral palsy. The explanation given by Piaget is that the perception of movement may substitute for the movement itself in children.

During the period from approximately two to four years of age language is a major developmental task. Educators, therefore, must include a great deal of understanding of language development and show the teacher how to help the children with language development.

The development of visual-perceptual abilities which Piaget calls the "intuitive stage" occurs from four to seven and a half years.

I cannot go into the different areas of development or the deficits which we find inherent, but we do feel, whether it is in reading or arithmetic or whatever subject we teach, it is exceedingly important that we make this exploration for each child and then for the class as a whole in order to know how to group the children flexibly all through the school day. In every area we feel that testing and remediation must be very specific.

There are so many difficulties which one really can't find. There are so many specific abilities that one doesn't know how to train them. But there is fortunately the treatment for these difficulties, if systematically applied, which is quite successful. In the treatment we do not treat the little things separately, but we treat them as a group. We treat them as integrated with other abilities. And just as there are many kinds of disabilities, there are also many abilities which a person has, and we have to teach through them.

With a child who cannot communicate, we must teach oral communication first, because to forget oral communication means you don't get anywhere.

We have to teach a child who cannot move how to perceive movement, how to perceive space without movement. Similarly, we have to use a great deal of sequential routine to help children who cannot read.

GALLAGHER: I think one of the things that would be an implication for training of teachers is to spend more time thinking about diagnosis or identification of functional defects. The teacher might spend more time on developmental processes; he might study Piaget more closely than you would study typical educational psychology. He would spend more time on remedial techniques and methods in working with individual children on specific deficits.

This approach has implications in the area of curriculum development. It does no good to tell somebody that a youngster is functioning at the four-year level in the auditory-vocal sequential subtest if you can't tell them what to do about it, or if you can't give the teachers a sequence of exercises that they can carry through as a result of this information. For the diagnosis to be complete, you must lay out rather specific remedial practices which follow from that diagnosis.

FREIDUS: But we're not talking about remedial work, really, when we are talking about the education of "these children." We're talking about starting from scratch before you need to do anything remedial. We're talking about laying so thorough a foundation that they learn with pleasure.

FROSTIG: We have found out in teaching spelling that there are many children who have difficulties in visualization. If we help the children to develop visualization through different techniques, they can learn to spell. The teacher must be oriented to this point of view.

GROSSMAN: We are dealing with a lot of information that unfortunately has been around for a number of years and primarily is the outgrowth of clinical observations of adults who lost the ability once attained for certain functions. This has to do with the phenomenon of word blindness which we see in adults who had certain lesions of the brain and with aphasia. I think, unfortunately, what has happened is that a great many of these observations have become incorporated into certain theoretical models and incorrectly applied. There is certainly a uniqueness about these problems in children which makes them quite different from those seen in the adults. One of the most important things is that in children we have an organism that is growing and changing considerably. The phenomenon of maturation is not properly considered in some of these theoretical models that people talk about, and particularly when they deal with these problems in children. Unfortunately, most people simply try to apply knowledge that has been gained in adults to the problems that they see in children or vice versa.

What we need are more approaches similar to Dr. Frostig's, where there is a developmental concept. Something that is perhaps similar to and also different from the problems seen in the adults.

CRUICKSHANK: In Dr. Frostig's paper she stresses a point which is exceedingly important and needs to be thoroughly elaborated, namely, the relationship between communicative disorders and reading disabilities (or it might be number disabilities or handwriting disabilities).

Somehow or other in the training of teachers of brain-injured children, we have to bring to them the interrelationship of the disability and its impact on a wide variety of learning areas. It's true that what we may see in a communicative disorder may also be the same as or may be basic to what is happening in the number-concept disorders. The child's inability to conceptualize auditory stimuli may be the reason he can't spell or he can't read or compute. This concept needs much amplification in the future basic training of teachers of brain-injured children.

Chapter 7

The Needs of Teachers for Specialized
Information on Number Concepts

ELIZABETH S. FREIDUS

EDITORIAL NOTE.—Mrs. Freidus' long experience and many
years of direct contact with brain-injured children provides
her with a background for authoritative statements in considering their education. While this paper deals with a segment of
the educational program, Mrs. Freidus would be the first to
insist that the educational program of the brain-injured child
must be conceptualized as a unity. Reading, discussed in Chapter 6, and number concepts, discussed in this chapter, have been
arbitrarily selected as two examples in the total teaching program which demonstrate the specialized competencies required
of teachers of brain-injured children. The points of view taken
by the two authors of Chapters 6 and 7 must apply indeed to all
areas, i.e., spelling, handwriting, and as well, often to a marked
degree, in other areas of learning which are based on the previously mentioned four fundamental skills, as for example, social
studies.

ELIZABETH S. FREIDUS prepares teachers for the education of neurologically impaired children at Columbia University's Teachers College and at New York University's School of Education. She supervises the Special Problems Program at Lexington School for the Deaf, and is educational director of The Gateway School for children with learning disabilities, both in New York City. From its inception in 1964, she has been program director of the Research and Study Center of the New York Association for Brain Injured Children, at Kerhonkson, New York, a summer camp facility for the study of brain-injured children and their families.

Mrs. Freidus studied at Hunter College and Cornell, Columbia, and New York Universities and completed a teaching internship under the late Dr. Alfred Strauss and Dr. Laura Lehtinen at the Cove Schools. In 1952, she served as educational director of the Henry Hudson School in New York, the first school for such children in the East.

Her writings include: "The Child with Brain Damage," in the *Proceedings of the 1959 Annual Meeting of the Association for the Aid of Crippled Children;* her chapter in *The "Brain Injured" Child;* and her chapter on "Methodology for the Classroom Teacher," *The Special Child in Century 21.*

Chapter 7

The Needs of Teachers for Specialized Information on Number Concepts

ELIZABETH S. FREIDUS

> . . . Education must essentially be the setting in order of a ferment already stirring in the mind. . . .
>
> ALFRED NORTH WHITEHEAD

Five little boys who might be first or second graders are sitting around a table with their teacher, who is about to cut an apple into pieces for sharing. "How many pieces do we need, Steven?" But Steven is halfway across the room to check on a truck he heard passing. He takes a quick look over his shoulder and says, "Five," as he takes off again.

"How many do *you* think, Paul?" Paul shifts into gear laboriously, looks, points, counts, starts all over again from the beginning several times. Finally he asks, "Six?"

Robert is next. He is ready with, "Do I know how to do that? Is it easy? No, I don't want to do it," and starts to whine. He is encouraged to try, then chants the numbers from one to ten, without regard for where his finger is pointing. There is no attempt to match numeral to child.

When Gregory is called on, he responds with, "My Daddy went fishing yesterday." He is reminded, "We're talking about this apple. How many pieces do we need?" Pointing to one child after another, but not in any particular sequence, he says, "One for him and one for him, . . ."

At last it is Peter's turn to share a discovery. Jumping up and down with excitement he shouts, "Paul and Steven are both right. Paul counted boys and Steven counted people. That's why Steven's was more. Five boys and six people. They're both right!" Peter is the youngest in the group.

The boys are in a class for brain-injured children. No two have had

113

the same kind or amount of schooling. No two have been placed in the class for the same reasons. No two approached the problem of the apple armed with the same elements of readiness for solving it. Their common need is individualized help in organizing their patterns of learning.

THE PROBLEM

Most children arrive at school having already succeeded in teaching themselves how to learn independently or with a minimum of help from adults. They find ways of filling gaps for themselves, almost in spite of the quality of teaching to which they may be exposed. Others, those with whom we are concerned, come to school without having established consistently effective learning patterns. Each one needs help in clarifying, strengthening, reorganizing his style of learning.

A common characteristic is anxiety, born of gaps in ability to deal with an inconsistently perceived environment. The anxiety expresses itself in many undesirable ways, generating chain reactions of avoidance mechanisms. The child who resists any experience that might expose an inadequacy deprives himself of opportunities to remove the very inadequacies that threaten him. It is a self-perpetuating pattern of deprivations built upon deprivations.

The child being considered needs help in: (1) receiving sensory information reliably, (2) processing it for meaning, (3) organizing and executing an appropriate response, and (4) monitoring the response to determine how it should be stored for future use. In other words, he needs help in learning how to learn.

If a teacher is to build an individualized educational program in number concepts for each of these very different children, his training must insure competence in several interrelated areas:

1. The ability to analyze the subject matter to be learned into its basic components. *What is involved* in being able to use a dial phone? —to make change?—to tell time? For teaching number concepts, this ability implies a thorough understanding of the structure of our number system and the processes by which it can be manipulated.

2. The ability to "read children," that is, (a) to decipher each child's habitual approach to the demands of his environment, as well as (b) to determine the elements of readiness that he brings to a specific learning task. He approaches the task with a spotty, unique accumulation of learning gathered from previous interactions with his environment. He functions at several different levels, some well above and others far below his mean. Therefore, nothing can be assumed. Every aspect of his readiness needs to be checked.

3. The ability to (a) assemble an extensive repertoire of teaching

methods, learning materials, techniques, skills, games, and other aids, and (b) evaluate and select from among them those best suited to meet specific needs as they arise.

4. The ability to create and maintain a classroom atmosphere conducive to learning by (a) constructively manipulating the timing and physical arrangements of the room, (b) providing leadership and guidance in human interaction, setting limits, and (c) taking full advantage of the resources to be found in the children's own families, in the school, the community, and in the contributions of allied disciplines.

If a teacher can discern what a child is trying to do in his informational interaction with the environment, and if that teacher can have on hand materials relevant to that intention, if he can impose a relevant challenge with which the child can cope, supply a relevant model for imitation, or pose a relevant question that the child can answer, that teacher can call forth the kind of accommodative change that constitutes psychological development or growth.

JOHN MCVICKER HUNT

THE SUBJECT MATTER

Every teacher has been exposed to arithmetic in elementary school. This does not imply an understanding of how our number system is structured or of what is involved in being able to learn it. Most adults of today, teachers included, have been taught arithmetic by rote, with no attempt to present underlying structure. Rote learning relies upon recall of a single pattern, neither necessarily part of a larger whole, nor necessarily related to anything else meaningfully. Rote learning lacks a diversity of memory hooks, of associations for recapturing meaning. Teaching that aims toward an understanding of a subject's basic structure is far more effective than is teaching for isolated skills or facts, learned by rote.

In teaching number concepts one needs primarily to recognize that arithmetic is a way of thinking about the quantitative aspects of life, and that it is also a language for expressing and dealing with them. It is a language with which to describe, measure, manipulate, and record quantitative relationships and operations.

The symbols out of which any language is built, if they are to be useful for thought and communication, must derive their meaning from reality. The more solidly they are based upon concrete experience, the more readily, the more reliably, can the meanings they express be abstracted and manipulated, and the more accurately can they be remembered.

This is especially true for children whose style of learning is inefficient. They need to base their understanding upon a greater variety of
concrete experiences, offered in more detailed steps, than do most other
children. Rather than needing drill, they require opportunities to make
the same discovery in a great many different concrete ways, all of which
they are helped to integrate into an applicable generalization. The more
firmly and broadly a generalization is rooted in experience, the more
flexibly can the child make use of it, and the more easily will he be able
to move from concrete materials to pictured representations, then finally
to spoken and written number symbols.

When comprehension makes possible the substitute of symbols for
reality, with meaning, then and only then is facility developed by repetitive practice, or drill. It is a final step based upon a solid foundation of
meaning.

Sets and Matching

An important requisite for understanding the meaning of numbers,
so clearly demonstrated by Peter at the table, is the ability to group
objects into sets so they can be counted. A child cannot match objects
for grouping without first being able to organize figure and ground so
that a single object may be focused upon and studied. When a second
object is then focused upon to be matched to the first, the concept of
"the same" must be ready to be applied. For this, the criterion for
matching needs to be held firmly in mind. "The same" may have to do
with color, size, form, function, or any other chosen characteristic. It
may even have to do with a combination of characteristics. A set may
be composed of children with blue eyes, boys with freckles, chairs made
of wood, or any other items sharing a bond of likenesses which the
child must be able to keep in mind.

Some children require a greater number and variety of experiences
in matching than do others before they can operate in terms of sets.
There are many possible reasons for this, which a teacher must learn to
identify and deal with, but whatever the reason, practice can be provided
in materials and at levels to suit the needs of the individual child. For
example, he might look for the red beads in a box containing two colors,
or the spheres in a collection of cubes, cylinders, and spheres, or pictures
of cars in a magazine, or pictures of things with names that start with
the sound "m-m-m," or he might search the calendar for months that
have thirty-one days. Older children might match and sort real hard-
ware, table cutlery, dishes or laundry, hair rollers, or menu items.

Teachers who are clear about what they are trying to accomplish
need not limit themselves to commercial, ready-made teaching materials.

They can make creative use of the aids to learning that are found everywhere and that offer motivation without threat to children who have lived in expectation of failure.

Relationship Concepts

Matching and sorting prepare the way for comparing and relating. Normally, the formation of relationship concepts begins long before a child reaches school age, while he is learning to understand bigger-smaller, above-below, in front of–behind, nearer-farther, heavier-lighter, before-after, sooner-later, more-less. Teachers need to appreciate the cumulative quality of babies' experiences as they explore their environment—experiences, for example, like those which teach a baby about relative heights. He discovers that he can easily reach what is lying on top of the coffee table, while only when he stretches as high as he can is it possible for him to reach the edges of the kitchen table. When he tries to sit up after crawling under the tables, he bumps his head under the low one, but is able to sit up comfortably in the shelter of the other.

Children are constantly discovering relationships, confirming one discovery with another, using one sense to elaborate upon what another has learned. Teachers must learn to determine what kind of information has been acquired and how effectively it has been received and integrated for use in interpreting new situations.

Clarity in relationship concepts is basic to understanding number concepts. Some children approach school learning without having established this foundation strongly enough during their preschool years. They need opportunities to solve many kinds of problems involving quantitative comparison—opportunities planned to fill gaps left by experiences that are insufficient in number or inadequate in awareness or clarity of meaning.

Measuring and Pairing

Assuming that a child has assimilated what is required for grouping objects into sets, that he has learned to compare individual objects to each other, he can now begin to compare sets. At first this is done by estimation: Will this block fit into this space? Will the sand in this container just fill that one? Have we enough cookies for all of us? The estimation is verified by measuring (fitting the block into the space, pouring the sand into the container) or pairing, one to one: "Here's a cookie for you, a cookie for you, . . ." until everyone is served. Later, moving almost imperceptibly from concrete toward abstract, it becomes, "One for Jimmy, one for Mary, one for Ruth," as the cookies are dropped into the serving dish. This is in preparation for assigning one numeral to each object in the set, so they can be counted.

Counting

Most children learn to count before they come to school. Their counting may be no more than a chant using what might as well be nonsense syllables, since they probably express no clear quantitative relationships. However, the chant of numerals in proper sequence helps make it possible for a child to match each object to a number symbol, one to one, for true counting. He may not be able to do this by just looking at each object in turn, or even by pointing. He may need to move each object, slide it from one side of the table to the other, pick it up and put it down with a thud, or press it into the palm of his other hand, to emphasize the one-ness of it. Then, as he assigns a number name to each, one, two, three, what he really means is, first, second, third, in the series of items. Each is matched to a numeral until the last numeral in the series represents the total quantity.

Sequential Values

In our number system, numerals are arranged in a clearly defined sequential order, from which their values are determined. Accepting any unit of measurement as the meaning of one (an inch, a mile, a penny, a dime, a pound, a ton, a minute, an hour, a year) each numeral derives its value meaning from its sequential position in relation to one. Thus, since two comes next after one, it has the value of one more than one, three has the value of one more than two, and so on. The relationship is consistent, no matter what the unit of measurement may be. A great variety of concrete experiences are needed to make this relationship clear.

Having learned to estimate set size, then measure or count by pairing a numeral with each object, the child looks for sets of the same measurement or containing the same number of elements: two hands, two inches, two pounds, two hours. The more sets of like numerical quantity he can find, the more does he strengthen his comprehension of the quality of two-ness, three-ness, four-ness, in relation to each other, and the more easily can he then associate a number symbol, oral or written, to that quantity.

Then, making use of the various aspects of readiness that he has accumulated, he chooses a set, his family for example, and arranges its members in order of age, height, weight, or any criterion he chooses. This is complemented by experience with other sets composed of members with easily measured differences. The sequential differences may be in any dimension: size, weight, intensity of color, volume or pitch of sound, tempo, texture, and so on. It is through such activities that every numeral takes on a consistent relationship to every other one.

Relationship of Parts to Whole, Parts to Each Other

The child can now explore the relationship of parts to the whole and parts to each other, using self-correcting materials. Through them he discovers how very consistently two given quantities, when combined, always equal the same larger quantity. He learns how to record his discoveries in sentences or algorisms. He experiments with combinations and discovers that: given two parts, he can predict what the whole will be, or given the whole and one part, he can produce the missing part; he can even detach a small set from a larger one and determine the value of the remainder—with ever fewer occasions to seek concrete support.

Operations

All of these discoveries he records and confirms. Out of them grow generalizations with which he can manipulate discovered facts. When he is sure of those facts, he is ready to develop fluency in expressing and manipulating them. He has been learning to operate upon sets, not only concretely, but symbolically as well. The number facts up to ten are becoming an important part of his equipment for dealing with the quantitative aspects of life.

The Decimal System

The next step is to learn our system of numeration and notation beyond ten and upon the base ten, or the decimal system. Is the set made of single grapes or bunches of grapes?—of single sticks or bundles of ten?—of single cubes or rods measuring ten cubes in length?

When teachers themselves experiment with materials offered to children, they can truly understand the use and importance of a number line or track, a place-values box, a ten-square counting frame, dimes and pennies, sticks for bundling, poker chips or checkers for stacking, and other materials for demonstrating the structure of our decimal system. The dual role of zero, both as an expression of a quantity and as a place-holder, is easily made clear with the help of these materials.

After comprehension, facility in notation and in analysis and synthesis of large numbers is developed through individual and group games. Children enjoy experimenting with astronomical quantities, especially if they understand their structure.

If the child has come this far in his comprehension of the language of numbers, and if this has come about with concern for even the most elementary levels of readiness, he should be able to learn and apply the laws relating to operations upon sets, and from there to go on to new adventures in quantitative manipulation. He should most certainly not have the problem of the young man who complained that he could never remember, in multiplication examples, whether you add or subtract "when you get under the line."

A major weakness in teacher preparation has been that teachers have been insufficiently impressed with the importance of checking back far enough in a child's previously acquired learning to insure readiness for what now needs to be learned. Time and effort invested in building a firm foundation can prevent many of the difficulties that children experience as they try to move on to more advanced, more abstract arithmetical processes.

He [the student] first learns his mathematics as a way of thinking, not as a set of skills. . . . Once a concept has been established we practice thinking with the concept. . . . We finally symbolize it [this type of thinking] in the mature computational processes that become the tools with which we fashion any future thinking with these concepts. Then we practice or drill with the tools until they are efficient devices under our conceptual and manipulatory control.

HOWARD F. FEHR

UNDERSTANDING THE CHILD

If learning to understand subject matter is important for teacher preparation, learning to understand the child is at least equally important. One aspect of the art of teaching is sensitivity to the balance between the requirements of a situation and the complex of past experience which the child brings to dealing with it. It is the delicate balance between challenge and threat that must be maintained at the most productive level possible. The approach is not simply:

Did he or did he not complete this task successfully? Specifically:

What did this situation require of him?

What strengths or weaknesses, what skills or disabilities did he bring to the solution of this problem?

How did his adaptations to deficiencies affect his approach to this situation?

What other tasks does he approach in the same way?

What is common to them all?

In what respects is his readiness for this type and level of activity adequate?

In what respects is it incomplete or inadequate? What other activities might be constructively inflenced if the readiness for this one is strengthened? How effectively does this child make use of previous learning in his approach to new situations? In what ways has this experience added to the child's fund of possible solutions to future problems?

Diagnostic teaching is built upon the answers to questions such as these. Knowledge about both the process of learning and the individual child makes it possible for the teacher to custom-build a flexible program for each child, to meet the requirements of both his unique learning style and his readiness for mastering a particular subject or increment of learning.

The Background

The process of learning is most profitably studied in relation to normal child development, particularly in the earliest stages when patterns of learning are being established. *For this, there is no substitute for hours of observation of babies and young children. Further, there is no substitute for interacting with children as they go about the business of teaching themselves to deal with their environment.*

To be digested most effectively, such observation and interaction require a great deal of discussion and sharing of personal reactions to children's ways of solving problems. They require careful introspection into one's own learning patterns. Only when the conclusions of others are seen through the eyes of personal experience does usable knowledge result. Only after the ideas of others have been assimilated in relation to one's own experience can they be used in situations requiring more than rote application. Only then can they be put to use flexibly, intelligently, constructively. Preparation for creative teaching, therefore, involves a combination of lectures and reading, observation, practice, and discussion. Theory, enriched by reality experienced in many different ways, then forms the basis for flexibly applicable generalizations.

Diagnostic Teaching

Familiarity with the earliest stages in the development of learning patterns is important because that is where the gaps are most often found in children who have learning disabilities. By the time the children arrive at school, those gaps, though still interfering with progress, are usually hidden under a precarious, not necessarily constructive, overlay of adaptations and compensations.

Therefore, in addition to normal child development, teacher preparation must include an overview of the known range of primary disorders and of their many possible influences upon a child's progress as a learning, adapting organism. This should be followed by intensive study, both theoretical and practical, of the secondary disabilities that grow out of them, the chain reactions of self-defeating mechanisms for avoiding failure and embarrassment. The power of secondary deprivations and disabilities to turn a minor disorder into a major handicap, and thus impair the total development of the child, deserves special consideration.

Children who have lived all their lives in the shadow of chronic failure become sensitive to anything that might draw attention to their inadequacies. The brighter the child, the more ways will he find to avoid or hide embarrassment, the more cleverly will he resist the possibility of another failure. He may want desperately to learn, to be like other children of his age, but he can't risk the failure he is convinced is inevitable. For him, learning must be approached in new ways—unthreatening, yet challenging enough not to humiliate him by seeming too simple.

The diagnostic teacher makes use of avoidance behavior by learning to recognize its habitual manifestations in each child. For example, when a child begins to clown or disrupt, it is possible that he anticipates failure and is trying to avoid it. If he deliberately breaks up an activity, preferring to risk punishment rather than exposure of an inadequacy, the activity must hold great threat for him. His problems are elusive, but his behavior has offered a possible clue to one of them. Similar behavior recurring in other situations may reveal the kind of threat they hold in common. The hunches derived from such comparison are then further checked against other activities.

What is learned in this way provides direction for the next steps in educational planning for this child. The teacher offers activities designed to build the readiness he needs, using materials that in no way remind him of his failures. His response to the offered activities provides clues to their appropriateness. It indicates whether and how they need to be modified, restructured at a different level, or presented in a different form through different materials.

It is unrealistic for teachers of brain-injured children to expect people other than educators to provide them with educational direction. The findings of practitioners in allied disciplines deserve careful attention. They are often helpful, as are the comments of parents, but they must be regarded as pieces to fit into the constantly evolving jigsaw puzzle of the child, rather than as the solution to the entire puzzle. It is the teacher's responsibility to coordinate all that can be learned about the child and to use it constructively as the basis for creative educational planning. This is a continuous process, ever subject to reevaluation, ever changing in response to changes in the child.

Teacher preparation, particularly for special education, would do well to emphasize the process of learning and the effects upon it of primary disorders and their secondary overlay. Rather than learning a specific method for each subject to be taught, teachers need to learn how to analyze the structure of subject matter so they can identify the readiness components for mastering it, then evaluate methods and materials for filling gaps in readiness and for meeting the requirements of each learning style.

EDUCATIONAL TOOLS

Having learned to analyze subject matter into basic components and having learned to evaluate a child's specific readiness for each task, the teacher needs to have available a variety of tools for implementing the educational program that follows. Obviously, no one approach can meet the needs of all the children, each of whom has a different combination of problems. For this reason, it is important that teacher preparation encourage and implement an appraising attitude toward educational tools. Armed with a set of basic principles, the teacher can learn to evaluate each method, each material, each activity, for the purpose it must serve.

The writings of Maria Montessori (1964, 1965) are helpful in their emphasis on self-teaching by means of self-correcting materials. For example, when working with a form board, the child does not need to rely on the authority of the adult to tell him whether or not a form matches a space. Through his own efforts to replace each form into its matching space, he strengthens his ability to separate figure from ground, to confirm with his hands what his eyes are learning to perceive, to make use of feedback from his own mistakes, then to store what he has learned so it is available for future use.

Among commercially available materials that are based on sound educational principles, perhaps the most effective for the development of number concepts are those included in Catherine Stern's Structural Arithmetic Program.* These manipulative materials are designed for discovery, experimentation, and corroboration of quantitative relationships. They lead the child in clear, logical steps from concrete experiences to abstract numerical concepts based upon them. The workbooks that accompany them are unusually well programmed. They make liberal use of two-dimensional representations of the three-dimensional mate-

* The Stern Structural Arithmetic materials can be obtained from the Houghton Mifflin Co., 110 Tremont Street, Boston, Mass. 02107.

rials as a bridge toward the use of number symbols for computation and problem-solving.

They share with other workbooks, however, the risk of being expected to do more than they were designed to do. Workbooks are for reinforcement of what has already been discovered, rather than for new learning. They can never replace live, diagnostic teaching. This is especially true in the case of children with learning disabilities.

Almost all of the arithmetic workbooks currently available require considerable modification for use with such children. One common fault is crowded, visually confusing pages, which need to be cut into sections or masked off for children with problems of figure-ground reversal. Another is that they move along too rapidly from one concept or process to the next. However, a teacher who understands the structure of the subject matter to be taught can easily find a wealth of pump-priming ideas in workbooks, without relying on them to do all the teaching.

Group games as well as teacher-made work pages are helpful for filling gaps in the transition from the concrete to the abstract, and for providing the necessary practice for fluency. Games may be simple, but they must be paced at a tempo that keeps every child involved to the extent of his ability. Even the simplest of games can offer different values to each child in the group according to his needs. Learning how to evaluate and make use of games for their multiplicity of values is an important aspect of teacher preparation.

A resourceful teacher brings his own hobbies and interests to school with him. Here again, understanding the structure of the subject matter makes it possible to find ways of using music, dance, crafts, sports, cooking, graph-making, or any number of other activities, for teaching number concepts.

An assortment of supplementary browsing materials belongs in every schoolroom. For number concepts, many different kinds of scales, rulers, containers for liquid measurement (these can be used with sand, in a deep tray), old clocks, thermometers, boxes and jars of various dimensions, sticks, checkers, poker chips, and other materials offer opportunities for matching, sorting, arranging, for estimating, comparing, and measuring.

It would be useless to provide teachers in training with lists of all available materials for developing number concepts. Rather, teachers need techniques for evaluation and selection, so that, as new developments appear, they may decide for themselves whether to use them, with or without modification.

CLASSROOM MANAGEMENT

It is valid to assume that a class for brain-injured children is made up of children who have been placed there because they were not learning according to expectation, or because their behavior could not be tolerated in a regular class, or for both reasons. It is not valid to assume that the tension generated by an atmosphere of noisy confusion needs to be accepted as inevitable. Even before the nature of each child's problems has been deciphered, there is much that a teacher can learn to do in order to create and maintain an atmosphere conducive to learning.

The teacher must be prepared: to determine what is acceptable behavior; to formulate rules clearly and adhere to them consistently, offering acceptable patterns to replace unacceptable ones; to set the general attitude of respect for each child's efforts to cope with his confusions, and for his right to achieve the most complete development possible for him; to arrange the schoolroom equipment so that it is most conducive to attentive learning; and to time activities so that everyone is constructively engaged at all times.

Everything that a child learns is in some way influenced by his family and home. This is especially true of children who, because of their inadequacies, have greater need of adult support than do others. Such children have the power to disrupt a family, tyrannizing unmercifully. In turn, they are often held back in their development by poor management at home.

Most parents of brain-injured children find it hard to be anything but confused and exhausted by their children's problems. It may be that they have been bombarded by conflicting advice, even contradictory diagnoses, until they have no confidence in professional opinion. They deserve all the skill that a teacher can be prepared to bring to creating a good working relationship with them, a mood of cooperative effort toward understanding the child so he can be helped to learn.

The teacher who recognizes that no one person has all the answers to a child's problems is well on the way to solving some of those problems. Teacher preparation must include some understanding of the work of allied professions, their scope and limitations, their tools, how they operate and how they communicate their findings, some of their problems, and their roles in relation to education. This can be accomplished with the help of guest lecturers and, even more effectively, through visits to clinics.

Much goes on in any school, in a community, in the world, that involves quantitative concepts interesting to children at some level.

Bringing the outside world into the classroom broadens a child's horizons while helping him learn what his culture demands that he learn. A teacher's awareness of this can make the difference between a dull approach to the teaching of number concepts and an exciting one that makes numbers live.

The education of the children with whom we are concerned requires far more than rote understanding of educational techniques or subject matter. Rather, teachers in this difficult, almost uncharted field need to be prepared, by knowledge and attitude, to learn as they teach, constantly evaluating the results of their work, making constructive use of their own mistakes, and becoming increasingly skillful as they deepen their understanding of children's problems. Their training must prepare them for continuous growth in professional competence.

SELECTED REFERENCES

Bruner, Jerome. *Process of education.* Cambridge, Mass.: Harvard University Press, 1962.
Fehr, Howard F. "Reorientation in mathematics education," *Teachers College Record,* 1953, 54, 430–439.
Freidus, Elizabeth. "Methodology for the classroom teacher" in *The special child in century 21.* Seattle, Wash.: Special Child Publications, 1964.
Gesell, Arnold. *The first five years of life.* New York: Harper, 1940.
Getman, G. N. *How to develop your child's intelligence.* Luverne, Minn.: Announcer Press, 1962.
Kephart, Newell C. *The slow learner in the classroom.* Columbus, Ohio: Charles E. Merrill, 1960.
Montessori, Maria. *Dr. Montessori's handbook.* New York: Schocken Books, 1965.
———. *The Montessori method.* New York: Schocken Books, 1964.
Piaget, Jean. *The child's conception of number.* New York: Humanities, 1952.
———. *The origins of intelligence in children.* New York: International Universities Press, 1952.
Stern, Catherine. *Children discover arithmetic.* New York: Harper, 1949.
Vygotsky, Lev S. *Thought and language.* New York: John Wiley, 1962.

Comment

FREIDUS: I think the first thing that any teacher needs to think about and build into himself is the ability to look at his task and decide what's involved in being able to do it. What's involved in being able to bring a spoonful of soup to your mouth without dropping it on the way? What's involved in being able to dial a telephone? What's involved in being able to tie a shoelace? You can have all the theory in the world behind you, but if you can't face the child who can't tie his shoelace and figure out what's involved in this so that you can help him through the stages to be able to do it, you're not teaching him. The subject matter has to be understood thoroughly, and the teacher has to be in a frame of mind in which it is habitual for him to break down what he is trying to teach. It's something like what occupational therapists do.

I don't think this is an impossible thing to expect of people. I think we're aiming too low in thinking about teachers. They have been hired help for too long, and I think we can raise teachers professionally—raise the level of their preparation and raise the level of our expectation for them. I think we can give them the dignity and the self-respect they haven't had. This is one way. We must get at the basic requirements of good teaching. The first requisite is being able to analyze what's involved in being able to do something, then asking the child to do it, and then, step-by-step, building toward it.

The second requisite is the ability to "read children." A number of us have been talking about intuitive behavior, built of generalizations that become so much a part of you that you can use them flexibly.

In order for this to happen, in order for teachers to have the understanding of children so that they can begin to use spontaneously what they know about children, they must have much experience with very, very young, normal children as they are developing and as they are teaching themselves. They must have this experience together with a great deal of discussion with a master teacher who can draw basic principles out of what they say and what they see. I think teachers have to have this kind of experience and introspection about their own reactions to children's behavior when they feel frustrated or inadequate as a result of the children's avoidance mechanisms.

Without this experience, discussion, introspection, and the sharing of reactions, teachers will not know what to look for. But we can give them what to look for. I have found that it is very effective to train teachers by means of a demonstration group of children. Children and their parents and the teachers are all in the same room; the children are worked with for an hour or two and then are taken out of the room. Then the parents and the teachers in training discuss thoroughly what everybody has learned from the experience.

BARSCH: I would like to discuss a practical question which exists for us at Madison now. All of the teachers in training within the program were trained in the traditional mathematics system. They are now adults; they add columns in the old style. All the children in the school system are now in a modern math program. All of the teachers, as they experience this in school, literally have to relearn mathematics.

If we now consider those children who have specialized problems as a result of their perceptual difficulties, do we invest in both systems of helping the teacher to acquire the basic design of modern math as well as encouraging him with whatever remedial techniques there might be? You see, they have not yet devised remedial techniques for modern math.

FREIDUS: Let's not talk about remedial; let's talk about fundamental. Let's lay a foundation so well that you don't have to do any remedial work later. The point is, if you go far enough back and build the foundation solidly enough, you don't have gaps in it later on. Modern math is supposed to be built on the structure of our number system instead of on the rote method that we used to learn, which fell flat because we didn't have any memory hooks in it.

I think in dealing with number concept, again, we come back to the first point—what's involved in it? In thinking about sets, for example, one of the bases of our number system, sets of one, sets of ten, sets of a hundred, you have to start from the developmental level in children. Can a child look at something, pick it out of the background and look at it sufficiently to see what are the criteria on which he can match something else to it, so that he can form a set, to be counted?

So many people try to teach number concept through number symbols without going all the way back to what is the basis for understanding numbers, sets, and spatial relationships—namely quantitative relationships of all kinds.

Chapter 8

Communication and Communicative Disorders
MIRIAM PAULS HARDY, Ph.D.

EDITORIAL NOTE.—It may appear strange to the reader that communication and communicative disorders have been placed in a section dealing with educational competencies. This has been done purposely to emphasize the teacher's total responsibility in all aspects of communication: written, spelled, spoken, or communication of a visual nature. The emphasis for the reader is on the competency of teachers in the communication process. This paper is not concerned with the preparation of the speech pathologist who, as a specialist on the interdisciplinary team, will have quite a different role from that of the teacher dealing with brain-injured children. The paper is concerned with the competencies which teachers must have from the discipline of speech and communication.

DR. MIRIAM PAULS HARDY is an audiologist and speech pathologist with a unique background in special education. Since 1949 she has been on the staff of The Johns Hopkins University and Hospital, Baltimore, Maryland, as Associate Professor of Otolaryngology and Environmental Medicine. Her major professional interest is differential diagnosis and management of children with communicative disorders.

Dr. Hardy received her B.A. degree from Harris Teachers College and is a graduate of the teacher training program of Central Institute for the Deaf. She received her M.A. degree from Wayne State University and her Ph.D. degree from Northwestern. She has been a teacher of children, a teacher of teachers, as well as a clinician and researcher. She has lectured extensively and has numerous publications. She has served on a variety of national committees, among them: The National Advisory Committee on the Education of Deaf, the Medical Services Committee of the National Project on Children with Minimal Brain Dysfunctions, The Communication Sciences Study Section (N.I.N.D.B.), and The Hearing, Language, and Speech Sub-Committee for the Perinatal Collaborative Project (N.I.N.D.B.). She is a Fellow of the American Speech and Hearing Association and was Vice-President in 1959.

Chapter 8

Communication and Communicative Disorders
MIRIAM PAULS HARDY, Ph.D.

IMPORTANCE OF COMMUNICATIVE DISORDERS

Learning to listen, to hear, to comprehend, to remember and recall, to formulate and express in speech a symbol code, and eventually to read and write this same code, is probably the most difficult and complex task the young child undertakes. It is subject to many interferences—anatomic, physiologic, neurologic, psychologic, cultural and environmental. Its development on a "normal" time schedule is dependent on reasonably intact sensori-motor systems and demands the most refined integration and function of the entire central nervous system. It must be encouraged and developed by good stimulation in the minute-to-minute activities of daily living. Its mastery undergirds all future academic learning.

There is good evidence that delayed (and/or retarded) language and speech development is one of the earliest and more sensitive indicators of the child "in trouble." It is not casual that most children who are categorized as "brain-injured" or "neurologically impaired" have in common a history of delayed language and speech, as well as parental concern about "listening" and "hearing." It is usually for these reasons, and not for reasons of aberrant behavior, that parents start the diagnostic rounds in the preschool years. The majority of these children enter school with residual communicative disorders that require the expert help of a sophisticated language and speech clinician as part of the daily program. The more profoundly affected children require a special educational program geared to the communicative disorder as the major disability.

It seems strange, with this common background of delayed communicative development, that relatively little stress has been put on hearing—the major input modality for learning language and speech, and for effective participation in the classroom. In the thinking about, and planning for, the CNS-involved child, great emphasis is put on vision, visual

131

perception, visuomotor skills, and motor training. A similar kind of emphasis needs to be put upon hearing and listening and ways of helping the child learn through his auditory difficulties.

Many of these children may not have hearing losses, but do have serious problems in managing auditory information in temporal and pattern sequence (auding) which are not always recognized. When hearing tests show no loss in sensitivity for pure tones, it is taken for granted that the child "hears"; an investigation is too seldom made of *how* he hears. The conclusion may be that the difficulties in listening can be attributed solely to distractibility and hyperactivity. While attentional peculiarities interfere with learning and must be brought under control, breakdowns in the auditory integrative system enact even greater penalties. For some of these children, auditory discrimination may be poor, but for many more, auditory rote memory is significantly below the expected norms for digits, isolated words, and repetition of sentences. They simply cannot follow and retain what follows what in a verbal sequence. As a consequence, language and speech development are delayed; and after onset, expressed language and speech are characterized by immature syntax, disorganization, cluttering, and often severe articulation problems. These children can comprehend short conversational units, but are confused by long, detailed verbal exchange. They become "word snatchers" and inexpert guessers of context, and restless in any situation that puts a premium on listening.

There is some research by Birch (1964) to support the idea that poor readers have difficulty in translating auditory tapped patterns into visual patterns. Certainly, many CNS-involved children have just as much difficulty in managing brief-exposure auditory events as they do with brief-exposure visual events. There is much clinical evidence to support the idea that the sensory systems are closely interlinked and that breakdown in the management of intersensory information is one of the major problems of the CNS-involved child.

In addition to problems in temporal integration, some CNS-involved children have mild-to-severe incapacities in learning, remembering and/ or formulating, and using a verbal symbol code (childhood aphasia). Language is not readily learned and is not stable. Memory and recall are the core of the problem.

Others may have an auditory disorder, alone, or in combination with other difficulties. This may be a conductive and/or sensori-neural loss from mild to profound degree (hypacusis), or a complex auditory disorder (dysacusis), that we do not as yet know how to describe adequately. There are a few with agnosia—an "unknowingness to sound" with what seems to be no loss in hearing sensitivity.

Some may be dyspraxic with an inability to recall and execute a motor speech pattern, yet can execute the same motor movement in eating, or other reflexive activity. Still others may not be able to imitate a motor pattern that is presented visually, but can readily reproduce the pattern once he has learned it by being led through it motorwise by the instructor.

Many exhibit subtle incoordination in fine and/or gross motor movements which may also be manifested in the speech pattern. Others are more frankly involved and have a specific motor involvement of the articulators (dysarthria) as well as a mild to severe motor palsy.

Any of these symptoms may appear alone, or in combination, in the child with CNS dysfunction. They can and do interfere with the acquisition and refinement of communicative skills and cause the language deficits that impede curricular learning. The communication program for a particular child must be designed to help him learn through his specific combination of sensory, intersensory, memory, and/or motor problems.

Therefore, teachers need an operational framework to help them understand the human communication system as a whole and the complex interrelationships between hearing, language comprehension and expression, seeing, speech reading, reading, speech, written language, and spelling. They will then be better prepared to develop total programs that are effective in meeting a child's capacities and incapacities, and will not be led down the garden path of beguiling but randomly selected devices and techniques that are supposed to be a panacea for "brain injury," or continue to think of language and reading solely as "school subjects."

While the charge to the contributors to these discussions is to plan "for the child whose CNS dysfunction does not produce gross motor, or sensory deficits, or generalized impairment of the intellect, but who exhibits limited alterations of behavior, or intellectual functioning," it cannot be overemphasized that large numbers of children who are the concern of special education, have CNS dysfunctions concomitant with their other handicaps. A significant proportion of "deaf," "hard-of-hearing," "aphasic," "mentally retarded," and "motor palsied" children exhibit these same symptoms of behavioral and intellectual dysfunction and for the same reasons. There are good reasons to question historic expectancies for neat, clean diagnostic entities that will fit into traditional subareas of special education.

Some of these children have suffered traumatic influences which have caused specific and/or diffuse breakdowns, but others show developmental lacks, or lags (developmental aplasia), which may be genetic or biochemical and are not as yet describable. The former may be described as "damaged organisms"; the latter appear to be "intact," but functioning suboptimally. The prognosis for the two groups may well be different.

It must always be borne in mind that the problems with a child are not static, as one is dealing with maturational and organic changes in a plastic, emerging organism. Unfortunately, there can be degenerative processes operating as well. This demands continuous reappraisal if the best interests of the child are to be served.

The importance of close and continued liaison between medicine and education in the diagnosis and long-term management of the child with CNS dysfunction and related communicative disorders cannot be overstressed. The earlier a child in trouble is found and an appropriate preschool program of management launched, the better the prognosis. Each child requires a thoughtful medical and paramedical work-up prior to educational placement. This work-up should provide the description of the child's capacities and limitations and indicate the special program that is required. However, the best diagnostic work-up can only delineate the problems, and only long-term, imaginative, diagnostic teaching can reveal how this child can best learn through his difficulties. It is out of these combined observations that the hand-tailored program to meet each child's specific needs is evolved. This demands that the teacher be a strong contributing member of the team with knowledge and competencies that enable him to fulfill his role.

KNOWLEDGE, COMPETENCIES, AND SKILLS REQUIRED IN THE AREA OF HUMAN COMMUNICATION

The teacher of children with CNS dysfunctions needs a broad, eclectic background of information that affords understanding of the all-pervasive, underlying nature of the communication process. He needs to know how to adapt his program to meet a child's particular needs and how to coordinate his efforts with the specific attack of the communication specialist. Among the knowledge, competencies, and skills required are the following:

1. The development of an operational framework for understanding the communicative system as a whole, so that the complex, intricate interrelationships between hearing, language comprehension, language expression, speech, seeing, speech reading, reading, written language, and spelling are grasped.

2. Knowledge of how children learn to listen and to hear, to learn language and to talk; and to have a grasp of the normal developmental expectancies for the emergence and refinement of these skills from birth to adolescence.

3. Some awareness of the kinds and degrees of hearing, language, and speech disorders that may occur alone, or in combinations, and their effect on communication skills and cognitive functions; as well as an appreciation that, for many of these children, the communicative disorder is but another symptom of the CNS dysfunctions.

4. An introduction to the anatomy, neurophysiology, and pathology of the ear and VIII nerve system, the eye and the visual system, the speech-production system, the brain and the central nervous system.

5. Some grasp of medical and paramedical terminology, such as aphasia, apraxia, agnosia, dysarthria, dyslalia, cluttering, echolalia, disinhibition, perseveration, distractibility, and so forth.

6. An appreciation that what is needed for (and from) a diagnostic evaluation is information about the child's capacities and limitations—rather than concern for diagnostic labels.

7. Experience in sharing medical and paramedical diagnostic reports and translating these findings into an appropriate habilitative program for the child.

8. An introduction to psychoacoustics (loudness levels, the speech spectrum, distortion) so as to be able to read an audiologic report and to understand what it means in terms of the child's ability to hear speech and to function in the classroom.

9. An introduction to a simple, organized system of English phonetics such as the Yale Charts. The aim should be some understanding of how vowels and consonants are said, how they look, how they sound, and how they are written in common English spelling. This is fundamental knowledge for interlocking speech, spelling, and reading.

10. Firm normative guidelines for critical evaluation of a child's language facility for both oral and written language comprehension and expression; to develop the ability to analyze a child's *oral* and *written* language in terms of the kinds of interferences it may manifest.

11. Grounding in a system (such as the Fitzgerald Key) for teaching language principles and grammatical sequence for children with hearing and/or language disorders in addition to the other CNS dysfunctions.

12. Experience in analyzing textbooks for vocabulary and language principles that need to be taught *prior* to introducing the textbook to the child with vocabulary and language deficits.

13. Ability to create, and program, language drill materials that are interesting, effective, and appropriate to the disability.

14. To understand that reading is but one aspect of the total communicative process and a specific reading disability may be related to other communicative disorders.

15. To recognize when a child is having difficulty with language memory and recall, and/or the formulation and expression of language, so that he may be referred for an intensive special program, for without specific help directed to memory and recall, he cannot gain language facility.

16. An understanding of the concept of "auding" (the management of auditory events in temporal and pattern sequence) and the effects of breakdowns in this system on language and speech; to be able to recognize it as a factor in a child's dysfunction.

17. Ability to create specific exercises and devices aimed at improving auditory memory, span, and sequence, as well as discrimination.

18. Skill in making informal diagnostic observations in the course of the daily program that further delineate and illuminate the child's capacities and limitations; to be able to organize these observations into succinct, meaningful reports to be shared with others on the diagnostic-management team.

19. To be able to use imaginatively and effectively various kinds of instrumentation: tape recorders, teaching machines, the Language Master, tachistoscope, and so on.

SELECTED REFERENCES

Barry, Hortense. *The young aphasic child; Evaluation and training.* Washington, D.C.: Volta Bureau, 1961.

Beasley, Jane. *Slow to talk: A guide for teachers and parents of children with delayed language development.* New York: Columbia University Teachers' College Bureau of Publications, 1956.

Birch, Herbert G., and Belmont, Lillian. "Auditory and visual interpretations in normal and retarded readers," *American Journal of Orthopsychiatry,* 1964, 34, 852–861.

Denes, Peter B., and Pinson, Elliott N. *The speech chain: The physics and biology of spoken language.* Baltimore: Williams & Wilkins Science Series, 1964.

Hardy, William G. "On language disorders in young children: A reorganization of thinking," *Journal of Speech and Hearing Disorders,* 1965, 30, 4–16.

McGinnis, Mildred A. *Aphasic children.* Washington, D.C.: Volta Bureau, 1963.

Streng, Alice, *et al. Hearing therapy for children.* New York: Grune & Stratton, 1958.

Templin, Mildred. *Certain language skills in children. Their development and interrelationships.* Minneapolis: University of Minnesota Press, 1957.

Travis, Lee Edward, *et al. Handbook of speech pathology.* New York: Appleton-Century-Crofts, 1957.

Woods, Nancy E. *Delayed speech and language development.* Englewood Cliffs, N.J.: Prentice-Hall, 1964.

PART III

COGNITIVE, PERCEPTUAL, AND
MOTOR COMPETENCIES

Chapter 9

The Needs of Teachers for Specialized Information
on the Development of Cognitive Structures

RILEY W. GARDNER, Ph.D.

EDITORIAL NOTE.—Nowhere has the problem of cognition and
cognitive structure insofar as brain-injured children are concerned been adequately discussed in the literature. Dr. Gardner
in this paper does the profession a unique service in bringing
together, not only his significant thinking on this matter, *but*
also the contributions which have been made, often as by-prod-
ucts, of other research interests and findings. The need for teachers to understand the role of cognitive development in normal
as well as in brain-injured children is clarified in the paper of
Dr. Gardner. Current work by the author referred to in this
paper is supported by Research Grant M-5517 and research
career program award K3-MH-21-936 from the National Institutes of Health, Public Health Service.

DR. RILEY W. GARDNER, a Senior Psychologist in the Research Department of The Menninger Foundation, Topeka, Kansas, received his B.A. degree from Yankton College in 1945, his Ph.D. from the University of Kansas in 1952. He has been a staff member of The Menninger Foundation since 1951.

Dr. Gardner has published works on clinical testing for brain damage and on the group process in outpatient evaluation, and an extensive series of papers and monographs (published in the United States, England, Mexico, and Japan) on studies of individual differences in cognition and other aspects of personality organization. His publications include *Cognitive Control: A Study of Individual Consistencies in Cognitive Behavior.*

Dr. Gardner has been director of The Menninger Foundation's Cognition Research Project since 1958. He is president of the Kansas Psychological Association for 1965–66.

Chapter 9

The Needs of Teachers for Specialized Information on the Development of Cognitive Structures

RILEY W. GARDNER, Ph.D.

It is generally recognized that the incidence of brain damage is greater than has often been assumed (Bell, 1965) and that even mild brain damage may have notable effects upon the cognitive structures formed in the course of human development. In advance of the discussions to follow, it should be noted that the cognitive effects of brain damage may be more appropriately stated in quantitative than in qualitative terms, once the relevant parameters of cognitive functioning involved are isolated (e.g., Reitan, 1959), and that no sharp distinction can be made between the effects of mild and more severe brain damage on cognitive structures. In spite of the fact that a good deal of evidence points to a correlation between severity of brain damage and severity of behavioral sequelae, the central nervous system is so complex that injuries to it produce a bewildering variety of both generalized and specific behavioral effects (Teuber and Libert, 1958). In addition, some children with brain damage show no detectable cognitive consequences.

The teacher should not conclude that the incidence of brain damage and its many effects on cognitive structures enforce a hopeless outlook upon the learning disorders involved. The untenability of the common assumption that the behavioral effects of brain damage are irreversible should be emphasized. Even at the present stage of understanding of the cognitive processes affected by brain damage, it is evident that either special training or spontaneous development of alternative cognitive strategies by the brain-damaged child may in part overcome the cognitive deficits. As the understanding of cognitive processes increases, we shall have ever-increasing resources for the development of effective training methods.

The variety of relatively enduring aspects of cognitive organization that could be subsumed under the general rubric, "cognitive structures," is great and ranges at least from single memories to the cognitive control structures that have been the focus of recent explorations of individual differences in the development of cognitive functioning (see, for example, the summaries by Gardner, 1964, and Witkin et al., 1962). The present paper is devoted largely to these enduring patterns, programs, or strategies of cognitive control, their variations in normal adults and children, and the known or hypothesized effects of brain damage upon these complex patterns of cognitive functioning. Certain other aspects of cognitive structure have been explored extensively by earlier students of brain damage. The effects of early and late brain injury upon language structure have, for example, been the major focus of a considerable number of studies. Still other aspects of cognitive structures remain to be conceptualized and/or explored.

It is well known that normal adults and normal children show wide ranges of individual difference on various dimensions of cognitive control, including defense mechanisms. These complex cognitive structures —for example, those involved in selectivity of attention, the deployment of attention, categorizing behavior, memory formation, attitudes toward confirmable versus unconfirmable experiences—have direct implications for perception, learning, remembering, thought functioning, generalized reality contact, and even the characteristic nature of consciousness itself. In combination, the individual's array of cognitive controls has been referred to as his over-all "cognitive style." In discussing the effects of even mild brain damage upon these highly and subtly organized behavioral control mechanisms, the present paper will deal not only with the growing body of research upon such controls themselves, but also with work on brain damage per se and other studies directly or indirectly relevant to the cognitive processes considered.

From the standpoint of the teacher, the major purpose of the following discussions is the development of a more complete conceptual framework with respect to some of the cognitive functions that are inevitably involved in the school learning situation. It is not assumed that these discussions or further study of the literature briefly referred to will prepare the teacher to diagnose mild or even severe brain damage. Accurate diagnosis is difficult even for experts, and the effects of mild brain damage are easily confused in individual cases with the effects of other limitations upon the development of cognitive structures. The principal focus here is upon the control processes themselves. The intent is to extend the conceptual tools the teacher employs in observing the cognitive performances of all his students—brain-damaged and normal alike.

EFFECTS OF MILD BRAIN DAMAGE ON ATTENTIONAL PROCESSES

The parameters of attention have never been fully explicated. Several major dimensions of attentional control have been dealt with rather extensively, however, and will be considered herein. Such potentially important but relatively unexplored aspects of attentional behavior as its characteristic intensity and its phasic intensity in certain pathological conditions will also be considered.

Effects on the Momentary Span of Attention

A key characteristic of the performance of some brain-damaged persons is a rather severe limitation of the momentary span of attention, i.e., the amount of ideational material that can be held in consciousness at any one time (Mayman and Gardner, 1960). The development of sensitivity to this all but hidden aspect of cognitive functioning (which is often not apparent in, for example, intelligence test scores) was of considerable help in the writer's clinical diagnostic work. When the brain-damaged person is required to keep two or three ideas or images in mind at the same moment, one or more of them may suddenly "disappear" from consciousness. There is evidence that the "lost" elements have actually been registered in memory and can be recalled under other conditions. This cognitive deficit is understandably anxiety-arousing and has some unfortunate effects on the ongoing thought functioning of some brain-damaged persons. This deficit makes it particularly difficult to deal with relationships among several ideas. While attempting to solve an arithmetic problem, for example, a child so afflicted may have the unnerving experience that one of the elements has disappeared from consciousness while he is trying to organize his thoughts about the other. He may become extremely anxious over this disruption of his thought processes but may have learned to conceal this anxiety.

This attentional deficit has obvious effects on memory functioning and may also show itself in the child's inability to achieve certain kinds of spontaneous organizations of material. When required to draw a person, for example, he may (if observed with great care) be seen to proceed from segment to segment, rather than to deal with the entire figure and the component parts at the same time. He may manage to draw a roughly adequate picture of a person, but only with difficulty and by a method different from that of the normal child. Momentary attention span is, of course, generally more limited in children than in adults. The brain-damaged individual, however, may suffer from a degree of deficit that produces relatively severe—but often difficult to observe—

fragmentation of the ongoing stream of thought. Or, the child may resort to confabulatory filling of the "gaps" in his conscious experience. Certain sporadic "memory lapses" may also be attributable to this attentional deficit. The idea that the momentary attention span is limited in cases of severe brain damage is, of course, a time-honored one that can be found in the writings of the early Greek physicians and that has often been emphasized in subsequent reports. The intriguing fact is its importance in many cases of mild brain damage and its frequent concealment by inelegant but partially effective restitutive maneuvers.

Effects on Selective Attention

Some of the most subtle and adaptively important features of cognitive control surround the facilitation and inhibition of cognitive processes that can be described as attention. Impairment of the capacity to attend selectively is one of the most thoroughly studied sequelae of brain damage and has also been explored extensively in recent work on cognitive controls. This capacity is (1) a major aspect of the capacity to differentiate certain aspects of experience, (2) a major component of one intellectual ability factor measured by modern tests of "intelligence," (3) determined to a relatively great degree by heredity, and (4) largely independent of verbal ability. In addition, it is one of the aspects of cognitive functioning most severely affected by any degree of brain damage. A. A. Strauss, who has made distinguished contributions to the education of the brain-damaged, has stated that the most serious thinking handicap of the brain-damaged child is this impairment of selectivity, that is, the inability to distinguish the essential from the nonessential (Strauss, 1944).

As discussed elsewhere (Gardner, 1962), recent work in neurophysiology provides a remarkably effective neural model for this critical set of adaptive operations. This model is a three-level one involving the cerebral cortex, the reticular formation of the midbrain, and the peripheral sensory organs. Interrelations among these structures, including complex patterns of feedback, are involved in the control of sensory input. Recent experimental evidence (e.g., Burks, 1957) supports the view that damage to the area occupied by the reticular formation has direct effects upon such attentional control.

The child who suffers from an organic impairment that interferes with the complexly organized controls guiding sensory intake can be expected to have certain characteristic difficulties in perception, learning, remembering, and thinking. There is clear evidence that impairment of the selectivity of attention affects both the perception of objects and the recall of memories, particularly when a single memory must be retrieved from a matrix of memories of relatively similar events. One general suggestion for the education of the brain-damaged child is that he can perform more easily when presented with clearly discriminable stimuli, rather than highly similar stimuli which he must differentiate attentionally. If such a child were to listen, for example, to a discussion of an historical sequence in which a number of persons were described in relatively similar terms, he could be expected to show an exaggerated difficulty in selective recall. If the material were presented in smaller and more discrete units, his organization of it might be considerably better.

Effects on Sustained Attention

Another aspect of attentional contact with internal and external reality is the capacity to maintain an effectively consistent level of attentional intensity. This is, unfortunately, one of the areas in which it is most difficult to distinguish between the effects of brain damage and the effects of psychotic thinking or other thought disturbances. It seems clear, however, particularly from the recent work of Rosvold and associates (1956), that this defect of attention is rather widespread among the brain-damaged. To the writer's knowledge there is as yet no direct evidence of a relationship between this waxing and waning of attention and the limitations of attentional span discussed above. General observations by students of brain damage suggest, however, that these phasic surges of attentional intensity may be of somewhat longer duration than the apparently momentary limitations of attention span.

Phasic variations in intensity of reality contact can, of course, lead to bafflement on the part of a teacher: a child who performs well one day may be completely unable to perform a similar task on another day. Such variability of behavior leads with unfortunate ease to the assumption that a motivational problem is the causative agent.

The possibility that some brain-damaged children may also suffer from a generalized reduction of attentional intensity has not been fully explored, in part because of the difficulty of developing adequate measures of intensity. It is conceivable, however, that the various forms of interference with the complex controls of attention referred to above could cause an over-all reduction in attentional intensity leading to reduced clarity of experience.

Effects on Extensiveness of Attention Deployment

An aspect of individuality in cognitive control that has been explored in some detail (see Gardner, 1964) is the extensiveness of scanning persons engage in before making decisions about stimuli. For example, in simple size-estimation tests requiring the subject to match the size of a standard stimulus by adjusting a variable stimulus, individual adults and children differ greatly in the amount of scanning they perform before making their final adjustments. It is intriguing that in normal children the degree of scanning seems independent of accuracy. The degree of scanning may be affected by the impulsivity of children in general and the still greater impulsivity so often characteristic of the brain-damaged child. It is thus conceivable that, in addition to the other potential effects of brain damage noted above, some brain-damaged children also suffer from impaired perception because they scan the environment too minimally, or too erratically. Any short-circuiting of the scanning process must limit the clarity and detail with which the external and internal environments are perceived.

A General Inference

Although this study has by no means dealt with all the important aspects of attentional control that may be interfered with by brain lesions, it is clear that the brain-damaged child's essential difficulties in complex learning situations are not all referable to peculiarities of ideation per se. Many of his difficulties are attributable to faulty operation of the structural mechanisms involved in the *processing* of sensory data. Adequate functioning of all the attentional controls referred to is necessary for coordination of anticipation to action, effective scanning of the inner and outer world, differentiated intake of internal and external stimulation, maintenance of an adequate number of ideas in consciousness, and achievement of effective contact with reality. The primary disorders are in the "machinery" of the brain, rather than in the "materials" of thought, although these may also be affected. As a number of investigators have pointed out, the brain-damaged child's attempts to cope with his deficits may lead him to unusual constructions that seem superficially like the thought peculiarities of disturbed children.

EFFECTS OF MILD BRAIN DAMAGE ON THE CATEGORIZATION OF EXPERIENCE

Every act of perception (at least following the earliest phases of cognitive development) implicates a categorizing process. This is as true of internal as of external perception. In the course of experiencing ourselves in interaction with the external world, we also produce, even in early childhood, elaborate, hierarchical arrangements of concepts that organize our memories in ways amenable to economical conceptual activity in subsequent thinking. The act of categorization, and individual styles of categorization, are therefore of critical importance to thought functioning. Some recent studies of categorizing behavior (see, for example, Gardner and Schoen, 1962; Gardner, 1964) have shown wide ranges of individual differences in categorizing style along several dimensions.

Effects on Conceptual Differentiation

One dimension of individual differences evident in the categorizing behavior of adults and children is the degree of "conceptual differentiation" imposed upon arrays of heterogeneous objects, persons, and events. Some normal adults and children consistently arrange the objects and events of their experience in many small categories. Others (who seem to be more concerned with similarity than with difference) arrange their experience in large categories containing many items. It can be inferred that their normal states of consciousness are characteristically different in this respect.

It is known that even mild brain damage may have severe effects upon concept formation. The brain-damaged child may focus upon isolated elements in the stimulus field. This can add to his other difficulties in abstracting principles from stimuli that are similar in some respects but different in others. In attempting to cope with these limitations, he may resort to circuitous reasoning leading to unusual formulations.

Impairments of the capacity to categorize and abstract effectively are sometimes among the most easily observed sequelae of brain damage. The writer recalls, for example, administering a categorizing test to a subject in a study of cognitive style whose performance was notable for its "fragmentation," the unusually small groups formed, and the reasons given to account for groupings. His unusual responses led to the hypothesis that he was suffering from long-standing brain damage, around which he had built a variety of coping devices. On pursuing this hypothesis, the writer found that he had suffered a birth injury but had developed compensatory coping strategies so effective that he was about to receive his bachelor's degree from a reputable university. His partial triumph over serious obstacles must be considered an almost heroic achievement, but it is probably not so unusual among brain-damaged individuals in whom some aspects of cognitive functioning are impaired but others are relatively unaffected.

In the school situation, the combination of difficulties affecting concept formation may have some traumatic effects. It may be difficult for even the mildly brain-damaged child to understand, and especially to remember, relationships among superficially dissimilar ideas. He may adopt a piecemeal approach to concept formation in which some abstract relationships tend to fall by the wayside. He may seem to grasp certain relationships (in which a capacity for concrete association can be substituted for true abstraction) with remarkable ease but fail to grasp other relationships that appear superficially to be equally simple.

EFFECTS OF MILD BRAIN DAMAGE ON MEMORY FORMATION

An aspect of cognition directly relevant to learning and remembering is that of the cognitive controls involved in memory formation. Certain aspects of cognitive control in memory formation can be explored as discrete entities or dimensions. Although knowledge in this area is as yet quite limited, individuality in one dimension of memory formation has been explored to a considerable extent. This dimension, referred to as "leveling-sharpening," was originally explored by Holzman and Klein and has been further investigated in a series of studies of adults and children (Gardner, 1964). The dimension is one of individual differences in the degree of interaction between new percepts and memories of related percepts registered earlier. To put it crudely, individuals differ grossly in the degree to which their new perceptions are colored or contaminated by related memories of earlier experiences. It is obvious, of course, that persons who are extreme in leveling (that is, in the contamination of new and old experiences) perceive new experiences differently from persons who may be called "sharpeners" and that they also form more contaminated memories of new experiences. In previous work, it has been shown that individuals differ consistently in this aspect of memory formation, that the cognitive operations involved overlap, in part, with those involved in the defense mechanism of repression, and that an extreme tendency toward leveling is associated with other aspects of inadequate reality comprehension. It should be noted, however, that, in the normal samples of adults and children used in these experiments, no strong correlations between leveling-sharpening and intelligence test scores have appeared.

In this area, there is direct evidence of the effects of brain damage. A study by Mathae (1958) has shown that brain damage notably increases the degree of leveling. This finding adds to the evidence from attentional and other studies indicating that the percepts and ideas recorded by the brain-damaged person are less differentiated and less adaptively effective than those of the normal individual. In the classroom, as elsewhere in his life, the extreme leveler, particularly if this aspect of his cognitive functioning is enhanced by other cognitive correlates of brain damage, can be expected to recall certain prior events in a relatively undifferentiated way. Because of this, it may also be difficult for him to recall certain experiences at all, especially when they are highly similar to other experiences he has recorded. These effects may often be relatively subtle and difficult to detect by ordinary means.

EFFECTS OF MILD BRAIN DAMAGE ON ATTITUDES TOWARD CONFIRMABLE AND UNCONFIRMABLE ASPECTS OF REALITY

There is not sufficient space here to survey the many contributions describing the literalness of the brain-damaged child, or the correlated difficulties in abstraction and imaginative thinking. It is well known from clinical and experimental studies that the brain-damaged person is limited in ability and willingness to experience events that are not conventionally confirmable. A dimensional aspect of cognitive control (called "tolerance for unrealistic experiences") has been formulated, and to some extent experimentally confirmed, that deals with individual differences in normal adults and children with respect to willingness to experience events that are unconfirmable (i.e., that are "unrealistic"). Some normal persons are consistently literal. Others delight in novel organizations of stimuli. It seems clear, without further experimental confirmation, that even the mildly brain-damaged child is relatively intolerant of such unrealistic experiences. This limitation presumably has its major effects upon certain aspects of abstraction (particularly those that require psychological distance from literal fact), on imaginativeness, on spontaneous creativity, and on related self-organized activities in the classroom. For all the reasons discussed above—such as attention and concept formation—as well as his relatively literal approach to reality, the brain-damaged child may have particular difficulty with tasks requiring spontaneous production of novel stimulus organizations.

EFFECTS OF MILD BRAIN DAMAGE ON THE CONTROL OF CERTAIN IRRELEVANT MOTORIC RESPONSES

Another dimension of individual differences that has been explored in normal adults and children and that seems to have obvious implications for the performances of mildly brain-damaged children is that of the control of certain irrelevant motoric responses in the course of certain types of intellectual tasks. The experiments thus far seem to indicate a meaningful dimension of individual differences in the capacity to inhibit irrelevant motoric responses in a unique verbal task and in a variety of related adaptive situations. The criterion task requires the subject to name colors printed in incongruous color words. Rapid color-naming in this challenging test requires effective, flexible inhibition of the overlearned tendency to read the words in which the colors are printed. Although all the necessary studies have not yet been done, the evidence of deficit in generalized motoric control in cases of brain damage, plus the evidence of unusual impairments of performance when complex inhibitory and facilitatory controls are simultaneously evoked, suggests that response to such tasks would be interfered with to an extreme degree. This dimension is a component of over-all adaptive capacity not ordinarily examined. Like the controls of attention referred to earlier, the capacity to inhibit irrelevant motoric responses is an important aspect of cognitive control in learning and remembering tasks. This kind of selective inhibition is apparently not correlated with the kind of selective attention that was described earlier. These findings support the general observation that selective inhibition (like selective facilitation) has many parameters in human development, parameters that are not necessarily correlated or referable to common determining factors.

SOME PROBLEMS FOR FURTHER RESEARCH

It is the general thesis herein that further understanding of the cognitive processes affected by brain damage will ultimately lead to more effective training procedures. Studies of individual differences in cognitive structure formation and the cognitive functions involved should therefore be extended to many more facets of cognitive behavior. Further insight into the cognitive control structures discussed briefly in this paper should contribute to better understanding of the total pattern of possible cognitive deficits, methods of detecting these deficits, and educational techniques appropriate to them.

Needless to say, further development of diagnostic techniques by specialists in that area is also needed. The work of Halstead, Reitan, and others may serve as a model in this area (see, for example, Reitan, 1959). In a collaborative study with Phillip Rennick and his associates in the writer's laboratory, the Halstead-Reitan battery is being administered to one hundred twins to whom large batteries of other cognitive tests were given previously. The concern of this study is with the importance of heredity to each of the aspects of cognitive functioning sampled and the particular cognitive operations involved in the diagnostic tests developed by Halstead and Reitan.

Further experimental studies of the performances of brain-damaged persons in learning situations are needed. A recent study by Jensen (1963) exemplifies the value of experimental studies of the performance of brain-damaged versus normal individuals in particular kinds of learning situations. He not only found that a key verbal difficulty was central to the problems brain-damaged children experience in a certain type of learning situation, but also was able to introduce a corrective set of instructions that notably improves their performance. Such studies can contribute directly to the improvement of training methods.

Not the least of the research problems remaining for further study is that of the dimensions of learning in the school situation. It is a considerable step from the laboratory to the classroom learning situation. Another area of research calling for further development is that of the personal interaction of the teacher and the brain-damaged child. Even the mildly brain-damaged child may experience severe anxieties and control difficulties that require special understanding and special help for effective cognitive growth to occur. It seems likely that certain instructors are more naturally suited to this general kind of interaction than others, although the others may be equally capable of normal classroom teaching. A frequently overlooked aspect of work with children who have cognitive defects is the unusual demands they place upon the teacher. We know too little, also, of the effects upon the learning process of similarities and differences in the cognitive styles of teachers and learners, and of any special features of cognitive style that may characterize teachers who are most effective with brain-damaged children.

SUMMARY

A number of dimensions of cognitive control have been explored in recent studies of individual differences in cognition and in experimental studies of the processes underlying these individual differences. Because of their complexity and subtlety of operation, these control structures may be peculiarly susceptible to the effects of even mild brain damage. Spelling out the nature of certain control dimensions and the known or hypothesized effects of mild brain damage upon them may alert the teacher to aspects of classroom behavior that would be more difficult to perceive clearly without the framework provided by the concept of complex cognitive structures. At many points, the individual-difference studies are closely related to earlier studies of the cognitive defects of brain-damaged children. The studies of individuality extend these earlier results and delineate some new aspects of cognitive impairment referable to mild brain damage. Several potentially fruitful but largely unexplored areas of cognitive functioning are indicated, as are some important research problems concerning the interaction of teachers and brain-damaged children.

SELECTED REFERENCES

Bell, R. Q. "Developmental psychology" in *Annual review of psychology*. P. R. Farnsworth, Olga McNemar, and Q. McNemar (eds.). Palo Alto, Calif.: Annual Reviews, 1965.

Burks, H. F. "The effect of brain pathology on learning," *Exceptional Children*, 1957, 24, 169–172.

Gardner, R. W. "The development of cognitive structures" in *Cognition: Theory, research, promise*. Constance Scheerer (ed.). New York: Harper & Row, 1964.

———. "Organismic equilibration and the energy-structure duality in psychoanalytic theory: An attempt at theoretical refinement." Unpublished manuscript, 1962.

Gardner, R. W., and Schoen, R. A. "Differentiation and abstraction in concept formation," *Psychological Monographs*, 1962, 76, No. 41 (Whole No. 560).

Jensen, A. "Learning ability in retarded, average, and gifted children," *Merrill-Palmer Quarterly*, 1963, 9, 123–140.

Mathae, D. F. "Figural aftereffects, weight judgment, and schematizing in relation to 'cortical conductivity'." Unpublished doctoral dissertation, University of Kansas, 1958.

Mayman, M., and Gardner, R. W. "The characteristic psychological disturbance in some cases of brain damage with mild deficit, *Bulletin of the Menninger Clinic*, 1960, 24, 26–36.

Reitan, R. M. "Impairment of abstraction ability in brain damage: Quantitative versus qualitative changes," *Journal of Psychology*, 1959, 48, 97–102.

Rosvold, H. E., *et al.*, "A continuous performance test of brain damage," *Journal of Consulting Psychology*, 1956, 20, 343–351.

Strauss, A. A. "Ways of thinking in brain-crippled children," *American Journal of Psychology*, 1944, 100, 639–647.

Teuber, H.-L., and Liebert, R. S. "Specific and general effects of brain injury in man," *American Medical Association Archives of Neurology and Psychiatry*, 1958, 80, 403–407.

Witkin, H. A., *et al. Psychological differentiation: Studies of development.* New York: John Wiley, 1962.

Comment

GARDNER: I have discussed in my paper some dimensions of individual differences in certain complex aspects of pattern that we call "structure," and I don't mean physicial structure which seems to emerge in the course of human development. We talk of these structures as aspects of personality organization. I was mentioning some of the dimensions of attention and categorizing memory formations, and so on, that have been studied in normal adults and children. It wasn't possible in a brief paper like this to deal with some of the supporting experimental studies of the practices per se that seem to be involved in these behaviors. Understanding of organized cognitive structures is only partial as yet, but we do study the relationship of sporadic areas of function of mild brain damage to these particular aspects of cognitive organization.

I have offered the speculative type of hypotheses because of their complexity and subtlety. These cognitive controls or patterns or strategies of information processing may be peculiarly susceptible areas because of their complexity, of course, to effects of brain damage. These control strategies or structures have led us to do studies which cut across the old categories such as perception and memory. We have been able to demonstrate, for example, that people who are unusually capable of selective information processing in the intake phase are capable of doing this whether the information originated outside themselves and has gone through rational processes or whether it consists of complex memory structures. We like to think that control strategies may turn up here, there, and everywhere within, of course, a limited set of situations and operations. It helps to break down some of the classifiable categories a bit, and in the paper I refer to the possibility that a difficulty in the attentional control strategies could effect the categorizing behavior. We might go on from there to other behaviors, I think, other versions of the development of cognitive structures. I have discussed with many at some length the possible relationship between an educative approach and the general group kind of approach to the development of cognitive function. I think I have been successful in doing some studies of individual differences to see how this generation will look when one looks at the wide variations that you see in individual children.

I have focused here primarily on a, by now, sizable but grossly inadequate and incomplete group of studies by us and others, largely in this country, of those complex, enduring, overtime strategies for processing, organizing, or controlling input and output or mediating the expression of impulses and purposes in adopting behavior. I have focused on the studies stemming from the interest in personality organization and in individual differences in cognitive organization as an aspect of personality organization.

I would just say again we are strictly placing emphasis on the areas of individuality. We haven't studied the effect of brain damage or other physiological conditions on the structures in systematic practicalities. I look forward to the day when we begin to see some differential sort of synthesizing with different kinds of deprivation, brain damage, and other disorders, but this is largely in the future. I see this material as perhaps interesting general background material for a teacher or teacher's teacher who is interested in cognition. The emphasis has been on the need for future understanding of processes, so that we can more effectively specify what it is we are trying to treat in the various kinds of cognitive insufficiencies, disorders, and defects.

We have struggled a great deal with process concepts. All of the process concepts that we have in our own work are purely hypothetical conclusions. It isn't even possible to validate some of them except as working tools. I should say also that we have found this work exciting and fascinating and interesting, and it seems to be opening up some new avenues of approach on cognitive organization and a somewhat more complex level of pattern. We have taken great pains to demonstrate the overwhelmingly enduring quality of these patterns in adults, and the results with children seem to confirm this. We don't know yet how early patterns of cognitive control strategy are laid down, so that we can again do more systematic developmental studies.

FROSTIG: It has been brought out in the paper on problems of development how important it is that children are unable to keep an idea in mind while they manipulate other ideas. We have some children who can't learn because of this difficulty, but what is important to us is that we find out what is the relationship between the difficulty which a child has in perception, the difficulty which a child has in different language functions, and the difficulties in cognitive functions.

Chapter 10

The Needs of Teachers for Specialized Information on the Development of Visuomotor Skills in Relation to Academic Performance

GERALD N. GETMAN, O.D., and
HOMER H. HENDRICKSON, O.D.

EDITORIAL NOTE.—The relationship between visual perception and the development of both gross and fine motor movements has become a matter of major concern to psychologists, neurologists, and educators in relation to the education of brain-injured children. Dr. Getman, here and elsewhere, has made a series of significant statements on this phase of education. Here he incorporates his ideas as an important competency required of teachers of these children.

Dr. Getman's paper in this Seminar was edited and completed by Dr. Homer H. Hendrickson, O.D., Temple City, California. Dr. Getman's sudden illness prevented his participation in the Seminar, and Dr. Hendrickson very graciously substituted as a participant to represent Dr. Getman's point of view.

DR. GERALD N. GETMAN is well known to teachers in both primary and special education departments for his contributions to work on visuomotor perception and its relation to academic progress. He started his study of vision development in preschool children with Dr. Arnold Gesell at Yale University in 1945. These early studies were extended into laboratory and clinical research on visual performance problems of children unable to learn by standard academic programs. Dr. Getman has worked with Professor Emmett Betts, at Temple University; Professor Samuel Ranshaw, at Ohio State University; and with Professor N. C. Kephart, at Purdue University. He has conducted many teachers' workshops and seminars at major colleges and universities in the past ten years. He served on the summer school faculty at Texas Woman's University in 1964. In the summer of 1965 he assisted the State of Hawaii in the organization of their visual screening program under Project Headstart.

Dr. Getman presently serves as consultant to several private schools and to several state departments of education. He has provided many monographs for intraprofessional publications; his book, *How To Develop Your Child's Intelligence,* has become very popular with parents and is used by numerous universities and colleges as a supplemental text.

Chapter 10

The Needs of Teachers for Specialized Information on the Development of Visuomotor Skills in Relation to Academic Performance

GERALD N. GETMAN, O.D., and
HOMER H. HENDRICKSON, O.D.

It is strangely interesting that visuomotor skills and their development continue to be misunderstood by clinicians and educators. In spite of all that has been written and all that is in the process of publication, visuomotor skills and clearness of sight, at distance and near, are continually presented as equivalent performance areas. Evidence of this lies in the frequent references to distance sight acuity in the same breath with discussions of visuomotor disabilities.

A few examples of this confusion will illustrate this point. In early May 1965, a one-day seminar was held at Rutgers University on the perceptual problems of the slow-learning child. The major speaker presented within his discussion specific comments about the importance of the basic oculomotor skills, their primary relationship to visuomotor skills, and the ultimate relationship to the visual performance involved in learning to read in standard academic programs. Another speaker, who served on the discussion panel, devoted his alloted time to questioning the relationship between oculomotor skills and learning performance. Amazingly, this same authority has published extensive research which shows that 92 per cent of those who demonstrate learning problems also demonstrate visuomotor problems. Another instance is a new public health service publication on amblyopia ex anopsia. This bulletin repeatedly stresses the importance of clarity of sight as the criterion for this condition, and states that it is a common cause of "blindness" throughout the world. Every clinician knows that an amblyopic eye is not a blind eye. It is merely incapable of standard acuity on a symbol chart. The third and most extensive indication of the confusion between visuomotor skills and acuity is shown on the government-issued screening forms for Project Headstart. Here, an entire program designed to screen out problems that would contribute to learning difficulties listed

155

acuity on a chart at twenty feet as the only test necessary. The eight-day Gemini 5 flight conducted an experiment on visual acuity, and it points up the paradox of the 1965 use of the 1865 Snellen acuity test. Targets were constructed on the ground, based on the angle of arc sub-tended at the eyes of the astronauts, to test their acuity. If Mrs. Gordon Cooper had written "I love you" in the grass of a mountainside with a lawnmower, her husband would have been able to read it!

Literally hundreds of similar examples could be quoted. The im-portant point is not the frequency of misunderstanding; our concern lies with the fact that classroom teachers or teachers of brain-injured chil-dren cannot be expected to understand "visuomotor deficiencies" or the need for the development of visuomotor skills until such confusions as those illustrated are eliminated.

Frequent workshops, seminars, and interprofessional discussions with educators of the past five years prove that the classroom teacher has a better understanding of visuomotor skills than most clinicians suspected. These are the first people to ask, "What are we to look for after we receive the clinician's report stating: 'There is nothing wrong with this child's eyes; he has 20/20 acuity'?" It is the teacher who knows that today's curriculum places a high demand upon vision, as a process, and the ability to interpret and comprehend all information expressed by printed materials.

Before an attempt is made to answer the teachers' question, and their next most frequent question ("What can we do in the classroom to develop the child's visual skills?"), definitions of vision, as the term will be used in this paper, are in order.

There must be an understandable differentiation between the terms, sight, acuity, and vision. This differentiation is necessary if there is to be a more realistic appraisal of visual performance by the teacher in the classroom.

Getman defines *sight* as the response of the eye to any light that enters it. The eye will align with the light source to gain the most even distribution of light across the retina; the pupil of the eye will dilate or constrict according to the intensity of the light that is entering the eye. Sight is the "alerting process" that allows the eye to set itself in readiness for seeing. *Acuity* is the result of all the sensori-motor actions that take place in the end organ (the eye) that will provide for the clarity of the light pattern that strikes the retina. The two eyes align and the dioptric systems of the eye adjust to bring the most adequate light distribution across the retina for the most adequate "sign" of the pattern or object seen.

Vision is the learned ability to see for information and performance,

Vision is the ability to understand the things we cannot touch, taste, smell, or hear. Vision is the process whereby we perceive space as a whole.

Vasco Ronchi (1957) states:

There is a body emitting radiation . . . . Impulses are generated by way of the optic nerve . . . to the brain . . . then the mind goes into action . . . inferring whatever it can [from the data received] with regard to the form and position of the emitting body. . . . The mind portrays the conclusion with an *effigy* which it then places outside the body at the distance deduced from the data received— it endows this effigy with form and colors. . . . The mind then confronts the luminous colored effigy (which it has created) and says it "sees the object."

It is only by vision that spatial relations of objects (or symbols) outside the body, and at a distance from it, are rapidly and efficiently dealt with in detail, in terms of economy of time and movement.

Vision is a closed energy sequence in an open energy system of the body. Vision is a process and an output. Vision consists of a coded, patterned input (which can be modified with lenses) that is matched (integrated) with the past experiences of the organism as well as the immediate inputs of the other sense modalities and is manifest by operant behavior. Vision, which utilizes a sense receptor for radiant energy, extends far beyond the confines of the mechanism of that receptor. Vision, which is the dominant process of development, could, when the responses within the organism are distorted, impose that distortion back upon the receptor and so further distort the stimulus and itself. This will be discussed later.

The development of vision has been elaborately traced by Gesell *et al.* (1949). As the infant establishes manipulative skills of his body for the exploration of the objects in his world, he learns the use, purpose, and value of these body parts in relation to the objects. He establishes skills in movement of himself through space, learning the body schemes for action. He learns *general movement* patterns *for action*— learning to use and move his head, body, arms, hands, legs, and feet to explore his world—and learns to guide these movements by using his *eyes* as the steering mechanism.

There is a direct relationship between how well a child moves about in his world, in organizing his actions into total behavior patterns, and how well he interprets his world through his visual mechanisms. His

Herrick (1956) says, "Motility is the seed bed of the mind. Motility experiences are dependent upon movement.

is the organized, integrated, directed, rhythmic behavior of the organism." Movement is essential for visual development.

Special movement patterns of action are learned when the child uses his body parts concurrently to control and manipulate the things in his world. He learns to use these manipulations to develop the movements of eyes and hands, or eyes and legs, or eyes and arms in combination. *Eye movement patterns* are learned *to reduce action* for quick, accurate, efficient visual inspection and interpretation of his world. This allows him to learn to use vision to obtain information about his world without the movements previously needed for exploration and manipulation.

The child learns to use his visual and movement experiences for communication with others, by developing *communication* patterns *to replace action.* There is established a visual and language relationship which permits the exchange of information through speech. *Visualization patterns* are learned *to substitute for action,* speech, and time. He learns the visual interpretation of likenesses and differences, finally in words and numbers, to gain further information about his world from printed materials. He relates and understands these symbols by visualization of actual or similar events in which he has participated, is participating, or will participate.

The child's ability to interpret the world and his place in it visually is learned. Hence, visual perception is learned. It is adequately and properly learned only to the extent of a child's action and interaction with *his* world. These actions and interactions are not always spontaneous and must be encouraged and/or arranged by adults. Thus, ultimately and ideally, adequate visual abilities are learned by the child.

Since visual abilities are learned, the teacher needs to: (1) know those visual abilities and how they are related to academic performance; (2) acquire competency in recognizing visual inabilities in a child which may adversely affect the academic performance; (3) know what performance in certain visual abilities is indicative of need for professional remedial visual care, and (4) know how to enhance certain of those visual abilities within the teacher's sphere of competency and training.

Five specific and highly related areas of information on vision for the teacher can be described. These five areas are especially related to academic performance and will assist the teacher to gain a far better understanding of all that is being written about visuomotor disabilities.

FIVE VISUAL SKILLS RELATED TO ACADEMIC SKILLS

Three of these visuomotor skills are visual action patterns that should be learned by the majority of children before they reach school age. They are: eye movement skills, eye teaming skills, and eye-hand coordinations. Unfortunately, many children have not gained these skills to a degree that is adequate to the demands of the primary grades, and the teacher's first observations should be directed to these three. The other two visual performance skills are products, or resultants, of the first three. They are visual form perception, and refractive status of the eyes. Although these two skills are not visible in explicit movements of the child, his observable performances in the visual tasks of the classroom will permit the teacher to make some valuable judgments of his abilities (or disabilities) in these two areas.

The following are the perceptual purposes of these visual skills, the academic pertinence of each, the signs of inadequacies, and the indications for referral.

Eye Movement Skill (Ocular Motilities)

This skill consists of being able quickly and accurately to align both eyes on an object, at the same time and place in space; to release and move in a controlled manner to another object; or to maintain alignment on a moving object. This skill provides a consistent visual input to be matched to other sensory inputs and the experiences of the organism.

The purpose of eye movement skill is to provide rapid, accurate visual scanning and visual inspection in all areas of classroom activities. The accurate and fluid horizontal movement of the eyes is requisite to movement of eyes across the lines of print in a textbook as well as to rapid, accurate return to the next line of print. Vertical eye movements (up and down, and some far to near–near to far movements) are used, for example, from desk to teacher and chalkboard or for columns of numbers. Diagonal eye movements are required in visual scan of worksheets and visual inspection of tridimensionality on arts and crafts materials.

Inadequate ability in eye movement skills is observed by the teacher when there is head turning by the child instead of eye movement, short attention span, frequent loss of place on the page, omission of words and phrases, confusion of left and right directions, poor orientation of writing or drawings on the page, or stumbling and clumsiness in playground activities.

Improvement of this skill will be noted when these problems decrease: for example, head turning reduces and the child no longer loses his place. The need for professional visual care is indicated when the child continues to avoid visual materials whenever possible, confusion continues in left-to-right directionality and he cannot think his way through a "direction" question, attention span shortens on visual materials but is notably increased on craft materials, or fatigue rate is higher on symbol materials. This visual ability is not identified by any standard screening tests used by most school nurses or teachers. If the visual problem continues beyond the first six weeks of school, the child should be referred.

Eye Teaming Skill (Binocularity)

The purpose of this skill is to provide speed and effectiveness of visual identification and interpretation of printed details. Children must learn and establish excellent teaming of the two eyes if accuracy of visual grasp of words is to be achieved. The accuracy and speed of "focusing" is dependent upon the degree of eye teaming the children achieve.

There are two aspects to be observed by the teacher: (1) horizontal teaming—alignment of both eyes so that they are in position to inspect the same symbol at the same instant (to provide singleness and clearness of all materials) and (2) near to far–far to near teaming—immediate clarity and accuracy of recognition of objects or symbols at all points in the classroom.

Inadequate abilities in eye teaming are indicated by complaints of seeing double, repetition of letters within words or words in the same sentence, omission of words or numbers, closing of one eye, extreme head tilt or working off one side of desk, poor orientation of writing or drawing on paper, total postural deviations that continue at all desk activities, excessive blinking, comprehension lower than apparent abilities, or extreme fatigue on all visual materials.

Improvements should be noted after a few weeks of school as the child becomes acquainted with the instructional program. Body posture will improve; attention span will lengthen; placement on the page will improve; fatigue on visual materials will notably decrease. Need for professional visual care is indicated when one eye turns in or out upon looking up from desk activities, when a finger or marker is required to maintain eyes on visual materials, when copying is inaccurate, when fatigue rate increases on visual materials, or when more clumsiness than usual is noted in visually demanding tasks with *less* needed on the playground.

Problems in eye teaming *may* show up on some screening tests. Often the 20/20 test is passed but one eye may turn in or out under the cover while the other is used to read the chart. Delay in visual care will either deter the child's academic progress or allow him to learn to ignore (suppress) one eye. He may continue to do quite well in the subjects where he can learn by listening, but he will show extreme inadequacies in any independent reading or writing skills.

Eye-Hand Coordination Skill

This skill consists of the eyes steering the hand(s) accurately and skillfully through the three coordinates of space, which are matched with the coordinates of the body and vision, for the purpose of manipulating tools or to form the symbols of the mother tongue. The purpose of this ability is to make visual discriminations of size, shape, texture, and object location. It is dependent upon use, practice, and integration of eyes and hands as *paired* learning tools. The skill and accuracy of eye-hand coordination for inspection of objects and making the written symbols are preparatory and basic to the visual interpretations of likenesses and differences of the words or numbers printed in work- and textbooks. The child's muscle awareness and his visual observations of his own hand movements in the reproduction of symbols (numbers, letters, words, forms, lines, formulas) assist him in acquiring the left-to-right concepts of his culture. This understanding of the cultural demands then assists him in gaining the left-to-right eye movements for the visual inspection of the printed pages of his textbooks.

Indications of a visual problem in this skill are: the need to feel things before any interpretive decision can be made; extreme lack of orientation on the page, as if the eyes were not used to "steer" hand movements; writing that is crooked, poorly spaced, not kept on ruled lines of paper; the need to use the hand or finger tips to steer eye movements across the page; or messy craft work in any grade after mid-first grade. If any of these problems persist after a short time in school, some degree of visual problem probably exists. Time alone will not eliminate this problem and special help must be given the child if he is to succeed in academic demands. In addition to professional visual care, the teacher should provide activities that will establish the eye-hand coordination.

Visual Form Perception (*Visual Imagery, Visual Memory*)

The skills of ocular motility, ocular teaming, and eye-hand coordination provide the perceptual information that permits the translation of object size, shape, texture, location, distance, and three-dimensional solidity into understandable pictures and words. The interpretation of these symbols (pictures and words) through the visual mechanism is a skill derived from the *visual* and *tactual* skills. Visual form perception is a derived skill—not a separate or independent skill. The ultimate purpose of this skill is the immediacy and accuracy of the visual discrimination of likenesses and differences so that comprehension can be achieved, and the appropriate action can follow.

Indications of a visual problem include any confusion of forms that indicates difficulty in the visual recognition of likenesses and differences, frequent return to use of the hands to determine likenesses and differences, any evidence of lack of skill in visualization, or any confusion or difficulty in the simple reproduction of symbols on paper. When there is opportunity for experience, the child demonstrates improvements by using his hands for reinforcement and clarification; drawings and writing become neater and erasures are made to improve accuracy. Specialized visual care is indicated when full use of hands does not produce observable improvements or when paper work continues to be erratic, with simple forms distorted, and the child becomes too quickly discouraged by his lack of ability to "make good pictures."

Understandably, the so-called normal child in the kindergarten and first grade should not be expected to demonstrate a high degree of skill in this area, but, if a child is obviously poorer than his group, he must be given special attention. If a reasonable degree of skill is not acquired by second grade, the lack of form-perception ability will be a hindrance in all academic areas, with the most difficulty being experienced in spelling and writing.

It must be stressed here that all training in form perception must be done in the basic underlying processes of ocular motilities and eye-hand coordinations rather than in repetitive practice on the symbols and forms themselves.

Refractive Status (Hyperopia, Myopia, Astigmatism, Refractive Problems)

This is really more than a skill area; it is, like form perception, a condition determined by the other areas of visual performance. This area of consideration is of such supreme importance, however, that every adult concerned with children and their academic achievement needs to be aware of any evidence of a refractive problem. Distortions or inadequacies of the eyes that alter the visual information signals (which the child must interpretively match with auditory and tactual signals every moment of every class day) can hinder the child's comprehension processes. Some of these ocular distortions can so completely override the auditory and tactual information signals that comprehension can be completely voided.

The indications of ocular refractive problems are many: loss of comprehension in any reading task which is continued beyond a paragraph or two, continued mispronunciations of similar letters or words, excessive blinking while reading or writing, holding the book too close or writing too close, avoidance of all near-centered visual tasks, any complaint of discomfort (eye ache or headache) or inability to learn in a task that demands consistent visual interpretations, closing or covering one eye while reading or doing desk work, frequent errors in transfer from chalkboard to paper or reference book to paper, squinting to see the chalkboard or moving nearer to see it, inflammation of the eyes after short visual activity, frequent rubbing of eyes, observable sag or fatigue after intensive visual activities.

These are the most obvious of the symptoms of a visual problem related to a refractive problem. There may be other, less specific symptoms, such as lack of interest, lack of motivation, or irritability. Only two or three of the trouble signs listed above will be verified, or even discovered, by the wall-chart test and other screening devices. When the child is given an "eye test," and the report of "full 20/20" comes back, there must be further examination of visual abilities by a more thorough examiner. The child who is to gain over 80 per cent of his knowledge through his visual mechanism, and who will spend the majority of his daily classroom time in visual tasks at his desk, must have the full benefits of the visual examination that gives adequate and careful consideration to the academic demands put upon his eyes. These problems will become worse with classroom demands. The child may become a nonachiever to avoid the increase in visual problem and discomfort, or he may sacrifice visual abilities and increase his ocular distortions to maintain achievement. In either case, he suffers the consequences.

The clinical evidence is rapidly accumulating that even ametropia (defective sight) is, in the large majority of cases, the result of an adaptation to continued stress and cultural impact. Thus, the less desirable conditions are, in a sense, also learned as the child does the best he can to cope with the demands placed upon him.

In recent years numerous investigators have shown that the effectiveness and availability of *all* sensori-motor body systems will influence *perception* and *learning processes*. Shipman (1955) states that "stress brings up a constriction of the perceptual fields, and the child observes less, sees less, remembers less, learns less, and becomes generally less efficient." Selye (1956) has demonstrated that when animals are under stress, confined, and their movement is limited, they develop various lesions and abnormalities. Perception is impossible without movement, and the examination of the structure of the end organ itself (ears, eyes, skin) is not adequate for the assessment of perceptual abilities. Hebb (1949), using an enclosing cubicle, brought about disturbances in space and size perception, such as illness, dizziness, hallucinations, and other perceptual deviations. Harmon (1958) has declared that the near-centered task brings on a response of avoidance through the involuntary nervous system.

It would appear that an important factor in symbol-interpretation failures that may have been overlooked was that of avoidance, the physiologic urge within the organism to preserve its own operational integrity by escaping from a threat to itself.

Speech is learned, and so is vision. Vision is usually acquired fairly well, in every aspect in the world around the child, until the culture faces him with the printed page and demands of him the supremely difficult task of matching that visual configuration with a far more developed speech-auditory system.

To create a congenial visual climate for learning to read, a method or means must be found to satisfy the avoidance response of the organism and yet allow continuity of learning to match visually recorded symbols (within arm's reach or nearer) with the speech-auditory experiences that the organism already has.

Skeffington (1930–65) has stated that a convex spherical spectacle lens has the property of doing this—it allows the organism to continue at the near-centered visual task. It provides satisfaction of the avoidance urge, that of avoiding or getting away from the containing task. Thus the organism can "achieve" and "avoid" at the same time.

Harmon's study at the laboratory of the Radiological Group in Austin, Texas, shows clearly the effects of avoidance responses on subjects in the act of reading. Convex lenses were applied in gradually increasing power. When the acceptable power was reached, the photographed subjects gave indisputable evidence that the total organismic revolt against the containment factor of reading was dispelled. Tensions in the muscles of the back were reduced; oscillation of the head and neck ceased; blood pressure, respiratory behavior, and galvanic skin reaction showed a strong tendency to return to normal.

Obviously, this can be considered a "visual problem" and not an "eye problem." Among those who have a "visual problem" there need be no loss of ability to *see* clearly, at a distance or near. In fact, there may be a heightening of the sheer acuity process. Only recently has the idea emerged that the stress of containment can cause the child to "observe, see, remember, and learn less." No other method of meeting this response to containment has yet been found, except through the use of convex spectacle lenses for all containing tasks. They are not used as a sign of an "eye problem"; there is no eye problem, as yet. They are used as "learning lenses" (for classroom use only), as a tool for the child's job of learning, to protect him against developing ocular defects. Unless such lenses are applied protectively and preventively, it has been found that by the end of the fifth grade about 80 per cent of the children will have developed a measurable "eye problem."

The question is raised, "Would you put lenses on every child?" It arises from the almost universal feeling that lenses indicate something already wrong with the eyes. The new approach is to ask, "Would you protect the learning ability of every child?" The answer is that there is little question that every child would benefit from the use of protective "learning lenses" in the classroom. Teachers need to know that, by modern optometric methods, children will be fitted with lenses when they can see without them, and significant gains in achievement will be noted. Some will be given dual-focus lenses, when added convex-lens help is needed at the reading distance and their distance sight would be blurred through that lens.

The teacher need no longer be fearful of "over-referring." Vision plays such a large part in academic progress and the validity of the teacher's observations has been so well established, it is time to state that the majority of "over-referrals" are really instances of "under-examination." The teacher and, of course, the parents of the child have every right to request a further investigation of visual abilities when the signs of visual difficulties persist even after some clinical care has been sought. As the teacher learns to observe the visual skills that are related to school demands, the parents will want to know whether or not the visual problem has been cared for—before it becomes a permanent hindrance to the child's responses in his learning opportunities.

THE DEVELOPMENT OF VISUOMOTOR SKILLS

Teachers can help children develop visuomotor skills and abilities. The teacher needs to become familiar with certain visual training theories, procedures, and techniques, and to know the limitations within which improvements of these skills may be effected in the classroom and school environment.

Optometric visual training is the term applied to the arranging of conditions whereby a child, or adult, may learn adequate degrees of freedom of movement to permit efficient visual functioning for the interpretation of light energy patterns.

The purpose of visual training in the classroom is to arrange conditions whereby a child may learn or improve the primary visual abilities —eye movements, eye teaming (binocularity), eye-hand coordinations, and visual form perception (visual imagery, visual memory). The purpose is not to strengthen eye muscles but to establish smooth, skillful eye control for a consistency of visual inputs; not to establish or change eye preference but to develop bilateral, binocular functioning to unify the inputs of the two eyes which are in turn to be matched with the experiences of the organism for information and action; not to change handedness or mixed or crossed dominance, or to establish ambidexterity, but to build bilaterality, freedom, and control of the hands, with the eyes steering and skillfully following or directing movements for productive achievement; not to learn specific forms and shapes but the ability to generalize and perceive and reproduce any form, or combinations of forms, and to visualize forms, places, things, ideas, concepts.

Specific activities and procedures have been elaborately described by optometrists (Getman, 1962), educators (Getman and Kane, 1964), psychologists, and others, for the development of visuomotor skills. Limitations of space will permit but a brief review of the philosophy and methods.

Practice in general coordination, in general movement patterns, provides the specific experiences in total body movement that many children miss, or because of some physical limitation do not have the opportunity to acquire. As skills are gained, the entire body becomes the supporting and contributing action system for the visual interpretations and comprehensions of the symbols of the classroom and the culture. If indeed, as Herrick says, "Motility is the seed bed of the mind," then the ability to move is paramount. The entire muscle system of the body may have even more influence on perception than any single receptor or combination of sense receptors.

Visual perception is dependent upon consistent matching of the immediate light pattern inputs of vision with the immediate inputs of the other senses *and* the past motor experiences (stored movement patterns) of the organism. The latter are more immediately available if, when they are experienced, they are also matched with the related visual inputs of the act. In other words, if when a child feels an object (moves his fingers across it, pinches or pokes it) he also looks at it, he will then be able, at a later time, to know more adequately what it feels like by merely looking at it. Ultimately, he will "know" what the object feels like by looking at a symbol (a picture or even a word) which represents it. Hence, it becomes important for movement, preferably all movement, to be related to, integrated with, and monitored by the associated light inputs of vision.

Eye movement patterns are trained for the purpose of producing consistent visual inputs to be matched with experiences of the oragnism for optimum localization and identification. Clinically, remedially, and developmentally, optometrists train pursuit eye movements with moving targets, and this can be accomplished in a classroom simply and in many ways. Ask each child to follow his own thumb nail as he moves it laterally, back and forth at his eye level, up and down on the midline, in circles, without head movement, seeing and noting as many objects as possible in his field of view. Have him look for colors, distances of objects, direction, and sizes. *Saccadic,* or side-to-side eye movements, should be trained as well as near-far-near movements. Many activities in the classroom lend themselves to this training.

Eye teaming (binocularity) skill is a result of bilaterality, total unity, and reciprocity of the total organism. As a foundation, the child needs to build an adequate body scheme, through tactile, kinesthetic, and visual monitoring. He needs to learn to move against gravity, the one most constant energy in his environment. By the use of the eyes to steer and monitor, all types of movement through space can be programmed for the purpose of gaining and storing information. Rolling, crawling, creeping, walking, hopping, jumping, or skipping are examples of movements the child should be able to execute, purposefully, in order to move, visually directed, through space. Targets for sight should be provided and peripheral visual targets introduced for accurate computing and localization by the child. Gaining, losing, and regaining, as well as maintaining, balance against gravity are a part of building bilaterality, binocularity, and a stable organism—a stable "launch platform" for purposeful eye-hand movements. Using the walk rail, teeter board, balance board, jump board, or jump rope, playing hopscotch, and many more activities can be programmed into the entrance and exit from the classroom and into every playground period and physical education class.

Practice in eye-hand coordination gives children the opportunity to learn how hands work together in pairs, in unity, and how to use eyes and hands as a team. The visual-tactual systems are a foundation for inspections and perceptions, a foundation upon which all symbolic interpretations and manipulations can be based. Chalkboard routines of bilateral circles, squares, rectangles, triangles, and so on, with the eyes guiding and monitoring the arm movements and chalk traces, build bilaterality, binocularity, rhythm, and awareness of size, direction, starts, stops, and changes of direction.

Visual form perception can be trained through such elementary gross or general movement activities as walking the sides of squares, circles, and triangles painted or chalked on the parking lot or sidewalk, or through special movements by combining movements of eyes and hands in template use, tracing forms, or reproducing forms. Templates are used at the chalkboard and at the desk on paper. They develop visual discriminations of figure-ground relationships, basic forms, perceptions of size, likenesses, and differences, and the motor-visual coordinations which underlie the basic acts related to reading, writing, spelling, and the manipulations of arithmetic.

SUMMARY

Vision is more than acuity. Vision is learned and trainable. Vision is the dominant process of development. Movement is essential for visual perception. Visuomotor skills should be trained by training general movement patterns and special movement patterns—always with the eyes participating. Teachers of brain-injured children can make significant contributions by training eye movements, eye teaming, eye-hand coordination, and visual form perception. Observation of children's visual performance, by the teacher, is one of the best methods of discovering visual problems and the need for professional vision care.

The needs of teachers for specialized information on the development of visuomotor skills, in relationship to academic performance, is summarized thus: (1) The teacher needs to know how visual abilities are related to academic performance. (2) The teacher should be able to recognize those visual inabilities that adversely affect the child's academic performance and that defeat the teacher's efforts and prevent expected academic progress. (3) The teacher needs to know what performance in certain visual abilities is indicative of the need for professional remedial visual care. (4) The teacher should know how to enhance the academically related visual abilities within her sphere of usual competency and training.

SELECTED REFERENCES

Gesell, A., Ilg, F., and Bullis, G. E. *Vision, its development in infant and child.* New York: Paul B. Hoeber, 1949.

Getman, G. N. *How to develop your child's intelligence.* Luverne, Minn.: Announcer Press, 1962.

———. "The primary visual abilities essential to academic achievement," *Child Vision Care.* Duncan, Okla.: Optometric Extension Program, 1964.

Getman, G. N., and Kane, E. R. *The physiology of readiness.* Minneapolis, Minn.: Programs to Accelerate School Success, 1964.

Harmon, D. B. *Notes on a dynamic theory of vision.* Austin, Tex.: published by the author, 1958.

Hebb, D. O. *The organization of behavior.* New York: John Wiley, 1949.

Herrick, C. Judson. *The evolution of human nature.* Austin: University of Texas Press, 1956.

Ronchi, Vasco. *Optics, the science of vision.* E. Rosen (trans.). New York: New York University Press, 1957.

Selye, Hans. *The stress of life.* New York: McGraw-Hill, 1956.

Shipman, V. I. Paper read before the Eastern Psychological Association, Philadelphia, 1955.

Skeffington, A. M. *Functional optometry.* Duncan, Okla.: Optometric Extension Program, 1930–65.

Chapter 11

The Needs of Teachers for Specialized
Information on Perception

NEWELL C. KEPHART, Ph.D.

EDITORIAL NOTE.—Dr. Kephart has had a long and close relationship with the psychoeducational problems of brain-injured children. An associate and colleague of Heinz Werner and Alfred A. Strauss at the Wayne County Training School in Northville, Michigan, Dr. Kephart's initial contact with this problem was with exogenous mentally retarded children. He contributes significantly to an understanding of the relationship between perceptual diagnostic procedures and the resultant educational corollary culminating in the "perceptual-motor match"—which understanding is an essential competency for teachers of brain-injured children.

DR. NEWELL C. KEPHART is Professor of Education and Executive Director of the Achievement Center for Children at Purdue University, Lafayette, Indiana. He received the B.A. and M.A. degrees from the University of Denver in 1932 and 1933 and the Ph.D. degree from the State University of Iowa in 1936. He served as Mental Hygienist at the Wayne County Training School and as Research Analyst with the United States Employment Service and in the United States Bureau of Naval Personnel before coming to Purdue in 1945.

Dr. Kephart is the author of *The Slow Learner in the Classroom* and co-author with Alfred A. Strauss of *Psychopathology and Education of the Brain Injured Child: Vol. II.*

Chapter 11

The Needs of Teachers for Specialized Information on Perception

NEWELL C. KEPHART, Ph.D.

One of the initial learning problems of the child is that of becoming familiar with the basic realities of the universe which surrounds him. Essentially, these basic realities are two—space and time. The child is confronted with the task, first, of making adequately precise observations on the various dimensions of space and time and, second, with combining these observations into a system or structure within which he can organize and integrate objects and events. It is through such a comprehensive and organized structure that events in the environment become comprehensible and by which the relationship between these events can be preserved. The great majority of brain-injured children have difficulty in making the adequate observations necessary to the development of a space-time structure and even more difficulty in organizing these observations into a comprehensive schema.

In general educational curricula and educational techniques assume such a schema as a point of departure for teaching. It follows that the brain-injured child can be expected to have difficulty with educational procedures inasmuch as the basic assumptions underlying the techniques and procedures are not fulfilled. Initial educational approaches with such children, therefore, should involve an attempt to establish these basic assumptions concerning the physical universe.

DEVELOPMENT OF MOTOR PATTERNS

The child's initial information concerning his environment is motor information. It involves experimentation with the various parts of his body and the movements of which they are capable. He observes these movements and the alterations in space involved in the accomplishment of these movements, and thereby develops an initial body of motor information about the environment. In this motor experimentation he encounters objects and manipulates them, thereby building up motor information concerning the nature of concrete objects.

Notice, however, from an educational point of view, the interest is in motor activities as sources of information and in motor functions as methods of exploration for the development of consistent information. The educator is not interested in motor performances per se nor in skilled motor activities which yield limited information. In the language of the physical educator, interest lies more in motor patterns than in motor skills.

A motor skill is a movement or a limited series of movements performed with high degrees of precision for the accomplishment of a specific end. A motor pattern, on the other hand, consists of a large number of activities performed with lesser degrees of precision but permitting the development of consistent information.

Thus, walking may be a motor skill. In this case the child places one foot in front of the other with high degrees of precision for the limited purpose of locomoting from one point to another. Locomotion, on the other hand, is a motor pattern. It involves many specific movements (such as walking, running, jumping, hopping) and permits the child to divert his attention from the movement itself to the exploration of the space between two points. Motor patterns, therefore, permit consistent exploration of the environment; whereas motor skills serve only limited purposes.

DEVELOPMENT OF GENERALIZATION

An extensive motor pattern or a combination of motor patterns leads to a motor generalization. Such a generalization is in all ways similar to the generalization on the concept level with which educators are more accustomed to deal. The motor generalization involves an initial datum which is elaborated through variation, the integration of these variations, and abstraction from this integration of a generalized principle. Thus, locomotion, in addition to being a pattern, may become a generalization. In this event the motor activities are completely subservient to the exploratory behavior, and a wide range of motor responses are called upon as the necessities of exploration, and particularly the necessities of *consistent* exploration, demand. During all such exploratory activity, the child's attention is devoted to the information-gathering aspect of the behavior, and it is not necessary to divert this attention at any time to the movements or the motor responses which are required.

There are four motor generalizations that are particularly important to education because of their relationship to the development of a space-time structure. The first of these is balance and maintenance of posture.

This generalization involves those activities by which the child maintains his relationship to gravity. The basis of space structure is the force of gravity. All objects in the universe are related to all other objects, but these relationships are relative. The only constant, for the human organism on the planet earth, among all these relativities is the force of gravity. For this reason, as Einstein has pointed out, the force of gravity becomes the point of origin of the three dimensions of Euclidean space.

Because of the relativity of spatial relationships, it is extremely important that a child learn to maintain an adequate relationship to gravity and that he be aware of both the point of application of gravity and its direction. It is only through this constant awareness of the gravitational force that a point of origin for the development of the dimensions of space is possible.

The second generalization is that of locomotion. It is through the locomotor generalization that the child observes the relationships *between* objects in space. He locomotes from one object to another, observing the relationship between them. If locomotion is a skill, then a child can only observe the beginning and ending of the explorations. During the intervening time his attention must be diverted to the locomotor movements. If, on the other hand, locomotion is a generalization, then observations of *all* the spatial relationships between the initial object and the final object can be observed consistently and thoroughly. In this latter event, a structure of the relationship between the two objects becomes possible.

The third generalization is that of contact. This involves those activities by which the child manipulates objects. Involved here are three basic stages: reach, by which he makes contact with the object; grasp, by which he maintains this contact while he observes the relationships within the object; and release, by which he terminates this activity and goes on to the next object. It is with these contact activities that the child observes relationships *within* objects. Out of extensive motor observations of this kind will later develop form perception, figure-ground relationships, and so forth.

The final generalization is that of receipt and propulsion. Receipt involves those activities by which the child makes contact with a moving object. Propulsion involves those activities by which the child imparts movement to an object. With the former the child investigates movement toward himself. With the latter he investigates movement away from himself. With a combination of the two he investigates movement lateral to himself.

With the first three motor generalizations the child has been able to make the necessary exploration to establish a structure among static objects in space. Many activities in his environment, however, involve the movement of objects in space. It is with this final generalization, receipt and propulsion, that he establishes a structure involving movement in space. It is out of this structure that an impression of a figure moving in front of a ground will develop.

This initial body of motor information is extremely important to the development of a consistent space structure involving the three dimensions of Euclidean space. For the development of such information, motor generalizations are required. Many brain-injured children have difficulty in the establishment of these initial motor generalizations. When their behavior does involve the motor activities necessary to such generalizations, it is frequently apparent that these activities are skills rather than patterns. As such they can not be used for the development of a consistent body of information. They give only specific information that is incongruent in both space and time and, hence, leads to marked difficulty in the development of a space-time structure.

It is important to remember that the educator's interest is not in the development of specific motor activities. There are no specific motor functions which are essential to the development of learning. Motor generalizations develop out of a variety of motor activities. No particular movement is *essential* to such development. What is required is a flexibility of motor performance which provides for variation and, hence, the abstraction of the generalization. It is the resulting generalization and not the specific motor movement which provides the consistent, thorough body of information necessary to the development of a structure.

In similar manner, it is not important that movements be performed in a certain fashion. In the development of a body of motor information, much distortion in individual movement can be tolerated. As long as the distortion is constant, it can be corrected for in the development of the information structure. It is the inconsistent distortion resulting from inadequate motor learning which makes the development of an information structure difficult or impossible. Thus, educators should not insist on particular patterns of behavior or particular forms of movement. Their concern should be with the consistency of the motor performance insofar as that consistency permits a similar consistency in the information that is being collected.

THE PERCEPTUAL-MOTOR MATCH

As the body of motor information becomes more adequate, the child begins to pay attention to the perceptual information that is coming into the organism at the same time. Perceptual information, however, becomes meaningful only insofar as it is correlated with previous motor information. Perceptual data enter the organism in a coded form. The external sense organ sends to the central nervous system a pattern of neurological impulses. This pattern of impulses, however, although it is related to a pattern of external energy, is unrelated to any activities of the organism or any information which the organism now possesses. In order to decode perceptual information it is necessary to compare it with the previous body of motor information which has been built up.

It is this process which has been called the perceptual-motor match. Perceptual information is matched to earlier motor information. Through this matching procedure perceptual data come to supply the same information that the previous motor data supplied. By this means a consistent body of information which can be translated back and forth between motor and perceptual abilities is established.

If the perceptual-motor match is not made or if it is made in an inadequate fashion, the child comes to live in two worlds: one a motor world in which he moves and responds, and the other a perceptual world in which he sees, hears, smells, and so on. Since these two worlds are not matched, they give information which can not be collated and the result is bizarre behavior resulting from responses based upon a different body of information than was the stimulation.

Perceptual information involves certain distortions. In the field of vision, for example, form constancy is a recurrent problem. A circular form is circular only if its orientation is vertical to the observer. If the form is rotated slightly so that it lies in a plane not directly vertical to the observer, the shape of its projection on the retina becomes elliptical. If it is rotated still further its retinal image becomes a straight line. The child learns to remove this distortion by comparing the perceptual data with motor data. Motor exploration in any of these planes results in a circular pattern. Through the perceptual-motor match the child learns to see a circular form regardless of its orientation in respect to his line of sight. In similar manner, size constancy is achieved through the perceptual-motor match.

It is therefore essential that the child achieve a perceptual-motor match and that this match be made in the proper direction. Perceptual data must be matched to motor data—not motor information to perceptual information. In the former case the distortions of perceptual data are removed as described above. In the latter case the child remains at the mercy of such perceptual distortions.

Just as it was important that motor explorations be consistent, it is equally important that perceptual manipulations be consistent. To insure consistency of perceptual exploration it is necessary that the child learn to control the external sense organ. Most significant here is the eye because it is the most mobile of our external sense organs. The child must learn how to control the visual input by controlling the direction of his gaze, and he must learn to identify the direction from which the visual data come by observing the direction in which his eye is pointed. He must learn to control the direction of his eye in terms of the perceptual information which is being received. It is not enough to control the eye alone, it must be controlled in terms of the information which it is producing. Thus, ocular control becomes an important problem in the establishment of the perceptual-motor match.

PRINCIPLES OF TEACHING THE BRAIN-INJURED CHILD

From what has been stated it follows that teaching for the brain-injured child should be developmentally oriented. Space-time structures arise developmentally. The initial body of motor information becomes the basis, through the perceptual-motor match, for the more extensive perceptual space-time structure. In similar manner the perceptual information becomes the basis of the conceptual structures which will develop later (these latter are beyond the subject matter of the present paper). It is important that each level of this development become solid and substantial before the next level is built upon it. If this has not occurred in the normal course of learning, then teaching should attempt to shore up those levels that are deficient before proceeding to more complex levels.

It is also apparent that teaching should be directed toward the development of generalizations. It has been repeatedly observed that the brain-injured child learns rote material with relative ease. The difficulty is to induce him to combine these rote materials into generalizations. This problem should be kept in mind and should form the basis of a major portion of the teaching techniques for such children.

Generalizations develop in the same fashion regardless of the level at which they may occur. Whether the generalization is motor, perceptual, or conceptual, its development follows the same pattern and only the data that are used are different.

Generalization begins with the acquisition of a datum. This datum is then elaborated by the acquisition of a large number of similar but not identical experiences. Such elaboration is accomplished through variation. The initial activity is performed in a large variety of ways, each of which produces similar but not identical experience. The normal child introduces such variation for himself. Given an activity, as Kurt Lewin has shown, he will spontaneously perform it in a large number of different ways. The brain-injured child, on the other hand, does not introduce such variation. He will continue to perform the activity in exactly the same way over and over again. Since this child is not able to produce variation for himself, the teacher must introduce it for him. Therefore, teaching should involve the continual introduction of large numbers of variations. These variations will need to be suggested to the child by the teacher since he is not capable of developing them for himself.

When the initial experience has been thus elaborated, the resulting variations are integrated and the similarities abstracted. These abstracted similarities become the generalization. Again, whereas the normal child spontaneously develops this abstraction, the brain-injured child has difficulty. Teaching must therefore be directed toward the development of the abstraction. Here the principle of redundancy is involved. The same material is presented in different ways at the same point in time. If the child cannot develop the similarity from the initial presentation, it is possible that he can observe it in the second presentation. Since these two presentations are simultaneous in time, the combined sources of information will present him with the required similarity. In practice, redundancy is customarily achieved by the use of various sense avenues. It is important, however, that the information be presented simultaneously in time with both sources of information active at once.

It is easy to assume that in the education of the brain-injured child one simply goes back developmentally to that stage where development broke down and recapitulates the normal development of the child. Such a simple solution to the problem, however, does not exist. The child has had to live during the intervening time and has therefore been required to make certain adaptations to his environment. The adaptations in part have been veridical and in part have been distorted. As a result, he has developed the rudiments of a structure but this structure is nonveridical and distorted in whole or in part. It is not possible to go back and teach as though this child were a normal child first encountering the developmental experiences presented. Whatever response he makes to these experiences at this point is colored by the rudimentary structure he has achieved.

For this reason, a third problem arises. One must try to determine the nature and extent of the child's present structuring, and then attempt to produce veridicality in this structure. In this regard, it will customarily be found that the child has areas of behavior that are stronger than other areas. Thus, he performs more easily and gains information more readily through one source than through another. Since the aim is to achieve veridicality in structure and since this must be done at the present point in time, it follows that it is desirable to use the strongest area of activity as the basis for establishing veridicality. It is therefore desirable to work in the child's strongest area of performance in order to insure correct structuring, while at the same time to work in his weak areas of performance in order to insure adequacy of structuring. It seems probable that much good teaching has gone astray because attention was not paid to the problem of establishing veridicality in the already existing structure.

Three major principles in the teaching of the brain-injured child have been suggested: (1) teaching should be developmentally oriented, (2) teaching should be directed toward the development of generalization, (3) attention should be directed toward the establishment of veridicality in the already existing body of the child's information.

THE TIME STRUCTURE

The problem of the development of a space structure has been discussed herein. It is essential that the child develop a similar structure on the dimension of time. The time structure develops in the same general fashion that the space structure developed. It begins with motor responses, continues with perceptual information, and eventuates in concept formation.

It would appear that there are three aspects of temporal learning that are important to education. The first is synchrony: the point of origin for a temporal dimension. The child can not appreciate events separated in time unless he can appreciate events that are simultaneous in time. Motor coordination and simultaneous motor activities are very important in the concept of synchrony.

The second aspect of the temporal dimension is rhythm. It is rhythm that permits the development of a unit on a temporal scale. The child must learn to appreciate equal temporal intervals.

The third aspect of the time dimension is sequence. Sequence means the ordering of events on the temporal scale. It is this aspect that frequently presents a problem in the classroom. The child is unable to perform a series of events in the proper sequence. (Consider, for example, the difficulty of teaching the sequential steps in long division.) This aspect of the problem, however, is more complex. The initial problems of synchrony and rhythm must be solved first before the child can develop a concept of temporal sequence.

The teacher of the brain-injured child should therefore: (1) understand the basic developmental sequences, (2) be able to observe breakdowns in developmental sequences, (3) understand the learning problems leading to generalization, (4) be able to *interpret* nonveridical responses, and (5) be ingenious in the devising of learning experiences adapted to the child with inadequate space-time structure.

Comment

KEPHART: I have chosen to discuss what I think is one of the unique educational requirements of the brain-injured child. I would say that this problem is unique to brain-injury (and possibly emotional disturbance) and indicates a rather different approach than is true in some other areas of exceptionality. One of the basic problems with the brain-injured child is the interference with the authority to organize or integrate, or as I have called it in this paper, *to generalize*. This was the central thesis of Strauss' second volume and has been indicated by a number of other workers.

Until recently, we have tended to feel that if generalization did not occur spontaneously, there was little if anything one could do about it. I think now we are beginning to feel that there are certain techniques by which we can aid generalization. We do not know as much about this as we should, and I suspect it will be a long time before we know anything really significant about it, but I feel that we should attack the problem.

One aspect here which I think has been frequently overlooked is that the problems of integration or generalization occur on all developmental levels, not simply on the cognitive or symbolic level, but on the perceptual level and on the motor level as well. [See also Chapters 9 and 12.]

Therefore, teaching for these children should be directed toward the problem of integration, regardless of the developmental level on which we are operating. If this is not true, we tend to teach in rote memory fashion on the symbolic level. We tend to teach in terms of perceptual differentiation and perceptual recognition on the perceptual level, and we tend to get into what is unfortunately quite common today, a sort of a perceptual-motor calisthenic on the motor level. I think all of these procedures have proved less than optimally successful.

We need to teach and we need to train teachers for the integration of these activities for the child. In the normal child this is not particularly vital, because he will make this integration for himself. In other words, I think that such integration with the normal child is compulsive; he can't avoid making some kind of integration. With the brain-injured child, however, this integrative function appears to be specifically interfered with and, therefore, we must aid in this integration.

When we speak of teaching developmentally in this area, we cannot think in terms of norms such as Gesell's, because we are dealing with a child who has disparities in development and disparities in level of ability. As a result, it could be expected that in his attempt to come to some satisfactory arrangement with the world around him, he would distort the developmental process. Consequently, developmental teaching for these children is different than would be the case with a normal preschool child whose chronological age is similar to the mental age with which we might be dealing. It is not quite as simple, therefore, as teaching normal developmental sequences in the normal sequential fashion.

I believe that another item to which we have not paid enough attention is the problem which I have called *veridicality*, by which is meant the child's organization in response to the fundamental physical laws of the universe. I think we should distingush between veridicality, which is an adjustment to the laws of the universe, and validity, which is an adjustment to social and cultural standards which may be taken by agreement. We tend to assume veridicality in the child's behavior, but in the event of distortions in development and particularly in the event of distortions in generalization, it is probable that this veridicality will also be distorted and the child's fundamental relationships to space and time will be disrupted.

Teachers should be sensitized to the problems of generalization, to the problems of distortion in veridicality, and to the problems of development.

Chapter 12

Teacher Needs—Motor Training
RAY H. BARSCH, Ph.D.

EDITORIAL NOTE.—An area of teacher preparation that has been completely ignored until now pertains to motor training. An aspect of child growth and development which usually needs only cursory attention in the normal child, it is a fundamental issue in the education of brain-injured children. This is a competency which will generally be lacking in the experience and background of teachers and one which must be developed if the teacher is indeed to be able to meet the needs of the brain-injured children who are entrusted to his skills.

DR. RAY H. BARSCH is the Director of the Teacher Preparation Program in the Area of the Physically Handicapped and the Neurologically Impaired in the Graduate School of the University of Wisconsin, Madison, Wisconsin. He is supervising the development of the experimental curriculum in three classes for children with special learning disabilities in the Madison Public School System. He also directs the Learning Disorders Clinic and the Laboratory for Research in Functional Vision.

For fifteen years prior to coming to the University of Wisconsin he served as the Director of the Easter Seal Child Development Center in Milwaukee, Wisconsin.

Chapter 12

Teacher Needs—Motor Training

RAY H. BARSCH, Ph.D.

The examination at this time of the need for teachers of the brain-injured child to be competent in motor training should lead to a profound understanding that a child's need to move is a constant and necessary variable in all learning.

Within the past ten years there has been increasing excitement in the clinical and educational fields, as the motor behavior of children came into sudden prominence as a significant component in the learning situation. Controversy even exists over whether it is more important to have children crawl proficiently as a foundation for reading or crawl proficiently for improving dynamic balance. The entire area of *movement* is enjoying unusual attention at the moment.

Sensori-motor learning has indeed been traditionally included in past consideration of child development, both in the literature of special education and in teacher preparation. But only recently has the concept become part of the more popular considerations such as physical fitness, psychosomatic medicine, perceptual disturbance, and neurological organization.

HISTORY OF INTEREST IN MOVEMENT

Perhaps the first lesson to be learned by the teacher is the recognition that present awareness and concern for motor efficiency is derived from a rich background of educational and experimental literature. It has not suddenly erupted as a new entity.

The heritage is rich indeed. The names of Periere, Montessori, Itard, Seguin, Piaget, and many others come to mind. Each in some manner has emphasized the significance of motor and sensory efficiency in learning. A rereading of these works through the lenses of current knowledge will enable the teacher to recognize the timelessness of their observations.

183

Just as more powerful microscopes now allow for probing tissue cultures more profoundly than in the past and thereby make possible insights which have contradicted or simply sharpened previous knowledge, the teacher must also recognize that when concepts of movement are viewed through the modern analytic lens, perspectives inevitably change. What has historically been called sensation must be changed to read sensitivity if most recent experimental evidence is to be counted. What has historically been called motor must be changed to read movement if the human performer is to be credited with dynamic capabilities. Motor is a mechanical word implying a fixed relationship of parts, denying the human potential to alter function under stressful conditions and, with the alteration of function, to alter structure. Such new perspective dictates a semantic change from the traditional label of sensori-motor to a more apt label combination which allows for the operation of human dynamics to be called movement-sensitivity. Old labels are difficult to erase, but if they serve to obscure understanding the erasure must be attempted.

The teacher must next adopt a new perspective for the word, coordination. The general literature reflects the connotation of clumsiness of hand and foot as being the symptom of a "coordination problem." Time-honored tests and observations of eye-hand coordination have rarely contained the *concept of coordination* since they have not discussed coordinates. Coordination is truly a matter of coordinates. The human organism moves on and around a set of three ordinates. He moves vertically, horizontally, and on the depth axis. Again seeking a label to describe more aptly the dynamic qualities of movement on and around the planes of these three dimensions, one utilizes the term, *triordination.* It is not simply a matter of putting two things together— it is a matter of harmoniously converging all three planes into a working relationship to guarantee movement efficiency. By usual terms, *everyone* has coordination, since there is no choice but to move on the coordinates. The question to be asked is whether or not the alignment of those coordinates within the individual promotes efficient or inefficient performance. If the performance is inefficient and does not comfortably advance the learner, then some effort must be made to modify alignment.

Movement and Alignment

The teacher who wishes to understand triordination must start with an understanding of gravitational fields and the challenge presented to the newborn organism seeking to identify himself in a world of erect, locomoting beings. Developmental momentum will force him to establish a system of dynamic balance to support and direct his movements into space. As developmental momentum forces a battle with gravity, some form of victory is achieved and the coordinates emerge. Out of this victory over gravity the individual builds his own unique set of triordinates. He moves according to his alignment of these triordinates. Objects, events, and activities on the terrain of his movement also may be analyzed in terms of triordinates. His movement efficiency depends on the accuracy with which he can align his triordinates upon the triordinates in external space. When any type of mismatch occurs, some form of warping takes place. The building of an efficient triordinate relationship requires the aid of many helpers. The human body is endowed with an extremely dynamic process for the achievement of properly aligned triordinates. The visual system, the auditory system, the proprioceptive, the tactual, the olfactory, and the gustatory—all have contributory roles to play in building alignment. Consequently, the teacher who wishes to understand movement must also recognize the unique manner in which each system of sensitivity contributes to dynamic balance, body awareness, and spatial awareness.

When the systems of sensitivity usually referred to as senses are viewed from the perspective of their "contribution to triordinate alignment," the true meaning of perceptual disturbance becomes clear. Any reduction in sensitivity to information in any of the six processing modalities must in some manner be manifest in the alignment of the individual if the logical intention of anatomical and physiologic design is to be fulfilled.

Two courses of teacher preparation are then clearly indicated if "movement training" is to be considered. First, a teacher must understand movement as transport in space through matching an internalized alignment of triordinates on an external world by projection in space. Second, the systems of sensitivity to information must be studied as interrelated to that alignment. Neither of these basic points of view are generally incorporated in teacher preparation programs at the present time.

The simple observation that a child walks, runs, climbs, crawls, and generally moves himself in space without bumping into doors, falling, or knocking over objects does not warrant the conclusion that he has no problem in movement. The question must always be asked as to whether or not these movements are well balanced, supported, visually directed, and accomplished in comfort and economy. When such a question is asked a surprising number of movement inefficiencies become apparent which in some manner interfere with the child's optimal performance. The more movement patterns in children are studied, the more does one come to understand the inevitable relation of movement efficiency to comfortable and economic processes in learning.

Perception emerges from movement. The efficiency of one's movement patterns dictates the efficiency of perception. Those performances among children which have so easily been labeled as evidences of perceptual disturbances might more aptly be viewed as problems in movement—thereby more appropriately defining the source of the difficulty.

EDUCATION OF TEACHERS IN "MOVEMENT ORIENTATION"

Educators are no longer faced with the question of whether or not concepts of movement belong in an educational program. The large number of school systems that have initiated, in both special and regular classrooms, some program of perceptual-motor or sensori-motor training give abundant evidence that such an emphasis is here to stay. The true question to be resolved is the type, manner, and amount of such emphasis.

Educators are now concerned with determining the methods for achieving a "movement orientation" in the teacher preparation process.

At the University of Wisconsin a distinction is made among three levels of sophistication in teachers with regard to movement training. The first group is classified as "movement exposed." This group has read the current books and some of the past books that relate to movement and sensitivity and they find it "all very interesting." They talk of movement, include related comments in term papers, but never quite absorb the concepts and never quite get around to buying the two-by-four walking rail. The second group may be called "motor converts." They have read the same books and have gone into action. They try this technique and that technique cavorting through the suggestions of the various authors gathering everything and anything. They refer to their approach as "eclectic," which gives a certain air of respectability to a theoretical smorgasbord. This group programs movement training into the curriculum as if the children were on a medication schedule and required a "motor pill" daily or perhaps every two hours. The third group is now labeled *movigenic* teachers—those who hold an abiding orientation to movement and see the necessity for using such an orientation as the foundation for all curriculum regardless of subject matter. For them the understanding of movement efficiency *is* the understanding of learning and the dynamic development of the learner. For them the child is a space-oriented being representing his spatial sophistication in language, possessing his own unique space world, constantly coming to dynamic balance, moving to act, organized at relative levels in processing modalities, and ready to take advantage of progressive increments to his efficiency if they are properly presented.

A movement orientation emerges from an effort to synthesize the experimental findings from a variety of sources. Various investigations which were pursued to answer certain perceptual and psychological questions among adult populations must be carefully studied for their possible practical implications for the task of the classroom teacher. All of the studies that contributed to the development of the sensory-tonic theory of perception are pertinent. The Witkin studies (1954) resulting in the concepts of "field dependent and independent" must enter the synthesis. The growing body of reports on sensory deprivation must be considered.

The fundamental purpose of programs of movement training at the kinetic level of rolling, crawling, and jumping is to improve the alignment of the learner on the three ordinates. Secondly, such a program must aim to achieve comfortable and economical movements in performance of tasks. Neither goal can be achieved without the recognition of the contribution of the six channels of sensitivity toward proper alignment, centering, and economy. Since alignment emerges from the dynamic synthesis of information from channels of sensitivity fed back through a proprioceptive system in the early development of locomotion, the same process of dynamic synthesis must enter into the development of movement training programs at whatever age levels they may be initiated.

The terrain of movement is space. The true understanding of movement efficiency must therefore be derived from a detailed investigation of space as a measurable and definable entity. As a model for conducting such an investigation to the benefit of each learner the teacher must learn to observe sensitively the child's relative efficiency of performance in the four meridians of *near, mid, far,* and *remote* space. His postural alignment, his response to stress, and his speed and accuracy of movement must be subjected to analysis in each of the space meridians to determine areas of weakness and strength. The "near-spaced child" may be subjected to undue stress when "far-space processing" is demanded by the lesson and the "far-spaced child" may be at a similar disadvantage in near-space tasks. The understanding of "meridians of efficiency" permits the teacher to plan activities intelligently to insure success and to organize carefully experiences designed to develop spatial efficiencies where they are lacking.

A teacher training program with a movement orientation comprises three basic units of preparation. The first is the study of the *developing learning organism.* Here the content focuses upon the physiologic readiness of the child, his postural alignment, the grace and ease with which he transports the full body or body parts into space for performance, and the individual and collective efficiencies of the six processing modes. The teacher learns to analyze the organization of the triordinates in each child and to utilize such analysis in planning activities to achieve optimum performance. His analytic attention is directed to fifteen dimensions in movement efficiency: muscular strength, dynamic balance, body awareness, spatial awareness, temporal awareness, visual, auditory, tactual, gustatory, and olfactory dynamics and kinesthesia, bilaterality, rhythm, flexibility, and motor planning. He learns the importance of each for efficiency in performance and comes to understand their interdependence and interrelatedness. These fifteen dimensions become the column headings for planning activities to help each child achieve the highest possible level of movement efficiency.

The second basic unit is devoted to the *study of environmental design.* Here attention is directed to the learning surrounding. Lighting, acoustics, thermal control, textures, contrasts, and physical positioning of the learning task become major topics of study. The study is further divided into two categories. One category refers to the physical surround in which learning takes place and concentrates upon the definition of an optimal learning climate in terms of appropriate lighting, adequate acoustics, proper seating, reduction of interference, concern for glare, textural modification, and so on. The second category refers to the design of materials to be used in the learning process. Critical evaluation of available materials in terms of perceptual ease, contrast, ease of movement, and so on is a necessary prerequisite to presenting materials to the child. General experience has shown that relatively few learning aids were designed for the child with a learning problem. Usually the teachers of these children find it necessary to design their own materials to resolve a particular dilemma faced by a child. In this independent design there are many rules of perception and movement which need to be taken into account. So long as it is likely that teachers will continue to construct their own devices, it is important that they learn some of the basic principles of design.

The design of learning materials must take into account the proprioceptive systems of the child so as to produce objects and tasks which insure positions and performances that reduce adverse stress and insure comfort and economy. Methods and techniques for setting content on paper or in solid form so as to avoid perceptual interference and allow for ease of performance must be considered a vital component of movement training. Arranging for children to perform table work while seated on a properly designed chair with adequate lighting upon the task surface constitutes a significant trio of variables to be controlled for body alignment, visual centering on the task, and movement ease. Since the customary image of a working learner is that of a sedentary being, movement training must be directed to achieving proper sitting balance and comfortable operation around the near-space triordinate planes on the work surface.

The third basic unit is the *study of symbolic competency.* Here the focus is centered on the nature of language as a system of communication rather than a mechanical organization of vocabulary units; on reading as a graphic system of communication for the advancement of thought and as a stimulant to movement rather than as a mechanical organization of a sight vocabulary and a phonic fluency; on spelling as a system of visualization of word space rather than as a mechanical organization of rote lists; and on arithmetic as a system of spatial relationships rather than the learning of numbers. A movement-oriented teacher incorporates movement concepts in *all* activities. Symbolic competency emerges from movement. The fifteen dimensions of movement efficiency lend themselves to incorporation in any activity where symbolic competency is determined as the major goal. Movigenic teachers continue to find more and more ways to improve academic functioning by using movement concepts to support, reinforce, and strengthen symbolic increments.

Course work must be developed to help teachers perceive the child as a dynamic organism gaining information from energy forms in the gravitational fields of space. The student-teacher must be permitted to explore the space worlds of physiology, anthropology, chemistry, physics, engineering, kinesiology, biology, zoology, and others, not with the intent to specialize in any of the fields but always to seek the answer to the same question: "What specific set of principles does each field contain which have direct pertinence for understanding the dynamics of the individual learner."

It is understandable that none of these fields has developed its body of knowledge from this perspective, but the true understanding of human performance resides in the utilization of any and all fields of knowledge. Some scholarly searching party equipped with insightful probing devices should find a rich reward from such an expedition. Selective sampling of pertinent data from each of these fields can structure a solid foundation for the understanding of human movement.

A second innovation would be the study of the dynamics of child development not as a series of composite norms reflecting an average process but rather as a probing into the long-range consequences of each step in the developmental timetable.

An orientation to movement efficiency may be acquired in part by a profound survey of past and present literature and, from that perspective, become a matter of "book learning," but this is only half of the preparation. The other half involves direct child experience. Live children who are dynamic representations of movement inefficiencies must be recruited to confront beginning teachers with the stress-laden dilemma of finding a comfortable, progressive learning climate for the children who are unaware of the symptom complex the textbook has already designated for them. This is the true laboratory of learning for the teacher—experience with the live child. Consequently, a teacher training program *must* involve direct child experience with movement concepts as an integral part of the preparation. The understanding of movement comes from empathy with a moving child—only the language of labels comes from the textbook.

Another significant consideration has emerged from efforts to immerse teachers in a movement orientation, that is, the personal movement efficiency of the teacher. His own composite of efficiencies and inefficiencies tend to influence the manner in which he plans and evaluates movement experiences for the children. Teachers who move inefficiently because of their own problems in spatial orientation avoid programming in areas that are blind spots for them. As a consequence, the acquisition of a movement orientation contains the element of personal analysis as a necessary part of understanding the learner. In some manner the personal development of the teacher toward movement efficiency must also be incorporated into the program.

Any program of teacher training and development must inevitably relate to the administrative realities of the manner in which school systems may elect to approach the general problem.

Programs with a movement orientation may be plotted along three lines of strategy: *developmental, corrective,* and *maintaining.* The first strategy—developmental—requires that knowledge of movement, alignment, triordination, centering, sensitivity systems, and so on be communicated clearly and succinctly to the parents of our nation, particularly to those whose children have been labeled in some manner other than normal. This knowledge must be brought to bear on child-rearing practices. Activity, opportunity, and experience sequences which will bring about the development of efficient movement patterns must be established and communicated by the one profession most vitally concerned with child learning. Consequently, the teacher must communicate his knowledge of movement to the preschool child as a preventive measure against learning failures. While this strategy is generally viewed as being outside the province of a community school system, boundaries of obligation must be made consonant with man's increasing knowledge. The developmental momentum of education will force the educators to this vital strategy if the full development of each child is to be promoted. The inherent difficulty of the first strategy forces upon teachers the more typical strategy of remediation. The child will reach the eligibility age for school in varying degrees of immaturity in efficiency—not ready to meet the curricular demands. Remedial strategy must be based upon seeking means to bring each learner to a level of optimum efficiency. A recognition of the vital relationship of movement and sensitivity to learning efficiency demands a shift in emphasis from an exclusively symbolically oriented curriculum to one that is movement oriented if one wishes to prepare the foundation structure to support the weighted complexity of the symbols which multiply incessantly with advancing years. Consequently, one should talk not of remedial reading, arithmetic, language, spelling, and so on, but rather of efficient use of space, establishing dynamic balance, becoming aware of feedback, processing bits of data, learning to visualize, learning to listen, and so on. Movement training is not for arms and legs; it is for alignment and balance. Movement training is not for muscle development but rather for kinesthetic awareness. Movement training must be designed to permit the greatest economy in the most comfortable relationship in the least time. Symbolic competence is a natural outgrowth of movement efficiency.

A program of correction or remediation must be derived from a set of physiologic principles aimed at modifying sensitivity and alignment through perceptual and cognitive experiencing. Under this heading the teacher may undertake two basic courses of action. He may devise various forms of activity for the practice of balance, kinesthesia, tactuality, rhythm, and so on to be experienced by the child, and he may so regulate the physical environment as to promote movement efficiency by lighting, acoustics, textures, thermal procedures, and so on.

The third strategy becomes a matter of further understanding the human response to stress and requires a consideration of techniques to achieve a "just right" concept of stress to promote movement without undue pressure that may disturb alignment. This becomes a matter of learning material design, changes in environment, pressure for achievement, and establishment of techniques for restoring balance.

SUMMARY

The preparation of teachers intending to specialize in the learning problems of the neurologically impaired child must be organized with a movement orientation. The neurology of impairment is secondary to the understanding of the dynamics of movement. The study of perception and symbolic functioning is but a second step in the sequence of learning to be preceded by a profound understanding of the structure of the human body.

Individual school systems may strategically choose to emphasize the developmental, preventive, remedial, or sustaining approach. The teacher must be prepared to adapt to whatever strategy may be elected. He must be prepared to work efficiently with individual children, groups of children, or with the parents of children with special learning problems. His competency must be in the field of learning at whatever level he may be asked to serve. The study of human movement is inseparable from the study of learning. As man moves he learns. If one wishes to understand the dynamics of learning, one must inevitably become involved in the understanding of movement. Movement and learning are reciprocal throughout the life of the individual. Therefore, the optimum efficiency of the teacher of the neurologically impaired child can only be guaranteed if his preparation has emphasized the profound and abiding orientation to the learner as a space-oriented being seeking to process, integrate, and express his adaptation in the most comfortable and economic movement possible. He must be truly movement oriented by inclination, collegiate orientation, and experimental validation.

Comment

BARSCH: We have a conceptual or cognitive machine at the University of Wisconsin which we have in a small laboratory, and it continues to ask the same question over and over; that is, how is this related to space, and whatever data we get and whatever we collect from literature all goes into that machine and it has to come out with that kind of an answer. That is the question that we are asking about all the data that we collect and everybody else collects in order to maintain some consistency in our own organization. We are looking at the individual— whether it is a brain-injured child, a cerebral palsy child, or a normal child—who is a space-oriented organism who has to survive in a spatial surrounding.

As a consquence, anything that happens to him must have some kind of spatial relationship. Thus we translate all our spatial processes into the concept that he must develop some kind of efficiency. Any of the learning problems that children have, we feel, stem from some form of inefficiency. There is a difficulty with their feedback process which forces them to rely upon other kinds of techniques in order to adjust.

As we see children, our question is: How did they make it so far? What's been going for you? What is working; what isn't working? We look upon the academic process in a school setting as a survival phenomenon. That is, each child who enters the kindergarten is supposed to survive in that academic world, and if he doesn't, he ends up in our clinic.

This leads us then to changing some of our orientations in relation to the teacher training process. We established one cardinal rule which says all of these children are developing organisms, dynamically organized, and they change from day to day. So don't be sure that you have anything pin-pointed on them, because by Saturday they have changed. This means that most of our measuring devices which establish certain numerical quantities must be somehow put on the basis of "it isn't going to be the same by next week."

This orientation of teachers to the process of whatever he is doing is a constant measuring process. That any effort he puts forth to the child is continually going to have to be evaluated by him means that there are no fixed rules or methods of teaching reading, arithmetic, or other subjects.

Another thing that is most important as far as we're concerned is that we have construed in elementary education and secondary education "sittingness" as being of great value. That is the usual orientation, in that a child comes into the school setting and is imprisoned in a two-by-two space that is the allotment of his desk. It's figured in cubic space around the room, and from five years of age until seventeen or eighteen that is his space of learning, and that's where he has to live. One of the major criteria for continued acceptance in the classroom is that he must sit. If you don't sit and the teacher has to chase you around the room or out into the hall you don't stay. So sitting has become a factor.

Sittingness requires that there be a fixed surrounding. That means that this becomes your learning space for your entire school life. This becomes vital then when we start talking near-point space, when we talk about vision, when we talk about addition, when we talk about kinesthesia, when we talk about actuality. This is where it has to happen, right in that little space. Children weren't meant to sit for that length of time. They are moving organisms, and somehow or other they have to establish control.

One of the reasons that we feel that they do not have the controls that we should like them to have is because we have architecturally blundered. In most of our units, design specialists have not taken into account the human factor. This involves the tilted desks; more adequate lighting in the classroom; and cubicles and various similar things considered as controls of space for the child. We're trying to educate our teachers to the concept of *environmental design* as being a variable with which they must deal in regular classes.

We extend the concept of design further to talk with new teachers about the fact that most of the things that they are likely to use with the children with whom they will work are noncommercial; that is, the teachers will be forever inventing something, running it off on the ditto machines, making special paper products—all this in order to work with the children. This means that they should have some understanding of design. They should have some understanding of how close together you put things on a paper; how can you make them stand out in foreground and background processes. We don't feel this has been included in most other teacher training programs, and so we are incorporating it as a special process with our teachers.

The next point, symbolic competency, which is a demand in a society that has dedicated itself to making all of its citizens literate, requires then that we put all of our symbolic processes (reading, writing, arithmetic, spelling) through that same machine, and the answer must be related to space.

We look upon all of the academic subjects as spatial orientations and feel that the competency required for good arithmetic, good spelling, or good reading is spatial efficiency. Our teachers have to relate all the academic work in which they may be involved to some form of spatial concept and motor pattern. They teach reading, teach spelling, teach arithmetic on a movement premise.

One of the things that we have also found is that the least likely place to find helpful information is in the educational literature. We have been forced to look through other bodies of literature in order to gain some insight into this. And again we keep asking the same question as we go to the literature of physiology and so forth: What relationship does what you know about the human organism have to space, and what is the learning phenomenon that we need to investigate?

We feel that one of the problems for teachers stems from their own limitations, that is, that they are going into a movement-oriented program. We discovered that teachers had a great deal of difficulty understanding some of the basic concepts in reading because they themselves were poor readers. They had a great deal of difficulty sustaining work. Many of them had their own visual problems, and many of them came in with one eye and went out with two in the process.

All of our teachers in training are also on a training program personally. They work with each other. They adapt for themselves the same techniques that they are going to try out with the children, and in that sense acquire some understanding of their own limitations. As they used the walking rail they were frightened to death, and, therefore, the teachers never programmed that into their child program because they could not handle it themselves. So we put it to the teachers on this basis:

we are not going to change you; we are not going to make you completely different, except that we want you to understand what your limitations are. At least do not deprive the children of those particular experiences.

KEPHART: I am convinced that we very much need physical education based on this principle: the development of motor patterns for the purpose of gathering information. We need this particularly at the elementary school level and we need it more especially in the case of the brain-injured child at the elementary school level.

We have been experimenting for two or three years with a physical education program with our clinic group. We have found that the program is very helpful in increasing school achievement as measured by the normal testing procedures.

We think that we have to go from your [Barsch's] initial approach, i.e., building on certain abilities and strengthening other abilities, to an individualized approach of this kind, to a more veridical approach in the second year in which we embody these things in games or problem-solving situations. Then we're ready to go into perceptual training and eventually into academic and symbolic training.

Chapter 13

The Needs of Teachers for Specialized Information in the Area of Psychodiagnosis

CHARLES R. STROTHER, Ph.D.

EDITORIAL NOTE.—The intimate relationship between psycho-diagnosis and teaching materials and methodology is being stressed more and more, if not with all children, then certainly with brain-injured children. The teacher of brain-injured children must have a clear psychological blueprint of each child with whom he will work which defines the child in great detail both from the point of view of psychological strengths and psycho-pathology.

DR. CHARLES R. STROTHER is Professor of Psychology and Professor of Psychiatry at the University of Washington, Seattle, Washington. He received his Ph.D. degree in clinical psychology and speech pathology from the State University of Iowa. He was appointed Assistant Professor of Speech Pathology at the University of Washington and director of the speech and hearing clinic. He returned to the State University of Iowa, Iowa City, as Associate Professor of Psychology, where he also directed the psychological clinic and served as chief psychologist at the University of Iowa Hospitals.

For several years, he was director of the Pilot School for Brain-Injured Children in Seattle and is currently director of a new Mental Retardation and Child Development Center.

He has served as consultant to the National Institute of Mental Health, the United States Office of Education, the Army, the Veterans Administration, American Foundation for the Blind, United Cerebral Palsy Association, Inc., and the National Society for Crippled Children and Adults.

Chapter 13

The Needs of Teachers for Specialized Information in the Area of Psychodiagnosis

CHARLES R. STROTHER, Ph.D.

The teacher confronted by a child with special learning disabilities has a choice of three alternative approaches: (1) he may rely on a formal curriculum which has been developed for classes of such children; (2) he may use some variation of standard methods or materials, or some special methods, on a trial-and-error basis, hoping to find a method which will be effective with the given child; or (3) he may utilize an experimental approach based on some systematic analysis of the child's behavior.

These methods are not, of course, mutually exclusive. Ordinarily, the teacher will use all of them in succession. He will begin with a standard approach which has proved to be reasonably effective with classes of children with special learning disabilities. If this method is not effective with a given child, then he will try whatever variations or special methods he knows or is ingenious enough to invent. If he has exhausted his repertoire of techniques and is still unsuccessful, he may then refer the child to the psychologist in the hope that psychological examination will identify the nature of the difficulty and suggest an effective remedy.

Too often, teachers complain that the psychological report is not helpful. These complaints have persuasive face validity. If a teacher feels that he has not been helped, he is probably correct.

There are a number of reasons for this unsatisfactory state of affairs. In the first place, until recently the tests available to the school psychologist have been too global to yield the specific information required by the teacher. While one may, for example, infer on the basis of a discrepancy between a verbal and a nonverbal I.Q. that a child is relatively deficient in verbal ability, or from a low block-design score that there may be a deficiency in visual perception, neither of these inferences may add anything to the teacher's knowledge of the child's problem or to her ability to devise an effective remedial program.

199

A second source of difficulty relates to the problem of communication between the psychologist and the teacher. Trained in a different discipline, the psychologist has developed a technical language which is frequently not completely intelligible to the teacher without special training. Then too, if the psychologist is to translate his findings into procedures which it is possible for the teacher to use, he must be reasonably familiar with the resources available to the teacher and with the classroom conditions within which the teacher must work. There are important implications here for the training of the school psychologist. The concern of the present study, however, is with the training of the teacher rather than that of the psychologist.

KNOWLEDGE TEACHERS NEED CONCERNING PSYCHODIAGNOSIS

Obviously, a knowledge of elementary statistics is essential if the teacher is to use psychodiagnostic information effectively. The teacher must be familiar with the concepts and procedures involved in frequency distributions, measures of central tendency and variability, sampling, correlation, and probability in order to understand the nature and mathematical significance of test scores. A knowledge of the various types of psychological tests that are available; of the problems and procedures involved in test construction, standardization, and validation; and some degree of familiarity with a few of the more widely used measures of general ability, of achievement, and of personality are generally considered indispensable for all teachers.

For the special education teacher, a general background in statistics and psychometrics is inadequate. The children with whom he works do not constitute a sample drawn from the populations on which most tests have been standardized; consequently, a somewhat different interpretation must be placed on the scores obtained by children with learning disabilities, or with sensory or motor or linguistic handicaps. Moreover, the general measures of ability, achievement, and personality to which the teacher is introduced in the usual survey of psychometric procedures are not adequate for the analysis of special disabilities.

To put the matter somewhat differently, the background considered essential for the regular classroom teacher is directed toward an understanding of methods of measurement and description of abilities, achievement, and personality in a normal population—in other words, to an understanding of psychometrics. The special education teacher, on the other hand, is problem-oriented. He is concerned with understanding the specific learning and behavior problems of an individual—and obviously deviant—child. In addition to the knowledge of psychometrics which is required for the regular classroom teacher, the special education teacher needs some understanding of, and training in, what may be referred to as *psychodiagnosis.**

Psychodiagnosis is similar in principle and process to diagnostic teaching. It begins with identification of some to-be-altered behavior, the systematic observation of that behavior, the ordering of these observations through some conceptual model of the structure of behavior, the formulation of an hypothesis, and ultimately the experimental manipulation of conditions designed to test this hypothesis. This process and concepts and procedures which may be utilized in carrying it out, both in diagnostic testing and in diagnostic teaching, can be made explicit and can be communicated to the teacher.

Almost all teachers are quite capable of identifying deviant behavior or of recognizing the occurrence of a learning difficulty. The demands of the social environment of the classroom and of the learning tasks presented to the child are so explicit that deviations from the expected standards are more or less self-evident. The teacher is, however, frequently unable to go beyond this initial observation and to analyze the behavior sufficiently to suggest any rational basis for effecting a change. He is most likely to fall back on some empirical rule, as: If a child is verbally aggressive toward another child, the teacher should . . . or, if the child is unable to perform this exercise satisfactorily, have him repeat the previous assignment. Some understanding of, and training in, the processes of psychodiagnosis would provide the teacher with a method of analysis that would lead both to greater understanding of these problems and to more powerful techniques of intervention.

TWO COMPLEMENTARY TRAINING PROGRAMS

For purposes of illustration, two quite different—but complementary—programs of training in psychodiagnosis will be described, either of which might well be included in the training of the special education teacher.

The first method to be described is referred to in the current literature as the "experimental analysis of behavior." It has developed from the work of B. F. Skinner and his students and is based on the general premise that behavior is controlled either by preceding stimulation (in which case it is termed "respondent" behavior) or by consequent stimulation (in which case it is called "operant" behavior). Following an introduction to the theory involved (Bijou and Baer, 1961), training begins with the selection and preliminary definition of some particular class of behavior—for example, hitting another child. The student

* The term, psychodiagnosis, as used here, is intended to include what is sometimes termed *educational diagnosis*.

tabulates the number of instances of such behavior that occur over successive intervals of time and compares his tabulation with that of another observer. Differences between observers are most likely to be due to a lack of precision in the definition of the behavior under observation—e.g., to a failure to distinguish between "hitting" and "touching." The definition is refined and other sources of difference discussed. When the student achieves a sufficiently high level of reliability in observing "hitting" behavior he extends his observation to the antecedent stimuli (i.e., what occurs just before the hitting behavior) and to the consequences of the hitting. He continues to record and analyze instances of hitting until he begins to observe some systematic relationship between the hitting and a given consequence. He then formulates the hypothesis that the hitting behavior is controlled by this consequence and if the consequence can be changed, then the behavior should change. The consequences are altered through the use of one or another of four basic "reinforcement" procedures. If the hypothesis is correct, the hitting behavior should become less frequent. To make sure that the change in frequency of the hitting is controlled by the reinforcement procedure that has been used, this reinforcement is discontinued and the behavior is allowed to have the consequences which it had initially. The hitting should increase. Reinstitution of the reinforcement procedure should again reduce the hitting and confirm the hypothesis. This technique of diagnosis and behavior modification is now being widely applied (Hart *et al.*, 1964) and training programs are being developed for teachers, attendants, parents, therapists, and others concerned with the behavior of children (Geis, 1965).

The second method to be described might be termed a cognitive approach to psychodiagnosis because it serves to systematize diagnostic information by relating it to a conceptual model of cognitive functions. It is, perhaps, surprising that the very considerable amount of experimental and statistical research that has been directed toward definition, analysis, and measurement of basic cognitive functions has had relatively little influence on clinical practice. The fate of Thurstone's Primary Mental Abilities Test is a case in point. School psychologists and clinical psychologists have generally preferred to administer tests of general ability—such as the Wechsler Intelligence Scale for Children—and then attempt to define specific dysfunctions by a detailed analysis of responses to subtests or to individual test items.

DIAGNOSTIC PROCEDURES BASED ON COGNITIVE MODELS

Recently, however, under the influence of trends in cognitive, developmental, psycholinguistic, and neurophysiological theory, there has been significant progress toward diagnostic procedures based on some model of cognitive processes. While many of the psychometric tools required for such an approach are still to be developed, those that are now available have clearly demonstrated their value (Frostig *et al.,* 1961; McCarthy and Kirk, 1963).

Psychodiagnosis, from this point of view, involves systematic examination of the following processes (and perhaps others):

1. Perception in the various sensory modalities (primarily visual, auditory, and kinesthetic).

2. Motor functions (such as equilibrium, coordination, and laterality).

3. Intersensory and perceptual-motor functions.

4. Memory.

5. Symbolization, concept formation, reasoning, and other "higher cognitive functions."

6. Response formulation (linguistic and motor).

7. Motor sequencing.

Other studies herein discuss the theoretical background required for such a systematic approach to psychodiagnosis. With this background, and with an understanding of the relationship of these psychological processes to the learning of reading, arithmetic, and other subjects (including the learning of social behavior), the student teacher is ready for a brief formal introduction to diagnostic procedures. This introduction should utilize demonstrations and case presentations designed to familiarize the student teacher with the techniques by which the psychologist attempts to analyze, for example, visual or auditory perception or language. The student would, for instance, become familiar with the Illinois Test of Psycholinguistic Abilities not simply as a formal psychometric instrument but as a way of assessing various functions involved in language comprehension and language use. If emphasis in both the theoretical courses and the course in psychodiagnosis is placed on the relationship of these basic psychological processes to school performance, the teacher and the psychologist are then able to communicate effectively with one another.

This method of analysis of the functions involved in a learning difficulty should contribute to the teacher's effectiveness in analyzing the child's problem and in modifying materials and procedures on the basis of some rational hypothesis as to the nature of the child's difficulty. If the teacher has seen a demonstration of the methods and materials used to test the child's auditory discrimination or auditory sequencing, he may be in a better position to understand the problem the child is having in

the classroom with auditory material. He may then experiment informally with a different way of presenting this material to the child.

Teaching materials based on this method of psychodiagnosis are
now beginning to appear in the literature (Frostig and Horne, 1964;
Kirk and Bateman, 1962; Levi, 1965). With some background in theory
and some familiarity with the diagnostic tests, the teacher is prepared to
use these teaching materials more effectively.

The major contribution of the method of training suggested here
is that it relates both diagnosis and teaching very closely to psychological
theory and research. Perception, cognition, language become meaningful
and important terms to the student teacher—terms which can be defined
concretely and analyzed operationally by diagnostic tests, terms which
are directly applicable to the teaching process and to the behavior of the
child in the classroom.

SELECTED REFERENCES

Bijou, S. W., and Baer, D. M. *Child development.* New York: Appleton-Century-
Crofts, 1961.
Frostig, M., and Horne, D. *The Frostig program for the development of visual
perception.* Chicago: Follett, 1964.
Frostig, M., Lefever, D. W., and Whittlesey, J. R. B. "A developmental test of
visual perception for evaluating normal and neurologically handicapped chil-
dren," *Perceptual and Motor Skills,* 1961, 12, 383–394.
Geis, G. L. "A short course (in the experimental analysis of behavior) for the
non-psychologist." Unpublished paper presented at the American Psychological
Association meeting, Chicago, 1965.
Hart, Betty M., *et al.* "Effects of social reinforcement on operant crying," *Experimental Child Psychology,* 1964, 1, 145–153.
Kirk, S. A., and Bateman, Barbara. "Diagnosis and remediation of learning disabilities," *Exceptional Children,* 1962, 29, 73–78.
Levi, Aurelia. "Development, assessment and remediation of higher cognitive functions." Unpublished paper presented at the American Psychological Association
meeting, Chicago, 1965.
McCarthy, J. J., and Kirk, S. A. *The construction, standardization and statistical
characteristics of the Illinois Test of Psycholinguistic Abilities.* Urbana: University of Illinois Press, 1963.

Comment

STROTHER: The only comment I want to make to supplement what
I've said in the paper is that the plea here is really for a rational approach
to psychodiagnosis and for the utility of having models for the organization of diagnostic information about the child. I would argue that at this
point no single model is apt. I'm arguing for three or four diverse models.

My concept of fruitful approach to psychodiagnosis at the moment
would encompass a Skinnerian analysis of behavior on the one hand and,

on the other hand, would encompass a cognitive analysis of behavior. I think those are at the moment complementary and both quite essential, and as Dr. Gardner's paper so adequately demonstrated, our models are constantly in the process of change.

I think the training of the teacher in psychodiagnosis should be approached on the basis of some temporary, incomplete rational model of the organization of behavior, and should look on psychodiagnostics only as a way of studying behaviors. The teacher can then apply it directly to the understanding of a specific incidence of behavior in a particular child.

CRUICKSHANK: Dr. Strother, I wonder if you'd consider this just a little further? In response to the question: to what extent, in view of the exigencies of reality in public schools in terms of availability of personnel, do you feel that the teacher himself ought to be familiarized and able to use certain psychodiagnostic tools, particularly those on which instructional concepts are based?

My approach to the education of these children is perhaps a little more mechanistic than that of some others, but I'm thinking, for example, of the intimate relationship between what the teacher does in the development of certain kinds of teaching techniques with a child and the presence or absence of the associated psychopathology that might very well appear on the Bender Gestalt Test.

Since it's my feeling that if dissociation, as a single example, is a factor in the child's behavior, the teacher has the obligation to either exploit that deficiency to the child's own adjustment or to find ways in which, through his teaching techniques, this aspect of psychopathology can be minimized.

Thus, he needs to know on almost a week-to-week basis the extent of this disability. The approach should be similar, I would think, in terms of the extent of the attention span and the length of the attention span under various kinds of circumstances. A teacher must know this constantly, or he cannot meet the needs of this youngster educationally. We could carry this through in a variety of other types of things.

Methods of measuring attention span, methods of determining the presence or absence of figure-ground pathology, and so on are elements on which I feel the entire initial curriculum, at least for this type of child, is built. I would be interested in your reaction as to the wisdom or the appropriateness of this.

STROTHER: If you work a psychometric instrument like the Bender Gestalt Test, it does several things. It provides a standard opportunity for observation, and it provides a way of classifying behavior. Hopefully, it provides some way of measuring that behavior.

These are the three functions of any psychometric instrument, it seems to me. If the child shows dissociation on the Bender Gestalt Test, he is also going to show dissociation in any schoolroom test, and I think it's more important for the teacher to understand what dissociation means, how it might be expressed on the Bender Gestalt Test, and how it might also be observed and expressed in other forms of behavior.

I would say that it's perfectly appropriate for the teacher to use any techniques of observation that yield significant information for him. But I'm not sure that some of these standard psychometric instruments are the most economical way for the teacher to make these observations in the classroom situation. And if the essence of a diagnostic instrument, a psychometric instrument, is standardization of the condition, then I would argue maybe this is a disadvantage to the teacher in the observation of the classroom, where the flexibility of the observation is important. But to understand the concepts that these tests are trying to measure and various informal ways in which they might be observed and tested in the classroom is, I think, the essence of the psychodiagnostic information that the teacher needs.

FREIDUS: There is something more. You mentioned measuring the attention span, that the teacher should learn how to measure attention span. I don't think you can measure it exactly. You can see that a child is not attending or has trouble attending, but you have to find out what distracts him from what, what can he attend to, and when and why. This is the job of the teacher, and all he is doing is putting together the jigsaw puzzle of the child's behavior. Test results are put together with the rest of the jigsaw puzzle. They are hunches which you have to check in other situations.

STROTHER: Achievement tests, of course, do contain a lot of material that is useful for diagnostic information even though they may not be used for that purpose. I've never been able really to understand the distinction that seems to be increasing between educational diagnosis and what I have called here psychodiagnosis, because I would choose to define psychodiagnosis so broadly that it would encompass educational diagnosis. I don't think they can be separated, and I think the attempt to separate them is an artificial one and an undesirable one. Teachers must also be sensitized to this view of psychodiagnosis.

Chapter 14

The Needs of Teachers for Specialized Information on Handedness, Finger Localization, and Cerebral Dominance

WILLIAM H. GADDES, Ph.D.

EDITORIAL NOTE.—As Dr. Gaddes so well points out, the problems of handedness, finger localization, and cerebral dominance have until recently received little attention. Dr. Norma Scheidemann included a chapter on handedness in her early textbook on the psychology of exceptional children. However, since then, except for an occasional scientific paper on one or the other of these problems, little consistent work had been done on the matter until Dr. Arthur Benton presented his excellent statement. In recent years these problems in relation to the total issue of perception and motor activity have received a great deal of attention. Dr. Gaddes brings these data together to demonstrate another area of understanding basic to teacher competency.

DR. WILLIAM H. GADDES has long been interested in classroom learning problems of children. He entered the University of British Columbia in 1930 and qualified as a teacher in 1935. In the public school system of British Columbia from 1936 to 1942 he taught most grades in the elementary and junior and senior high schools. In 1942 he joined the Royal Canadian Air Force. In 1945, after discharge from the Air Force, he entered the Canadian Army Medical Corps as a clinical psychologist, where he developed a strong interest in the cases of head wounds, traumatic aphasia, and perceptual disorders. Since 1946 he has taught psychology at the University of Victoria, British Columbia, and since 1948 he has been consulting clinical psychologist at the Victoria Veterans' Hospital. As a visiting professor he has taught teachers in several colleges in California and in British Columbia. In 1963 he established a Neuropsychology Laboratory at the University of Victoria where children with different types of brain damage and cerebral dysfunction are studied daily. Dr. Gaddes holds B.A. and M.A. degrees from the University of British Columbia and a Ph.D. from the Claremont Graduate School.

Chapter 14

The Needs of Teachers for Specialized Information on Handedness, Finger Localization, and Cerebral Dominance

WILLIAM H. GADDES, Ph.D.

A consideration of the competencies, skills, and knowledge that the teacher of brain-injured children will need for the special teaching responsibilities confronting him is a demanding task which requires a workable synthesis of neurological, psychological and educational knowledge. Drs. Gallagher and Rappaport in their comments, Birch in his book (1964), and others have described the difficulty of defining "brain damage" in children. The temporal, spatial, and multiple aspects of brains that dysfunction are so variable that a simple definition is impossible and a complex one is so inclusive as to be in danger of losing its definitiveness.

In fact, the problem is basically a philosophical one—the age-old question of the mind-body problem. In the past, educators and psychologists have tended to avoid the mind-body relationship and all its puzzling implications, by acknowledging only mental or behavioral phenomena in the learning process. Apart from recognizing the gross and basic requisites of rest and nutrition, most teachers have approached the process of learning, and still tend to approach it, in terms of superficial cognitive success or failure and social adjustment. Too frequently the child is fitted into a particular pedagogical habit pattern which may or may not meet his learning needs and skills. When it does not, he may be labelled mentally dull or noncooperative or both.

While Aristotle was probably one of the first to recognize the dependence of mind on body, and the mental impairment resulting from organic damage ("when the act of imagination is hindered by a lesion of the corporeal organ . . . we see that a man is hindered from understanding actually even those things of which he had a previous knowledge" (1952b, p. 139)), almost all of his discussion "On Memory and

Reminiscence" is devoted to images, concepts, recollection, and other purely mental phenomena (1952a).

Philosophers, until the nineteenth century, perpetuated this mentalistic emphasis. Descartes, in the seventeenth century, realized the essential importance of the brain and nervous system to thinking, but his explanations were neurologically naive (Murphy, 1949). The British and French philosophers and associationists of the eighteenth century continued the interest in reasoning, mental qualities, and association begun by Aristotle, and their studies also ignored any awareness of physiological correlates (Murphy, 1949).

Not until after 1800, when knowledge in biology and physiology began to develop rapidly, were scholars able to produce useful theories in neuropsychological problems. Boring, among others, has pointed out that "experimental psychology was getting its start within experimental physiology during the first half of the nineteenth century" (1957, p. 27).

With the increased understanding of the structure and function of the nervous system which occurred during the nineteenth century, there began to develop among neurologists the realization of various physiological correlates of mental behavior. Hughlings Jackson (1958) in 1872 in a lecture on "The Physiological Aspects of Education" urged a broader view of mind, to include not only the mentalistic aspects but also the correlated physiological processes.

Many of the psychologists of the 1920's, notably John B. Watson, E. L. Thorndike, Karl Lashley, and E. B. Holt, drew more or less on neurological knowledge in their attempts to explain behavior. A few clinical psychologists interested in the learning problems of children attempted to relate academic performances to certain endocrine deficiencies. A notable example of this last group was Florence Mateer (1935), a clinical child psychologist, trained by G. Stanley Hall, who expressed a physiologically theoretical bias by recommending gland feeding (largely thyroid and pituitary) to correct reading, spelling, and learning deficits in children. This view enjoyed some popularity at that time.

But these attempts have been spasmodic and few; educators and psychologists as a group are ignorant of the physiological factors in learning and largely indifferent to their use. The majority suffer from this mentalistic stress and an accompanying neurological neglect.

Tradition dies hard and only shows any change when new knowledge appears to challenge its questionable bases. The neurologists in the last hundred years and the physiological psychologists in about the last forty years have provided an increasing body of knowledge about the relationship of the nervous system (principally the brain) to behavior. As a result, there is a pressing need to apply this knowledge to teaching the brain-injured child and the child with cerebral dysfunctions. So far, only a relatively few teachers are making much use of it.

However, the breach between the neuropsychologist and the educator is still marked because each of these specialists is largely ignorant of the work of the other. The neurologist and the psychologist have gained each other's respect and cooperation in many hospital settings during the last twenty years, but this union, when it has taken place, has been effected by the members of each team working closely together and learning the basic knowledge of the other's discipline. This means then, that if the brain-injured child is to be helped by neuropsychological knowledge, the neuropsychologist and the special educator must learn to work more closely together and must begin a greater exchange of knowledge.

To communicate useful new knowledge to teachers is difficult, and to communicate highly sophisticated knowledge is almost impossible. The education of the brain-injured child requires the integration of the best judgment and skills of the neurologist, the public health nurse, the special teacher, the educational administrator, the neuropsychologist, and frequently the neurosurgeon, the radiologist, the audiologist, the speech therapist, the social worker, and other professional specialists. When so many professional people are involved, the effectiveness of their communication among themselves, as well as to the teacher, may be determined by the least competent of the group.

The able teacher may be one of society's most influential members, but, like most practitioners, he is asked daily to carry out procedures for which neither he nor anyone else may have any clear theoretical understanding. Like most, in this position, he will act either on prejudice, intuition, blind faith, or some strongly championed principle which for fortuitous reasons he has chosen to accept. When it happens that the principle and the practice are tenuously related, and his practices are successful empirically, no harm is likely to be done. But if he is provided with a half-truth, or a difficult type of knowledge which he perceives only dimly, then there is a possibility that he may simplify and distort his conception and impose ideas and skills on small children which include some deleterious effects.

In attempting to advise teachers of brain-injured children, one is caught between the two dangers of oversimplification, and hence distortion, and overelaboration, and hence confusion. How, then, are teachers to be helped with this knowledge?

The teacher of the brain-injured child is faced with three broad responsibilities. He must learn a certain body of knowledge pertaining to neurology, psychology, and education; he must learn to communicate successfully with parents, other educators, neurologists, and other medical specialists, social welfare personnel, and all persons concerned with the child's growth and education; and he may have to learn or develop some new specific teaching techniques.

KNOWLEDGE OF TEACHERS CONCERNING BRAIN INJURY

To investigate the first of these—the knowledge required—the writer administered a questionnaire to over two hundred teachers attending the 1965 summer session courses in three universities. Respondents supplied information from the University of New Hampshire, Whittier College in California, and the University of Victoria. While the sampling was uncontrolled, it did show a wide geographic coverage.

Some were special education teachers and some were preparing to teach "normal" children. The majority taught children in the primary and elementary grades. However, since Myklebust (personal communication) and others have estimated that up to 10 per cent of children in all "normal" classrooms probably suffer from some degree of cerebral dysfunction resulting in learning difficulties, it seems reasonable that all teachers may be better prepared with some knowledge of neurological structure and function.

Among a large number of questions, teachers were asked what they understood by the terms, brain-damaged or brain-injured, whether they would coerce a six-year-old to change from left-handed to right-handed writing, what they understood by cerebral dominance, the locus and function of some of the cerebral lobes, and the definitions of aphasia, alexia, agraphia, and mixed laterality.

While an item analysis was done on the results of the questionnaire, no attempt will be made here to report them in detail. In general, most of the teachers sampled had had little or no formal training in clinical neurology; a few had a planned approach in dealing with left-handed six-year-olds but most did not; only about one in six had any clear idea of cerebral dominance; only one in ten had a theoretical understanding of handedness, but there was little agreement as to reasons for it; only two thirds of them gave special instruction to left-handed children; most had no knowledge or a garbled concept of eyedness; most had little or no understanding of mixed laterality among hand, eye, and foot; and nine out of ten teachers did not think of relating neurological factors to reading disability. Between 87 and 98 per cent of those teachers sampled had no knowledge of the location of Broca's area, the occipital lobes, nor did they know the meanings of the terms, aphasia, alexia, agraphia, and mixed laterality.

While many educators might not expect a teacher of "normal" children to need to know these things, it probably means that the 5 to 10 per cent of his students with learning problems resulting from some type of neurological involvement will be taught with almost complete ignorance of the interaction of neurological and psychological functions. Because of this, it might be argued that since all behavior, including learning, is mediated by sensory, central, and muscular activities, all teachers, whether they teach "normals" or brain-damaged children, should have at least a basic knowledge of neurological structure and function and their relation to perception, cognition, and motor response. A further reason for suggesting the provision of rudimentary neurological training for all teachers is to attract and recruit a greater number of well-trained "special" teachers who might otherwise be oblivious to the interests, challenges, and practical uses of neuropsychology.

HANDEDNESS

The best sources of reliable knowledge on handedness appear to be in the writings of the neurologists and the experimental psychologists and not in the textbooks of psychology or education. Most of the professional educators either ignore the matter of handedness in their writings or mention it briefly and superficially. The experimental psychologists, prior to about thirty years ago, also approached the problem at a purely behavioral level, but in the mid-1930's, brief references to its neurological implications began to appear. Since so many motor performances depend on one or both hands, and since some degree of ambidexterity is so common, those attempts to define handedness by degree on a continuum recognizing a large number of manual performances seem to be scientifically most useful (Benton, 1962; Harris, 1958; Rife 1940).

In 1922, Rife proposed an interesting classification of three types of right- and three types of left-handedness which was descriptive and purely behavioral. In 1935, Dennis concluded from a controlled observation of one pair of fraternal twins that laterality preferences, including handedness, were due more to innate factors than social learning. He did warn, however, that the assumption "that hand preferences are due solely to asymmetrical structure of the cortex" is "unjustified and that a single cause or explanation of all hand preferences is unlikely to be correct." Lederer (1939) drew attention to the failure of most writers to provide an adequate definition of what they meant by handedness. "In many instances the criterion of handedness seems to be the hand used in writing," wrote Stoddard and Wellman in 1934 and too frequently this is still true. Some interesting infant studies have been designed to investigate hand preferences prior to the influence of social learning, but in spite of careful attempts to analyze observations statistically and to provide unimanual, bimanual, prehensatory, manipulatory, and postural activities for these infants (Lederer, 1939), handedness signs have not been clear. During the first year of life, handed status of the same infant evidently tends to change more than during the second year, and more frequently from left to right than the other way. Such findings suggest little predictive value in single or brief observations during the first year, and possibly a greater theoretical support for the influence of learning than heredity.

The work of Humphrey in England, and others, has shown "that hand preferences are in general very much less consistent among left-handed than among right-handed subjects, even among those who had always written with the left-hand." And, "the left-handed subjects were in general less consistent as regards foot and eye preferences" (Zangwill, 1960, p. 3).

Whether handedness is due to constitutional factors (such as inherited cerebral dominance, position of the fetus, visceral distribution, a Mendelian trait) or social learning (such as direct training, desire to conform, or, in the case of left-handedness, the desire to resist parental influence) cannot be proved at the present time. A review of the literature seems to indicate that psychologists with little physiological knowledge tend to favor the social-conditioning theory and that neurologists and neurosurgeons tend to draw on both physiological and psychological evidence in their theories. (Nielsen, 1962; Penfield and Roberts, 1959). This latter view is also true of the neuropsychologists (Benton, 1959; Reitan, 1959; Semmes et al., 1961), who are revealing interesting neurological correlates with handedness.

Reitan uses the Halstead Finger Oscillation Test to study lesions of the right and left motor strip and the cerebral motor structures. Kløve, with his interesting and relatively new motor steadiness battery (personal communication), is attempting to localize right and left cerebellar lesions and pyramidal tract damage. Teuber and Weinstein for some years have studied the neuropsychological relationships among pressure sensitivity of the two hands and the loci of unilateral somaesthetic cerebral injuries. There is a great mass of research data in the work of these and other neuropsychologists, but little attempt has yet been made to integrate this into a body of knowledge to understand handedness better in its relation to classroom learning or to help the teacher. Not only have teachers not been exposed to this knowledge, neither have most psychologists (Reitan, 1965).

FINGER LOCALIZATION

Finger localization, while an essential source of sensory input and hence an influential determinant in both tactual perception and learning, "is not a perceptual skill of any great cultural interest" (Benton, 1959) nor of any great research concern. It has had the clinical interest of Gerstmann in Germany since the early 1920's, but the normative genetic aspects of finger localization were investigated only as recently as 1938 by Strauss and Werner (Benton, 1959). Since 1940, increasing research, though still relatively little, has been carried on to study this sensorimotor function and its relation to other behavioral patterns. Gerstmann, by linking it with agraphia and acalculia implied its relation to the learning of spelling, writing, and arithmetical deductive reasoning. While he did not study this relationship primarily as an educator, other later researchers have revealed its nature, at least in part, and this information should be added to the knowledge and skills of the teacher of the brain-injured child. Benton, Hutcheon, and Seymour (1951) have shown a positive relationship between mental level and proficiency in finger localization. Ettlinger (1963) has found that some patients with parietal lesions tend to be inferior in finger localization, calculation, writing, and three-dimensional construction. Matthews and Folk (1964) have found in a study of mentally retarded subjects a positive correlation between success in finger localization and written arithmetic and all three Wechsler I.Q.'s. Hence, since it appears that mental age is a correlative of finger-localization ability, and since this appears to be related to somaesthetic cortical function, further research may reveal useful educational knowledge. Matthews has recently carried out interesting research which suggests that, among mentally retarded subjects, Wechsler Verbal and Performance I.Q.'s decline linearly as the total number of errors increase, but Performance I.Q.'s decline at a significantly faster rate. The percentage of subjects with VIQ ≥ PIQ increases as the total number of errors increases. Matthews has concluded, "The results suggested possible relationships between finger localization deficits and chronic-static encephalopathy in retarded subjects" (in press).

This and other studies point to fascinating possibilities in an almost completely neglected area of study. Benton (1959) has supplied normative data and to date has probably made the greatest contribution in this area, but relatively little research has yet been carried out to study the relationships between finger localization and competence in arithmetic, spelling, writing, constructional praxis, and other academic and perceptual-motor performances in normals. Most research so far has been done with mental retardates. Teachers will need to know much more about this particular sensory and manual function and its qualitative relation to classroom learning before they can integrate the knowledge into their professional theories and practices.

CEREBRAL DOMINANCE

Most teachers, like most psychologists, if they think of cerebral dominance at all, consider that the hemisphere contralateral to the preferred hand (and this is usually inferred from the hand with which the subject writes) is the dominant hemisphere. Any serious student of handedness and cerebral dominance knows that this simplified concept may or may not be true, and that many more behavioral functions than handedness depend on various cerebral areas which are not equipotential in their functions.

A little over one hundred years ago, Broca's discovery of the relationship between lesions in a particular part of the left frontal hemisphere and mutism and motor aphasia established the theory that the left hemisphere is dominant for speech and language. This has been corroborated many times by neurologists (Penfield, 1959; Russell, 1961) and neuropsychologists (Benton, 1963; Kimura, 1961; Kløve and Reitan, 1958; Matthews, in press; Reitan, 1959). So intensive has been the study of handedness and speech (Brain, 1945; Nielsen, 1962; Penfield and Roberts, 1959; Weisenburg and McBride, 1964; Zangwill, 1960), and especially speech and left-hemisphere function, that Benton has suggested, "Even today many people think of the concept [of hemispheric cerebral dominance] solely in these terms" (1965). In fact, cerebral dominance appears to determine many more activities than speech and hand preference, and it is these several activities that will be considered here in an attempt to integrate them into useful educational theory and practice.

Benton (1965) reports that in 1900 the German neurologist, W. Liepmann, was the first to define "apraxia," or the inability to perform a desired skilled act or series of movements, as a type of behavioral impairment occurring in patients with cerebral lesions. Liepmann's evidence suggested that "ideomotor apraxia" (e.g., making a fist on verbal command) resulted from left-hemisphere lesions, and subsequent research has supported this.

Although not corroborated with as clear-cut evidence, the constellation Gerstmann studied with its four behavioral traits (finger localization, left-right orientation, and the ability to write and calculate) seems to be largely determined by left-parietal function. "Thus we see here [left] hemispheric dominance for abilities related to the so-called body image or, at any rate, to performances that would seem to be 'orientational' rather than strictly 'verbal' in nature" (Benton, 1965).

Benton (1965), in his scholarly survey of the problem of cerebral dominance, has also provided research evidence that while the left hemisphere is dominant for language, even in most left-handers, the right hemisphere seems to show maximum control of visual space perception and memory, constructional praxis, praxis for dressing, auditory perception and memory, and motor impersistence. He points out that this "broadening of the concept of hemispheric cerebral dominance has been one of the most significant developments in human neuropsychology" (Benton, 1965).

That "aphasia is more frequently encountered and, at the same time, is likely to be less severe and of shorter duration in the sinistral with a unilateral cerebral lesion than in his dextral counterpart has fostered the conclusion that complete hemispheric dominance for language is more characteristic of the right-handed than the left-handed individual" (Benton, 1959). This evidence and the fact that representation of language in both hemispheres is rare in the right-hander but not in the left-hander have led Benton to suggest that "left-handedness may be conceived to be a form of immaturity, i.e. a *lack* of right-handedness rather than its opposite" (Benton, 1959). Penfield, in a somewhat similar vein, has suggested that "brain function and handedness may be unrelated except by disease" (Penfield and Roberts, 1959). Kimura's interesting work in this field has suggested, "It is clear that the ear opposite the dominant hemisphere is more efficient [in receiving verbal stimuli], irrespective of handedness" (1961) and that while the right ear is more sensitive to language, the left ear is superior in sensing melodies (1964). The fact that most right-handers tend to show a preference for the use of the right hand, but most left-handers tend to be more ambidexterous (Zangwill, 1960), suggests not only the continuous quality of handedness, but the probable presence of a mixed cerebral dominance depending on the particular manual skill or behavior trait being considered.

Not only does the cerebrum show a left-right dominance for verbal and spatial-perceptive-constructive functions, but it also seems to possess an anterior-posterior axis for specific registration and control of particular behavioral performances. Motor and somaesthetic functions obviously are subject to anterior-posterior control which is not normally considered a form of dominance in the usual sense. But, in addition, frontal dominant function for deductive and inductive reasoning (Halstead, 1947), recent memory (Jacobsen, 1936; Pribram, 1958), and self-control (Russell, 1959) have long been suspected. Serial-order functions (both receptive and expressive) have been thought by Pribram (1958) to be controlled by frontal-lobe function, and research in this writer's laboratory with visual memory for patterns presented serially is designed to investigate this hypothesis. Since reading, auditory cognition, spelling, writing, and almost all classroom learning include serial-order behavior, neuropsychological research of this function should have both theoretical and practical value.

In summary, a possible hypothesis of multiple cerebral dominance that includes both spatial and temporal dimensions has been presented. The evidence is strong to suggest left-hemisphere dominance for language and possible right-hemisphere dominance for certain nonverbal performances of a perceptual, constructional, and motor nature. Temporal dominance of the frontal lobes, from time to time, to dominate the activity of subsystems of the central nervous system, has been described by neurologists for some time (Russell, 1959). This means, then, that the matter of cerebral dominance is highly complex, and that the teacher who attempts to master much of this knowledge should be more sympathetic to and diagnostically more knowledgeable in his approach to the learning problems of his students.

PREPARATION OF TEACHERS

The preparation of teachers has traditionally not included any training in neurology or even attention to the physiological correlates of learning disabilities or response patterns that are fairly clearly determined by neurological deficits or dysfunctions. Even handedness, as already described, is seldom mentioned in textbooks of either psychology or professional education. While teachers of the brain-injured must analyze a child's classroom performances at a behavioral level, nevertheless he should have an understanding of the child's neural processes underlying his perceptual-cognitive-motor performances. In order to understand better what the child's limits might be, and to aid him in his predictions of the child's possible future behavior, he needs this knowledge. In the writer's laboratory, it has been found useful in understanding a child's perceptual-motor deficit on Benton's visual retention test and his difficulties in reading and spelling to know that the grade iii dysrhythmia in his left parietal and occipital lobes probably means a certain degree of chronicity of visual-perceptual difficulty. Not only this, but if his auditory and tactile perceptions are average or superior, these sense modes can be emphasized in his training program (Wepman, 1964), and the absence of any neurological signs in the temporal and anterior parietal areas tends to support this diagnostic approach.

The special teacher of the brain-injured child should understand that the brain reveals little asymmetry of structure (Bonin, 1962) but marked and complex differences in function, that man has at least "two brains" (Young, 1962), that the two hemispheres operate as a delicate, integrated energy system (Gazzaniga et al., 1965; Sperry, 1962), that brain lesions may cause chronic behavioral symptoms that interfere with normal learning (Hecaen, 1962), that cerebral dominance may alter depending on the particular function and time of observation, that the left hemisphere is usually dominant for speech and language functions, that the right hemisphere may have its own sphere of dominance, that handedness should be carefully defined (Benton, 1962; Rife, 1940), that finger localization has a specific role in classroom learning, and that dominance in hand, eye, and foot may be considered in planning remedial learning programs (Delacato, 1963; Hildreth, 1949).

Very few teacher training programs are either broad or thorough enough yet to prepare the teacher of the brain-injured child adequately. Too often teachers who are seeking frantically for quick answers to their problems of instruction will uncritically adopt methods with no scientific validity simply because they seem to provide a much-needed answer. Better programs of teacher training should help to protect children from possible damage resulting from this type of ignorance.

If an integrated graduate training program in clinical neurology, research design in neuropsychology, and special education can be provided, many of the problems facing teachers of the brain-injured child will be answered, at least in part.

SELECTED REFERENCES

Aristotle. *Great books of the western world. Vol. 8.* Chicago: Encyclopaedia Britannica, 1952a, 690–695.

Aristotle. Quoted in Chapter 56, "Memory and imagination" in *The great ideas: A synopticon of great books of the western world. II. Vol. 3.* Chicago: Encyclopaedia Britannica, 1952b, 133–157.

Baldwin, Alfred L. *Behaviour and development in childhood.* New York: Dryden Press, 1955.

Benton, A. L. "The definition of 'handedness' " in *Interhemispheric relations and cerebral dominance.* V. B. Mountcastle (ed.). Baltimore: Johns Hopkins Press, 1962.

————. "The problem of cerebral dominance," *The Canadian Psychologist,* 1965, 6a(4), 332–348.

————. *Progress report. Grant NB 00616 performance tests in cerebral disease.* Iowa City: Departments of Neurology and Psychology, State University of Iowa, 1963.

————. *Right-left discrimination and finger localization development and pathology.* New York: Paul B. Hoeber, 1959.

Benton, A. L., Hutcheon, J. F., and Seymour, E. Arithmetic ability, finger-localization capacity and right-left discrimination in normal and defective children," *American Journal of Orthopsychiatry,* 1951, 21, 756–766.

Birch, Herbert G. (ed.). *Brain damage in children: The biological and social aspects.* Baltimore: Williams & Wilkins, 1964.

Bonin, Gerhardt von. "Anatomical asymmetries of the cerebral hemispheres" in

Interhemispheric relations and cerebral dominance. V. B. Mountcastle (ed.). Baltimore: Johns Hopkins Press, 1962.

Boring, Edwin G. *A history of experimental psychology.* New York: Appleton-Century-Crofts, 1957.

Brain, W. Russell. "Speech and handedness," *Lancet*, 1945, 2, 837–842.

Cruickshank, W. M. (ed.). *Psychology of exceptional children and youth.* Englewood Cliffs, N.J.: Prentice-Hall, 1963.

Cruickshank, W. M., Bice, H. V., and Wallen, N. E., *Perception and cerebral palsy.* 1st ed.; Syracuse: Syracuse University Press, 1957.

Cruickshank, W. M., *et al. A teaching method for brain-injured and hyperactive children.* Syracuse: Syracuse University Press, 1961.

Delacato, Carl H. *The diagnosis and treatment of speech and reading problems.* Springfield, Ill.: Charles C Thomas, 1963.

Dennis, Wayne. "Laterality of function in early infancy under controlled developmental conditions," *Child Development*, 1935, 6, 242–252.

Ettlinger, G. "Defective identification of fingers," *Neuropsychologia*, 1963, 1, 39–45.

Frostig, M., and Horne, D. *The Frostig program for the development of visual perception.* Chicago: Follett, 1964.

Gazzaniga, M. S., Bogen, J. E., and Sperry, R. W. "Observations on visual perception after disconnection of the cerebral hemispheres in man," *Brain*, 1965, 88, 221–236.

Halstead, Ward C. *Brain and intelligence.* Chicago: University of Chicago Press, 1947.

Harris, Albert J. *Harris tests of lateral dominance: Manual of directions for administration and interpretation*, 3rd ed.; New York: The Psychological Corporation, 1958.

Hecaen, H. "Clinical symptomatology in right and left hemispheric lesions" in *Interhemispheric relations and cerebral dominance.* V. B. Mountcastle (ed.). Baltimore: Johns Hopkins Press, 1962.

Hildreth, G. "The development and training of hand dominance: III. Origins of handedness and lateral dominance," *Journal of Genetic Psychology*, 1949, 75, 255–275.

Jackson, Hughlings. "The physiological aspects of education (Hunterian oration, 1872)" in *Selected writings of John Hughlings Jackson. Vol. II.* New York: Basic Books, 1958.

Jacobsen, C. F. "Studies of cerebral function in primates. I. The functions of the frontal association areas in monkeys," *Comparative Psychological Monographs*, 1936, 13, 3–60.

Kephart, N. C. *The slow learner in the classroom.* Columbus, Ohio: Charles E. Merrill, 1960.

Kimura, Doreen. "Cerebral dominance and the perception of verbal stimuli" *Canadian Journal of Psychology*, 1961, 15(3), 166–171.

————. "Left-right differences in the perception of melodies," *Quarterly Journal of Experimental Psychology*, 1964, 16(4), 355–358.

Kløve, H. The motor steadiness battery (personal communication).

Kløve, H. "The relationship of differential electroencephalographic patterns to the distribution of Wechsler-Bellevue scores," *Neurology*, 1959, 9, 871–876.

Kløve, H., and Reitan, R. M. "The effects of dysphasia and spatial distortion on Wechsler-Bellevue results," *American Medical Association Archives of Neurology and Psychiatry*, 1958, 80, 708–713.

Lederer, Ruth Klein. "An exploratory investigation of handed status in the first two years of life," *University of Iowa Studies of Child Welfare*, 1939, 16(2), 9–103.

Mateer, Florence. *Glands and efficient behavior*. New York: Appleton-Century-Crofts, 1935.

Matthews, Charles G., and Folk, Earl D. "Finger localization, intelligence, and arithmetic in mentally retarded subjects," *American Journal of Mental Deficiency*, 1964, 69(1), 107–113.

Matthews, Charles G., Folk, Earl D., and Zerfas, Philip G. "The relationship of lateralized finger localization deficits to differential Wechsler-Bellevue results in mentally retarded subjects," *American Journal of Mental Deficiency*, in press.

Murphy, Gardner. *Historical introduction to modern psychology*. New York: Harcourt, Brace & World, 1949.

Myklebust, H. Personal communication.

Nielsen, J. M. *Agnosia, apraxia, aphasia: Their value in cerebral localization*. 2nd ed.; New York: Hafner, 1962.

Penfield, Wilder, and Roberts, Lamar. *Speech and brain mechanisms*. Princeton: Princeton University Press, 1959.

Pribram, K. H. "Neocortical function in behavior" in *Biological and biochemical bases of behavior*. H. F. Harlow and C. N. Woolsey (eds.). Madison: University of Wisconsin Press, 1958, 151–172.

Reitan, Ralph M. *The effects of brain lesions on adaptive abilities in human beings*. Indianapolis: Dept. of Neurology, Indiana University Medical Center, 1959 (mimeograph).

———. "A research program on the psychological effects of brain lesions in human beings" in *International review of research in mental retardation*. N. R. Ellis (ed.). New York: Academic Press, 1965.

Rife, D. C. "Handedness, with special reference to twins," *Genetics*, 1940, 25, 178–186.

Rife, J. Merle. "Types of dextrality," *Psychological Review*, 1922, 29, 474–480.

Russell, W. Ritchie, *Brain, memory, learning, a neurologist's view*. London: Oxford University Press, 1959.

Russell, W. Ritchie, and Espir, M. L. E. *Traumatic aphasia*. London: Oxford University Press, 1961.

Semmes, Josephine, et al. *Somatosensory changes after penetrating brain wounds in man*. Cambridge, Mass.: Harvard University Press, 1961.

Sperry, Roger W. "Some general aspects of interhemispheric integration" in *Interhemispheric relations and cerebral dominance*. V. B. Mountcastle (ed.). Baltimore: Johns Hopkins Press, 1962.

Stoddard, George D., and Wellman, Beth L. *Child psychology*. New York: Macmillan, 1934.

Weisenburg, T., and McBride, K. E. *Aphasia: A clinical and psychological study*. New York: Hafner, 1964.

Wepman, J. M. Discussion of "The modality concept" in *Meeting individual differences in reading*, H. A. Robinson (ed.). Chicago: University of Chicago Press, 1964, 26, 25–33.

Young, J. Z. "Why do we have two brains?" in *Interhemispheric relations and cerebral dominance*. V. B. Mountcastle (ed.). Baltimore: Johns Hopkins Press, 1962.

Zangwill, O. L. *Cerebral dominance and its relation to psychological function*. London: Oliver and Boyd, 1960.

PART IV

PSYCHOMEDICAL COMPETENCIES

Chapter 15

The Needs of Teachers for Specialized Information in the Area of Neuropsychology

RALPH M. REITAN, Ph.D.

EDITORIAL NOTE.—Dr. Reitan, a former student of Ward Halstead at the University of Chicago, has been engaged in neuropsychological research for his entire professional life. Placing his emphasis in this paper on competencies of the "genuine students of the nervous system as it relates to behavior," Dr. Reitan stresses competencies which have not heretofore been a significant part of teacher education. These, however, are considered essential for teachers of brain-injured children. The availability of instruction in this area, among others, supports the contentions of the Editor, as noted in Chapter 1, that locations of professional centers for preparation of teachers of brain-injured children must be affiliated and closely related to major interdisciplinary university complexes. This paper is based on research supported in the main by grants NB-1468 and NB-5211 from the National Institute of Neurological Diseases and Blindness and grant CD-15 from the Division of Chronic Diseases, United States Public Health Service.

DR. RALPH M. REITAN is currently Professor of Psychology (Neurology), and Director, Section of Neuropsychology, Department of Neurology, at the Indiana University Medical Center, Indianapolis, Indiana. He has been affiliated with this institution since 1951. He received his B.A. degree from Central YMCA College in 1944, and the Ph.D. degree in psychology from the University of Chicago in 1950.

Dr. Reitan has published numerous significant papers concerning the relationship of various forms of brain damage and behavior. He has been a member of the Neurology (A) Study Section of the National Institutes of Health, the Perinatal Research Committee of the National Institute for Neurological Diseases and Blindness, and the Space Medical Advisory Group.

Chapter 15

The Needs of Teachers for Specialized Information in the Area of Neuropsychology

RALPH M. REITAN, Ph.D.

Although investigative and clinical interest in the psychological correlates of brain lesions in human beings has existed for many years, the last two to three decades have seen a striking growth in recognition of the importance in understanding the limiting and facilitating effects of brain functions as they relate to specific aspects of behavior. The area of human neuropsychology is presently only in a formative phase, and rapid extensions of information and knowledge are in the process of being made. The questions which exist and problems which need to be solved are much more readily subject to identification than is a full and integrated body of knowledge which might be communicated to teachers.

As an idealized postulate it would be safe to say that teachers of children with brain lesions would appreciate advantages in their work in direct relationship to the fullness of their knowledge of the vast array of neurological conditions which may change the structure and function of the brain, the completeness of their knowledge regarding the ability and personality structure of normal children, and their understanding of the changes in ability and personality that may accompany brain lesions. Such an aim, however, is unrealistic in that it would require not only thoroughgoing training in psychology, with specialized training in neuropsychology, but well-rounded training in the neurological sciences as well. Rather than to propose criteria by which this idealized aim might be delimited to the basic needs of teachers, it is probably important to recognize at the outset that the problem relates to degree rather than kinds of training in neuropsychology, that the degree of training or information in this area must be balanced with the practical problem of obtaining information in other areas as well, and that the degree of emphasis in the area of neuropsychology will, in practical terms, vary from one location to another if only because of the emerging definition of neuropsychology itself. A consideration of the needs of teachers for knowledge in this or any other area will benefit from the extent to which it contains sufficient flexibility to achieve a realistic orientation, rather than to succumb to a rigid and narrow framework that leaves little room for change, growth, and considerations relating to the over-all balance of knowledge. There have been too many commitments to ideas representing inadequate bases for closure or generalization, too many adherents of particular "schools," too many disciples of single theories or methods, and too few genuine students of the nervous system as it relates to behavior.

Two points should be communicated to teachers, each of which embodies a great deal of specific information that may be dealt with in varying degrees of completeness. First, teachers should be given a realization that "brain damage" is a relatively meaningless term because it includes so many varied and diverse neurological conditions. The major categories of brain lesions include: (1) traumatic brain injury, (2) inflammatory damage of the brain associated with infectious diseases, (3) cerebrovascular lesions, (4) neoplastic lesions of the brain, and (5) developmental anomalies of the brain. Lesions of the brain may involve large areas or small areas and they may represent rather complete destruction in the areas involved or only a degree of damage or alteration that is reflected principally in abnormalities of function. A great deal of meaningful subdivision occurs in each of the five categories listed above. For example, traumatic injury may be relatively minimal or it may be gross with extensive penetration of the skull and widespread destruction of brain tissue. Neoplastic lesions cover a range of types of tumors from those that are congenital to ones that customarily occur first in early middle age; from lesions that directly involve and damage the brain tissues (intrinsic tumors) to ones that grow outside the brain itself but within the skull and exert an influence on brain functions as an adjacent space-occupying body (extrinsic tumors). These various types of brain tumors, while showing great differences from each other, also show a considerable degree of variability within specific types with respect to their pathologic characteristics.

In addition to the wide range of variation in types of brain lesions and the extent to which they have compromised normal brain functions, brain lesions may also involve different areas of the brain to varying degrees. Information has long existed regarding the special role of certain areas of the brain for sensory and motor functions as well as in speech and language. More recently, a considerable body of evidence has also accrued to indicate the special significance of lesions in other locations. Thus, the regional location of the lesion is another biological factor that is highly relevant to the psychological significance of brain lesions. Other biological factors are also undoubtedly of significance. The duration of a lesion is particularly relevant in considering traumatic injuries, in which reorganization of brain functions and a certain degree of recovery may occur, as contrasted, for example, with a progressive disease process in which increasing impairment of brain function may be expected. Finally, the age at which the lesion was sustained must also be considered. A traumatic lesion imposed on a relatively undeveloped infantile brain would certainly be expected to have different psychological effects than a similar lesion occurring in the brain of a young adult. In addition to the differences in impairment that must necessarily be a function of the differences in the behavioral repertoires of the young child and the young adult, another consideration relates to the particular effects of the brain lesion on the potential for psychological development of the child. In this sense, duration of the lesion and the age at which it was sustained imply a type of interaction in the child relating to psychological development that may be quite different in the adult.

In spite of the diversification and wide variation among brain lesions, it is interesting to note a recent research approach oriented toward identification of the particular significance of these many neurological variables (Reitan, 1962). Even at the present time the majority of psychological investigations into the effects of brain lesions are concerned with the general category of "brain damage." While such investigations are perfectly valid as a starting point in studying brain-behavior relationships, they are too often treated as if they provided final types of answers. The inadequacy of such an approach can easily be substantiated. For example, pronounced differences in psychological deficit have been shown as depending upon lateralization of cerebral lesions (Andersen, 1950; Fitzhugh et al., 1962, 1963; Hécaen et al., 1956; Heimburger and Reitan, 1961; Reitan, 1955; Reitan and Tarshes, 1959). In a study this writer made in 1955, a group of subjects with lesions of the right cerebral hemisphere obtained a mean score on the Block Design subtest of the Wechsler-Bellevue Scale (Form I) that was next to the lowest of the eleven subtests. A comparable group of subjects with lesions of the left cerebral hemisphere, however, had a mean score on Block Design that was next to the highest among the eleven subtests. Obviously, the cerebral hemisphere involved has a good deal to do with the nature of the resulting psychological deficit.

Mention is made at this point of the necessity to recognize the complex and variable nature of "brain damage" as a basis for aiding teachers to avoid mistakes of oversimplification and premature generalization that have hindered optimum progress in neuropsychology. It would be important for teachers to develop some understanding and appreciation of the complexity of the brain as an organ and of the great number of ways in which damage or disease may alter and impair the function of this organ.

The second major point that should be communicated to teachers is that the brain is the principal organ of behavior, both in persons with normal and in those with impaired brain functions. The initial reaction to this statement is that it is a truism—that everyone, with or without technical training, already knows it. There are, however, many different ways of "knowing" something, and the natural tendency to abstract, oversimplify, and categorize or "pigeon-hole" soon leads to the development of stereotyped and inflexible notions of how "brain damage" affects behavior. The history of psychological investigation, in fact, has been equally as guilty of oversimplifying "behavior" subserved by brain functions as it has been of oversimplifying "brain damage." This contention is readily subject to substantiation by even a very brief review of the various methods that have been proposed for inferring psychological deficit resulting from brain lesions. A popular method, which is still widely used by psychologists, depends upon a comparison of scores on tests that are supposedly minimally affected by "brain damage" with scores obtained by the same subject on tests that are adversely affected by "brain damage." Reference to the above paragraphs, which indicate the diversity of "brain damage," may initially provide the reader with a basis for criticizing this approach, but the point should be made here that if the brain is the principal organ of behavior, both normal and impaired, any method which proposes that behavior will be affected by "brain damage" in a unitary, constant, invariable manner can hardly be adequate. The problem has been that many psychologists have been motivated to find some simple, easy formula that is subject to routine application in differentiating human beings with and without "brain damage." The problem is not as simple as this, and those in the profession would probably never have engaged in so much effort which assumes that it is if the truism stated above had been borne clearly in mind. These experiences, however, may assist in avoiding a perpetuation of the difficulties when considering the information needed by teachers of the brain injured. The behavioral consequences of brain damage are not so constant and simple that they can be described in a sentence or paragraph. Many psychologists and teachers are distressed by this realization, since it complicates their view of the problem. If they would take time to realize that brain functions subserve their own personal abilities and behavior, complex, subtle, and varied though they may be, they would also have something to be pleased about.

The above points need to be made because of the recurring inclination among many psychologists and teachers to presume the presence of brain damage on the basis of simple observations and resulting one-word descriptions. The terms, hyperactivity, distractibility, and impulsivity, fall into this category. Even though many children with brain lesions demonstrate these characteristics, it is important to realize that many children with known cerebral lesions are passive, calm, and even withdrawn. Further, and even more important, is the realization that many children without anamnestic or neurological evidence of cerebral lesions also show these qualitative behavioral deviations that are so frequently assumed to characterize brain damage exclusively. Essentially, the concept of false-negatives and false-positives must be communicated to teachers together with some concept of appropriate standards for evidence on which to base conclusions. Two times recently the writer has encountered instances in which a disparity between hand and eye preference has provided the basis for a certain and unequivocal conclusion by teachers that brain damage was present. The simple realization that such disparities occur in a substantial proportion (according to the writer's data, probably about 30 to 35 per cent) of perfectly normal people, both neurologically and behaviorally, would dispel the tendency to attribute unequivocal neurological diagnostic significance to this finding.

In this context, mention should be made of the difficulties inherent in establishing definite and detailed diagnoses of brain lesions, especially in children. The Neuropsychology Laboratory of the Indiana University Medical Center has focused since 1951 on the problem of obtaining detailed but independent neurological and neuropsychological findings on individual patients, followed by careful comparison and joint study of the two sets of information. The files contain many instances of patients with unequivocal evidence of brain lesions in whom one or more of the standard neurological diagnostic methods provided negative results. For example, the physical neurological examination frequently is negative or noncontributory regarding a diagnosis even in instances in which brain injury has been actually seen or is definitely indicated by special diagnostic techniques. Electroencephalographic findings are also often negative, particularly in slowly-developing brain diseases or in instances of brain damage that are chronic, nonprogressive, and long-standing in nature. X-ray contrast studies, although providing unequivocal information regarding brain lesions in many instances, are not contributory in a considerable number of conditions of brain damage and, in accordance with preliminary findings, are frequently not performed because of the small element of risk that accompanies their use. The problems and difficulties involved in diagnosis and description of brain lesions by experts in the neurological sciences are still formidable in clinical practice, and the teacher of the brain-injured should have some appreciation of these problems.

The prediction can safely be made that as neurological diagnostic methods are more thoroughly applied and improve in accuracy and validity, damage to the brain, especially that which results from trauma and inflammatory damage, will be identified in many persons who presently remain undiagnosed. Many lines of evidence converge to support this prediction, but a recent report by Aguilar and Rasmussen (1960) may be cited specifically. These investigators studied pathological specimens of excised epileptogenic brain tissue in 449 consecutive seizure patients operated on over an eight-year period. Thirty-two of these cases, or 7 per cent of the total number, showed at least some histological evidence suggesting the presence of an active encephalitis. In most of these cases the presence of an active inflammatory process was unsuspected preoperatively. Twelve of the thirty-two cases, who showed uniformly severe histopathological changes typical of those seen in chronic encephalitis of proved viral etiology, were selected for detailed study of clinical data. The diagnosis of measles encephalitis had been made in one of these instances and suspected or presumed encephalitis in an additional two. Although febrile illnesses followed by neurological signs or symptoms had been present for several additional patients, the diagnosis of encephalitis had been made in none of the remaining nine patients. Obviously the frequency of patients who have had encephalitis far exceeds the frequency of proved diagnoses, but to what extent remains unknown. This point is of significance with respect to the problem of definition. At present a good deal of evidence suggests that a substantial number of persons have sustained brain lesions but that the definitive evidence is impossible to obtain for many individuals. This situation will continue to exist as long as adequate diagnostic methods which can ethically be applied to all subjects are not available. On the one hand, this situation implies that a rational basis for resolution of the questions relating to definition and terminology is not yet available, and secondly, it emphasizes the urgent need for additional research aimed toward identification and classification of these children. Neuropsychology may well have a contribution to make in this area.

A rather widespread notion exists that the prospects for improvement are limited if the diagnosis of cerebral damage is established. Parents of brain-damaged children, for example, have been known to hope desperately for a diagnosis of emotional disturbance or even of psychosis rather than brain damage, apparently because of an impression of finality and hopelessness associated with actual structural damage to the brain. This impression may have gained currency from the widely known statement deriving from neurophysiological research that functional regeneration of neurons does not occur within the central nervous system. This statement in itself is in need of many qualifications, as judged from the recovery of function in the hind limbs of many animals following complete transection of the spinal cord; but be that as it may, instances of remarkable spontaneous recovery of higher psychological functions over time following brain injury have been described (Reitan, in press, a).

Another influence which has contributed to the apprehension concerning the finality of brain damage has been the interpretation placed on observations of psychological deficit. Some investigators have implied that deficits resulting from brain lesions represent differences in kind rather than degree as compared with normal behavior. With respect to abstraction ability, for example, Goldstein (1940) has said, "Even in its simplest form, however, abstraction is separate in principle from concrete behavior. There is no gradual transition from one to the other." If such a contention were correct, quantitative scaling or measurement of behavior and comparison of groups with and without cerebral lesions on the basis of such measurements obviously would be meaningless. The prospects, in fact, for developing a scientific body of knowledge in neuropsychology would be dim.

Because of the importance of this question, a series of experiments (Reitan, 1956, 1957, 1958, 1959a, 1959b) was performed in the laboratory of the Indiana University Medical Center to determine whether or not the same abilities, measured in a comparable way, were being obtained in patients with and without cerebral lesions. Two groups composed of fifty paired subjects with and without brain lesions were used for this study. Comparison of the level of performance in the two groups showed consistent and highly significant quantitative differences between the groups. These quantitative differences by themselves were clearly not adequate to answer the question of differences in *kind* of mental functions in persons with and without cerebral lesions (even though the same test format was used), if the hypothesis was correct that different kinds of psychological functions existed in patients with cerebral lesions as compared with those having normal brain functions. It seemed reasonable, however, to assume that if different kinds of abilities were used by the brain-damaged subjects, the interrelationships or correlations between various tests would differ from the interrelationships shown by the group without brain damage. Twenty-five psychological test measures were available for each group. This number of variables provided for a total of three hundred coefficients of correlation when individual tests were arranged in all possible pairs. These coefficients were converted to Fisher's z-values, the standard error of the difference for z was found, and each pair of coefficients (brain damage vs. no brain damage) was compared for statistically significant differences. In addition, the extent of agreement of the correlation matrices for the two groups was determined by computing the correlation between them.

Variables from the Wechsler-Bellevue Scale provided ninety-one of the three hundred coefficients for each group. In comparing the groups, only two of the ninety-one coefficients were "significantly" different at the .05 level of confidence. Correlation of these two arrays of coefficients was 0.79, which further indicated the close agreement between the magnitude of the coefficients for groups with and without brain damage.

Of the 300 coefficients, 156 represented correlations between Wechsler-Bellevue results and scores obtained on Halstead's tests. Only 4 of these 156 pairs of coefficients showed differences which reached the .05 confidence level. Correlation of the 156 coefficients obtained in each group yielded a coefficient of .78. In comparing the 55 coefficients derived from interrelationships on Halstead's battery, only one pair showed a "significant" difference, and this barely reached the .05 level of confidence. A correlation of .64 between the matrices for the groups with and without brain damage was obtained. Correlation of the matrices of the total of 300 coefficients obtained for each group yielded .85.

These results provided some feeling of confidence that the scales were relatively appropriate and consistent over the area represented by groups with, as well as without, cerebral lesions. Further, the results provided a strong argument that the effects of cerebral lesions are not, as claimed by Goldstein (1940), "a totally different activity of the organism," but instead seem to represent quantitative deviations from normal levels of the same kinds of abilities as measured in subjects with normal brain functions.

An additional test of this general question was studied using results on the Halstead Category Test for groups of fifty-two patients with and without brain lesions (Reitan, 1959b). The purpose was to compare subtests 5 and 6 of the Category Test, since, even though the subject is not so informed, the subtests are based on the same organizing principle. The investigators wished to compare the absolute number of errors on each subtest for the group, the absolute improvement shown from subtest 5 to subtest 6, and the proportional improvement. The hypothesis was that the group with brain lesions would perform more poorly on each subtest, and that possible differences in type of abstraction abilities might be reflected by differences in the absolute or proportional degree of improvement from subtest 5 to 6. Of particular interest was the testing of Goldstein's (1940) contention that brain lesions caused an essential change through transforming abstraction abilities into concrete performances. Results showed clearly significant differences between the groups with respect to the number of errors made on each subtest considered individually. However, there was no significant difference between the groups in terms of either absolute or proportional improvement from one subtest to the other. Thus, while the brain-damaged subjects consistently performed more poorly than the group without brain damage, they showed the same pattern of error scores between the two subtests.

This same type of study was performed using data from the Halstead Tactual Performance Test (Reitan, 1959a). The group with brain damage was significantly poorer in comparison of the scores obtained with the right hand, the left hand, or both hands, as well as on the total time required for the three performances. However, there were no significant differences between the groups in any instance with respect to absolute or proportional amounts of improvement. The results suggested that the essential differences were quantitative ones in terms of level of performance rather than representing different types of performance in the two groups. Both groups showed clear improvement with practice, and the intergroup differences in this respect were not statistically significant. It should be noted that these results are not relevant to interpretation of intraindividual differences that may be obtained in patients with lateralized cerebral lesions, but instead are referrable to the general results obtained with heterogeneous groups of brain-damaged subjects. Results of this type of investigation should be communicated to teachers of the brain-injured. There is no influence so powerful in eliminating false impressions as the impartial results of controlled, scientific experiments, and the false impression of hopelessness and despair regarding the potential for improvement of brain-injured children certainly deserves to be exposed to the light of scientific inquiry. Even though many have learned from first-hand experience and observation of the potential for improvement that exists among brain-injured children, this area is still urgently in need of additional investigative work to identify the factors that subserve the improvement potential and that might serve most validly as a predictive index.

The content area of neuropsychology, to which teachers of brain-damaged children should have some introduction, is too extensive and varied to permit inclusion in this study. A considerable amount of information is available which relates neurological and psychological information regarding the condition of the brain. This information ranges from controlled comparisons of sensori-perceptual and motor measurements through higher-level ability measurements including complex psychomotor functions, intelligence, and concept formation, to detailed theoretical statements of brain-behavior relationships. A broad range of prerequisites in the neurological sciences, psychological testing and theory, and psychology generally are necessary for a fully comprehensive and detailed study of neuropsychology. The aim in this instance, however, should be to achieve a meaningful survey of the area rather than to achieve a degree of training that would permit fulfillment of a complete professional commitment to neuropsychology.

A meaningful kind of approach to the needs of teachers would be to devote a substantial part of their training in neuropsychology to consideration of characteristic types of problems manifested by children with brain lesions, and to place special emphasis on illustration of inappropriate as well as appropriate orientations and efforts in teaching. A brief survey of some of the writer's experiences suggests that the following types of special problems should be included in such instruction of teachers.

NEUROPSYCHOLOGICAL IMPAIRMENT OF BASIC ADAPTIVE ABILITIES

Generalization

Children with cerebral lesions will sometimes manifest neuropsychological impairment of basic adaptive abilities that considerably exceed expectation as based on conventional measures of general intelligence. If the teacher's reaction to the child is based principally upon intelligence test scores, without recognition of the impairment in other areas, the essential nature of the child's problems will be misunderstood and he will not receive training in the areas of his critical needs. As a result, the child's adjustment problems may be compounded rather than improved.

Illustration

G. M. was a boy ten years and four months old who was referred to a child guidance clinic because of behavioral problems in school, at home, and with his playmates. He was continually a disruptive influence in the classroom. His parents had serious emotional problems in their marital relationship, and their interactions with this child were inconsistent and often explosive. The child had shown an increasing tendency to withdraw from his peer groups. Rather than play with other children, he would withdraw into some type of solitary activity, frequently reading. The behavioral disturbances in the classroom were the basis for referral to the child guidance clinic.

Conventional psychological examination of this child indicated that he had results within the normal range on both the verbal and performance parts of the Wechsler Intelligence Scale for Children. Serious problems of emotional adjustment were apparent both from a detailed history as well as from additional psychological testing. A careful analysis of the child's behavioral problems indicated that he appeared to be much more reasonable and appropriate in his behavior in one-to-one situations, especially with adults, than in circumstances involving groups of people. The Bender Gestalt Test provided evidence suggesting the possibility of cerebral damage and the child was referred for neuropsychological testing.

The neuropsychological test battery administered to this child has been described and the evidence for its validity in reflecting cerebral damage has been reported elsewhere (Reed et al., 1965; Reitan, in press, b). Brain damage was strongly indicated by the results of this battery, with two major areas of deficit standing out clearly. First, the test results indicated that he had a great deal of difficulty and performed poorly in his initial attempts to adapt to unique or novel problem situations. On the second and third trials on similar tasks his scores improved sharply. Secondly, and most importantly, this child was severely impaired in his basic concept-formation ability and abstract reasoning. He had great difficulty in tests that required him to observe and respond rationally to recurring elements of an unfolding total situation (Category Test). He showed a marked inclination to respond differentially and inconsistently to the elements of the situation rather than to impose any organization and derive over-all meaning from the task as a whole. This deficit, which is common in persons with brain lesions regardless of the adequacy of intelligence test scores, probably represents an important key to his behavioral difficulties. Considering this deficit, it was not surprising that the history indicated distractibility and impaired ability to relate in a consistent and meaningful way to complex environmental situations. The child was, in fact, seriously deficient in his ability to select the essential elements of complex situations on the basis of which to form a meaningful concept of the situation. Since he was thus limited in his ability to "make sense" of his environment, it is hardly surprising that his behavior was often distractible, impulsive, and unrelated to the total purpose.

Instances of the type shown by this child raise the hypothesis that hyperactivity and distractibility in brain-damaged children may be the result of special impairment of concept formation with relation to other abilities. Failure to observe similar hyperactive behavior in adults with brain lesions, even though comparably impaired in concept-formation ability, may well be a result of the over-all context of psychological development in which this deficit is manifested. In fact, parallels in the behavior of adults with similar deficits may easily be drawn, although they are usually expressed within at least some of the constraints that are expected of adult behavior. An explanatory hypothesis for hyperactive and uncontrolled behavior of brain-damaged children has obvious implications regarding therapeutic approaches—in this instance centering around methods for developing improved concept formation and abstract reasoning. Although space limitations do not permit such a consideration here, teachers of the brain-injured child should receive information regarding the various methods that might be useful for this purpose.

TEACHER RESPONSE TO SENSORY AND MOTOR DEFICITS

Generalization

A tendency exists on the part of teachers, as well as many others professionally involved with children having cerebral lesions, to respond out of context and, therefore, sometimes inappropriately to the readily apparent sensory and motor deficits that brain-injured children may have. It is important to realize that cerebral lesions which cause certain sensory and motor deficits also have definite corresponding consequences with regard to neuropsychological deficits. The tendency to "excuse" performances limited by the sensory and motor deficits may thus, in at least some instances, deprive the child of practice and experience in the area of psychological functioning in which he is most impaired and in which he most urgently needs training in order to develop minimum competencies for successful living.

Illustration

A fifteen-year-old boy had a life-long history of serious impairment of visual acuity. Interpersonal problems between his parents had caused a good deal of tension in his early life, leading to dissolution of the family. He had formerly lived with foster parents. Although previous group intelligence tests yielded results in the low-average range, the child showed little initiative in cooperating with attempts being made to prepare him for an adult life. In fact, he would not make any effort to find his way from one place to another in town even though his visual functions were adequate for this. Because of the problems he was having in adjusting to his visual deficit, and the possible significance of early emotional trauma in the turbulent family situation, he was referred to a child guidance clinic. Results on the Wechsler Intelligence Scale for

Children (Verbal I.Q., 84; Performance I.Q., 40) and other psychological test findings raised a question of damage to the right cerebral hemisphere, resulting in referral for neuropsychological evaluation.

Neuropsychological examination yielded strong evidence of damage to the right cerebral hemisphere with corresponding findings of widespread and profound impairment in the area of spatial comprehension, organization, and integration. Review of the history indicated that because of visual impairment this child had been shielded and protected from activities requiring adaptation to visuospatial configurations—the very area in which the principal impairment would be expected, considering the location of the brain lesion. In fact, he had not even been permitted to learn to negotiate stairs. While his parents had started this "protective" behavior, it had been perpetuated by his foster parents and teachers. Although verbal and academic abilities had been developed fairly well, he was not at all prepared to adapt to the many requirements in normal living that depend upon temporal and spatial configurations. A program of simple training involving activities such as finding his way from one point to another inside buildings or finding his way about town was initiated and is reported to have resulted in a brightening of the child's attitudes toward his problems of adjustment within two months. The basic impairment, however, was severe and had been compounded by "experiential deprivation" over many years of childhood. The eventual outcome is thus subject to only a guarded prediction.

FAILURES IN ADJUSTMENT

Generalization

Various combinations of psychological deficits, resulting from brain damage, may occur which predispose the child toward various forms of aggressive as well as passive maladaptations to problems in living. These failures in adjustment are frequently viewed as arising from emotional problems in the child's environment. Indeed, they do represent adaptive difficulties with strong emotional overtones, but teachers need more information regarding the interactions of deficits caused by brain damage and the special stresses in adapting to environmental problems and interpersonal relationships that result.

Illustration

This fifteen-year-old boy had a history of serious behavioral disturbances over a period of years. He had caused such flagrant difficulties in his public school classes, with repeated recurrences, that he had finally been dismissed and not permitted to return. He was enrolled in a private residential school for delinquent and emotionally disturbed boys, but again he created so much conflict and disturbance that this school "gave up" on him and returned him to his family situation. Following this, he was admitted as a patient to an institution for the mentally retarded in spite of the fact that his intelligence level was clearly higher than that of the usual person who qualifies for admission to this institution. The patient was not satisfied with this environment and repeatedly ran away from the school. Finally, it became apparent that it was not possible to keep him as a patient at this institution and he was again returned to the family. The patient's mother had sought repeated help on a private basis from psychologists and psychiatrists who had postulated family difficulties and tensions as the basis for the boy's aberrant behavior. Finally, his mother had consulted a neurologist who suspected that this child may have sustained brain damage earlier in life and referred him for neuropsychological evaluation.

Although the mother of this child was relatively stable emotionally and very much concerned about the boy's welfare, the history of the family had not been conducive to the development of emotional stability on the part of the children. The father had been an alcoholic for years, absent from the family for extended periods, and extremely quarrelsome and inclined to punish during his presence. This situation had finally led to a divorce of the parents and this child had been placed in his mother's custody. Although the child had been in an automobile accident shortly before he began first grade in school and had suffered a head injury from which he was unconscious for a fairly extended period of time, the possibility of brain damage as a contributing factor with respect to his behavioral problems had not been considered seriously prior to the neurological examination. The tension and difficulties in the family situation had been considered an obvious adverse influence, and all explanations of the boy's behavior to the mother in the past had centered around such considerations.

Results yielded a Wechsler-Bellevue Verbal I.Q. of 80, Performance I.Q. of 105, and Full-Scale I.Q. of 91. Examination for aphasia, while not indicating definite organic language deficits, did give evidence of a mild central dysarthria. In addition to an impaired general level of performance on Halstead's neuropsychological tests, disparities in performances on the two sides of the body yielded evidence to indicate cerebral damage. For example, the patient was much poorer with his right (preferred) hand than his left hand on the Tactual Performance Test, and also was no faster on finger-tapping speed with his right hand than his left hand. These results in the context of other findings suggested maximal damage to the left cerebral hemisphere and were consistent with the disparity between verbal and performance intelligence levels. In addition, the patient performed extremely poorly on the Category Test, suggesting that he had a great deal of difficulty in organizing diverse stimulus material and drawing reasonable conclusions from his observations.

The particular combination of ability deficits, in the degree shown by this child, are strongly suggestive of a serious behavioral disturbance. It is suspected that the basic difficulty in instances such as this one relates to impairment of concept formation, abstract reasoning, and the ability to analyze situations with a sufficient degree of accuracy and reality to be able to exercise good judgment. In addition, this child showed clear impairment of verbal intelligence and the ability to use verbal functions for comprehension and rationalization of complex situations. Superimposed on these deficits, the results of the tests indicated, was a definite potential for good performance on manipulatory and performance types of tasks. These latter findings would be interpreted as suggesting a strong potential in this child's ability pattern for becoming involved in situations in an active way. With basic impairment of concept formation and reasoning processes, supplemented by impairment of verbal comprehension, the potential for active involvement in socially unacceptable ways was greatly enhanced. Thus, the results suggested that the particular pattern of deficits shown by this child as a result of brain damage were strong predisposing factors in the development of his serious behavioral disturbance. At this point one can postulate an habilitative approach based on specific training oriented toward improving the specific ability deficits which appear to underlie this child's predisposition toward socially unacceptable behavior.

NONACADEMIC PERFORMANCE AFFECTED BY BRAIN LESIONS

Generalization

As would be expected from the hypothesis that the brain is the principal organ of adaptive behavior, the psychological effects of brain lesions cover a wide range of abilities. Frequently, children are encountered with definite neurological and neuropsychological evidence of cerebral damage in whom training efforts have been directed explicitly and almost exclusively toward development of academic competence. Even when these efforts are successful, the child is still left with broad areas of deficiency. It is important that teachers have a familiarity with the many ways in which brain lesions may impair abilities. Practical performances in everyday life are rarely factorially pure, but require input of abilities from many aspects of the ability spectrum for successful completion.

Illustration

This child, seven years and six months old, appeared to be making satisfactory progress in school and was not a behavior problem in the sense of being disruptive. He had suffered suggestive signs of cerebral involvement with high fever accompanying a respiratory infectious illness in infancy although compelling neurological documentation of any brain damage was lacking. The child was regarded currently by his parents as somewhat clumsy in his movements, passive and lacking in motivation, and having difficulty in developing normal relationships and interactions with his playmates. Since the history contained information suggesting the possibility of mild cerebral damage and the stresses of family and other interpersonal relationships seemed within normal limits, the child was referred for neuropsychological examination.

The Wechsler Intelligence Scale for Children yielded a Verbal I.Q. of 111, Performance I.Q. of 99, and Full-Scale I.Q. of 106. The scaled scores for individual subtests indicated a fairly reliable difference between verbal and performance aspects of general intelligence, with the Performance I.Q. possibly being somewhat depressed. The Peabody Picture Vocabulary Test, also given to this child, yielded an I.Q. of 117. Neuropsychological examination suggested that this child had sustained some mild cerebral damage that appeared to be rather long-standing in nature and was of a chronic and nonprogressive type. Further, these tests suggested that the right cerebral hemisphere was somewhat more involved than the left. Findings supporting this inference included a number of deficiencies on the left side of the body as compared with the right. The child had clear difficulty in perceiving a tactile stimulus on his left side when a competing stimulus was given simultaneously on his right side. His finger-tapping speed, while in the normal range for both hands, was somewhat slow with the left hand as compared with the right hand. A sensori-perceptual component of this lateralized deficit was also present, since the child clearly was not as good in tactile form recognition with his left hand as with his right hand. He also performed more poorly on the Matching Test (a test of coordinated function) with his left hand than he did with his right hand. Finally, the child had special difficulty even in simple tasks dealing with the perception and manipulation of spatial relationships. Even though the adequate level of performance shown by this child on most psychological tests precluded an inference of any serious psychological deficit, the consistency of the above findings presented a convincing basis for inferring some mild and chronic damage of the right cerebral hemisphere. Additional test results suggested that very mild generalized cerebral dysfunction was also present.

The significance of these findings would appear to relate more to possible problems of future development than to the present adjustment capacities of this child. One would have expected from these results that his development in the school situation would be relatively normal because his ability level was good in most respects, his verbal intelligence specifically was adequate, and no really significant signs were present in the test results of damage to the left cerebral hemisphere. While adequate verbal and language abilities may be required principally for school success, adjustment to requirements later in life are likely to call more heavily for ability to deal with visuospatial and manipulatory performances in problem-solving types of situations. This is the area in which this child presently demonstrated deficiencies, consistent with indications of mild damage to the right cerebral hemisphere. Development of a normal ability pattern in this child will require that he be given every possible opportunity for improving his manipulatory and visuospatial skills. Normal experiences in everyday living frequently present opportunities for practice in this area, but the history material indicated that this patient tended to withdraw from such activities, probably because of negative reinforcement associated with the deficiencies described above. Assessment indicated that if a special effort were made at the present time to assist this child in the areas of his deficiencies, the prospects for normal later development appear to be excellent.

VARIABILITY IN LEVELS OF ACADEMIC PERFORMANCE

Generalization

Variability in level of psychological test performance, both within a battery of tests and between the same test administered at different times, that exceeds normal expectation is the rule rather than the exception with brain-damaged children. Similarly, intraindividual variability in the level of competence in academic performances must be expected, especially in accordance with the level of environmental stress which may be present.

Illustration

A child was examined in whom neuropsychological test results indicated a relatively mild lesion of the left cerebral hemisphere. The reason for referral related to inadequacies of academic progress in spite of normal intelligence.

Emotional problems were suspected as causative factors because of pronounced variability in level of academic performance in various situations. While some variability was present in the classroom, the child was especially poor in reading when in the less familiar environment of the speech and hearing clinic.

SUMMARY

The important point that needs to be emphasized for teachers is that the interaction of stress and performance, while present in the normal child, frequently becomes much more apparent in the child with mild impairment due to brain damage. Observation of the impairing influence of stress on performance is hardly a basis for presuming that emotional difficulties are the primary etiological factors. It is only logical to presume that the more tenuous grasp of a specific ability by a brain-damaged as compared to a normal child should be more readily subject to disorganization by any type of adverse influence. This is a basic principle of brain-behavior relationships and is expressed in many specific ways. For example, the writer recently had an opportunity to visit a laboratory in which monkeys with experimentally induced epileptogenic foci were being studied. When stress in the form of mild electric shock was introduced, under conditions in which the monkeys had previously learned to avoid the electric shock, the incidence of seizures increased 300 per cent!

A large body of knowledge has developed in the area of brain-behavior relationships. Much of this knowledge is pertinent for teachers of brain-damaged children, but because of its rather specialized nature only the rudiments of it are readily subject to inclusion in their regular curriculum. Special courses in the form of summer workshops and seminars would provide material benefits in preparing teachers in this highly complex area.

SELECTED REFERENCES

Aguilar, M. J., and Rasmussen, T. "Role of encephalitis in pathogenesis of epilepsy," *Archives of Neurology,* 1960, 2, 663–676.

Andersen, A. L. "The effect of laterality localization of brain damage on Wechsler-Bellevue indices of deterioration," *Journal of Clinical Psychology,* 1950, 6, 191–194.

Fitzhugh, K. B., Fitzhugh, L. C., and Reitan, R. M. "Effects of 'chronic' and 'current' lateralized and non-lateralized cerebral lesions upon Trail Making Test performances," *Journal of Nervous and Mental Diseases,* 1963, 137, 82-87.

———. "Wechsler-Bellevue comparisons in groups with 'chronic' and 'current' lateralized and diffuse brain lesions," *Journal of Consulting Psychology,* 1962, 26, 306–310.

Goldstein, K. *Human nature.* Cambridge, Mass.: Harvard University Press, 1940.

Hecaen, H., Penfield, W., Bertrand, C., and Malmo, R. "The syndrome of apractognosia due to lesions of the minor cerebral hemisphere," *Archives of Neurology and Psychiatry,* 1956, 75, 400–434.

Heimburger, R. F., and Reitan, R. M. "Easily administered written test for lateralizing brain lesions," *Journal of Neurosurgery*, 1961, 18, 301–312.

Reed, H. B. C., Reitan, R. M., and Kløve, H. "Influence of cerebral lesions on psychological test performances of older children," *Journal of Consulting Psychology*, 1964, 29, 247–251.

Reitan, R. M. "Certain differential effects of left and right cerebral lesions in human adults," *Journal of Comparative and Physiological Psychology*, 1955, 48, 474–477.

————. "The comparative significance of qualitative and quantitative psychological changes with brain-damage," *Proceedings*, Fifteenth International Congress of Psychology, 1957, pp. 214–215.

————. "Effects of brain-damage on a psychomotor problem-solving task," *Perceptual and Motor Skills*, 1959a, 9, 211–215.

————. "Impairment of abstraction ability in brain-damage: Quantitative versus qualitative changes," *Journal of Psychology*, 1959b, 48, 97–102.

————. "Investigation of relationships between 'psychometric' and 'biological' intelligence," *Journal of Nervous and Mental Diseases*, 1956, 123, 536–541.

————. "Problems and prospects in studying the psychological correlates of brain lesions," *Cortex*, in press, a.

————. "Psychological deficit," *Annual Review of Psychology*, 1962, 13, 415–444.

————. "Qualitative versus quantitative mental changes following brain-damage," *Journal of Psychology*, 1958, 46, 339–346.

————. "A research program on the psychological effects of brain lesions in human beings" in *International review of research in mental retardation*. N. R. Ellis (ed.). New York: Academic Press, in press, b.

Chapter 16

Psychopharmacology in Learning and Behavioral Disorders of Children

HERBERT J. GROSSMAN, M.D.

EDITORIAL NOTE.—Although the utilization of medication with brain-injured children is obviously a medical problem, it is essential that the teacher possess sufficient information regarding medications that he will be in a position to understand clinical records, anticipate behavior in children following prescription and report back to medical personnel observed behavior which may be the result of medication. This is a competency of teachers which has been ignored until now but which is essential in the interdisciplinary nature of this phase of special education.

For biographical information regarding Dr. Grossman, see Chapter 4.

Chapter 16

Psychopharmacology in Learning and Behavioral Disorders of Children

HERBERT J. GROSSMAN, M.D.

The search for drugs to influence behavior and learning, or to induce feelings of inner calm and contentment, extends far beyond modern pharmacology. Natural substances such as opium, atropine, alcohol, and mescaline have been used to calm and soothe, to increase acceptance of a poor situation, or simply to cause partial oblivion from sensory dullness. The cure, however, is often worse than the illness. Adverse effects of these drugs include habituation, addiction, and loss of personal control.

These early drugs failed primarily because they did not meet the necessary criteria of the effective "tranquilizer." An effective tranquilizer should produce rapid therapeutic responses in a majority of cases, without inducing tolerance or addiction. It should have a low incidence of toxic effects and side effects. Hopefully, it would not dull the senses, decrease perception, or interfere with mental alertness.

The first major group of synthetic drugs to be used in this way were the barbiturates. They offered considerable advantages over the "natural" drugs, but they had one major shortcoming. They dull the senses and blunt mental responses, for basically they are sedatives rather than tranquilizers.

Early in the 1940's some favorable responses to the administration of amphetamines were observed. These drugs were known for their stimulating effect on the central nervous system and for their effectiveness as appetite depressants. These compounds are better known commercially as Benzedrine and Dexedrine.

There was little additional work completed until the 1950's when Chlorpromazine was introduced by French investigators. Since that time the literature dealing with drugs that affect behavior has grown at an incredible rate. Numerous compounds have been developed, and some have emerged without careful investigative study. Unfortunately, to this day, there are few well-designed, controlled scientific studies to assess the psychological state of the patient, and its relationship to agents under study. The enthusiasm and optimistic results of many initial studies wane under a more rigorous evaluation in actual clinical use.

One of the biggest problems has been the assessment of the placebo effect. A placebo has no specific pharmacological effect; it contains no medicine. It is often given for its psychological effect and sometimes prescribed just to "humor" a patient. The placebo effect is defined as one in which certain responses occur for no apparent reason—certainly not the pharmacological reaction of an inactive agent. Certainly many studies have shown that when placebos were administered in a wide variety of disorders, involving pain syndromes as well as behavior, some response was shown in a given number of patients. One of the fundamental difficulties in dealing with pharmacologic research has been the need to assess this particular aspect.

The basic question is whether or not the agent used is directly responsible for an observed effect. This is particularly important in studying behavior where one must determine (1) the specific pharmacologic effect of the drug and (2) the reaction of the subject to nonspecific operatives. When any prescription is given to a patient, whether medication or a placebo, a relationship involving physician, patient, and family is established which in itself may modify behavior. There are also secondary, less tangible derivatives. For example, the teacher who knows that a hyperactive child is now receiving a drug "that will resolve" this problem may be reassured and therefore better able to deal with the child in the classroom situation. (On the other hand, the teacher might assume that medication indicates a strictly medical problem and subsequently discontinue special efforts to help the child.)

Another serious problem has been the way in which some psychopharmacological research has been carried out. Some studies have been done haphazardly with few controls. There are considerable differences between studies done in a well-controlled hospital setting and those using outpatients where a variety of social, emotional, and environmental factors must also contribute to the test results.

These comments refer primarily to studies performed with adults; the fact is that there are far fewer investigations of the effects of psychopharmacologicals on children. Those which reflect good design and sound methodology are even more scarce. We simply do not have the necessary data. Therefore, it is especially important to have an empirical attitude toward psychopharmacologic agents—particularly in respect to modification of behavior and/or learning. There is no question that these drugs may be of considerable value in certain instances, but they are of little or dubious help in other cases, especially in minor problems.

DIAGNOSTIC CATEGORIES FOR DRUG USAGE

Psychopharmacologic agents are not a panacea for learning and behavioral disorders. It is particularly important to categorize common symptomatology and then indicate those categories which might be amenable to management with pharmacologic agents.

Anxiety

Children and adults manifest anxiety in different ways. Adults usually have considerable subjective feelings of discomfort. Some children may experience this, but more exhibit restlessness and hyperactive or aggressive behavior. The youngster with anxiety may appear to be "falling apart at the seams." He may be constantly on the move, unable to settle down, have a very short attention span and a rapid rate of speech. The youngster may talk about real or imagined fearful situations and have excessive fears of places, events, and objects. These youngsters are often unable to function adequately because of this anxiety, and obviously they have more difficulty in relationships with peers as well as in play and school situations. Tranquilizers may be of value in helping to control the anxiety and tension, thereby allowing them to feel more comfortable with peers and in other relationships.

Chronic Aggressive Reactions

These children often have periodic outbursts of temper, are sassy and rebellious, and have explosive behavior. They are often provocative and tolerate frustration poorly. This pattern of behavior usually dates from preschool years. Tranquilizers are of limited value with these chronically aggressive children, who are usually more deeply disturbed than anxious children or those with stress reactions. In emergency situations, the tranquilizers may be helpful, however, in quieting an agitated, destructive child.

Neurotic Disorders

Psychopharmacological agents are rarely effective in neurotic disorders of children. In these cases psychiatric management is the preferred method of treatment.

Personality Disorders

For the various personality disorders in children, drug therapy is of limited value. A wide spectrum of drugs has been tried ranging from major tranquilizers to stimulant drugs, but the results are not conclusive.

Organic Brain Damage

Other youngsters are described as having organic brain damage. One must recognize the shortcomings of this particular diagnostic category. Diagnosis of organic brain damage is, in most instances, difficult and requires considerable skill on the part of people in a variety of disciplines. Certainly the mere observation of hyperactivity or aggressiveness in itself does not indicate brain damage. An "abnormal" electroencephalogram is not necessarily diagnostic of "brain damage." It is also important to realize that brain damage per se does not necessarily affect learning or behavior.

Some of the manifestations of organic brain damage in children are extreme degrees of increased motor activity, distractibility, short attention span, and impulsive, explosive behavior. Anxiety may be part of this picture, but it does not have the overwhelming quality that it does in the psychotic or primarily anxious child. In cases where organic brain damage has been reasonably well documented, some children do show improved behavior with certain drugs. Even when there is a successful pharmacological response, these drugs are at best an adjunct in total management. Drug therapy does not take the place of a carefully conceived program of management.

The basic pathophysiologic state in so-called organic brain syndromes and mental deficiency is not alterable by any known medication. For some reason not yet clear, these youngsters generally do not tolerate barbiturates well and may even exhibit accentuation of hyperactive behavior. Paradoxically, stimulants such as dextroamphetamine or methylphenide relieve the symptoms of hyperactivity and distractibility in many of these youngsters. However, drugs cause increased manifestations in some patients with organic brain syndrome, so that one cannot necessarily predict the specific effect. Some children in this group also have electroencephalographic abnormalities and may respond to anticonvulsant medication.

Behavioral Disorders

One of the most dramatic observations has been seen in children who have behavioral disorders manifested by hyperactivity, acting-out behavior, impulsiveness, distractibility, aggressiveness, or destructiveness. These children often react favorably to administration of the stimulant group of drugs—particularly the amphetamines and others such as methylphenidate. The response is rather paradoxical. In adults these agents have been used as antidepressants and energizers, but in many children with seemingly constitutional hyperactivity they act as sedatives.

Often even small doses of these drugs result in improvement in the behavior of such children. On the other hand, some children require rather high doses. It is interesting that they can handle these high doses with seemingly beneficial effects whereas most adults could not handle proportionate doses.

Psychoses

Tranquilizing drugs have their greatest usefulness as an adjunct in the treatment of psychoses in adults and in children. This is particularly true in early stages of these disorders. Children in the early stages of a psychotic process are likely to go one of two ways. They may tend to withdraw slowly and to have excessive fantasy, often becoming extremely quiet and uncommunicative. Tranquilizing drugs are not at all useful in these cases. On the other hand, they may handle the coming break with reality by neurotic mechanisms that involve hyperactivity or aggressive behavior. Youngsters may be described as coming apart—both physically and mentally—and trying to function wildly in all directions. Tranquilizing agents are of great value in most of these patients. The major tranquilizers of the phenothiazine family may be useful in checking impulsive and destructive behavior and thus make the child more accessible to psychiatric management. Children with psychotic disorders, however, do not respond as dramatically to currently available drugs as adults may.

DRUG CLASSIFICATION

The psychopharmacological drugs may be classified in the following categories.

Major Tranquilizers

The major tranquilizers, as the term implies, are the most potent. Most are in the phenothiazine category; chlorpromazine is the most extensively used. Reserpine and its derivatives are not used as much as drugs of the phenothiazine family primarily because their effect is not as predictable. These major tranquilizers are particularly effective in hyperactive, aggressive, and agitated states. They do have certain undesirable side effects. They potentiate the effect of barbiturates, thereby increasing the drowsiness associated with those drugs. The phenothiazines can also produce jaundice, blood dyscrasias, and extrapyramidal syndromes. Certain drugs in the phenothiazine family seem to produce even more side reactions, such as torticollis (wry neck), trismus (wry smile), and extrapyramidal seizures. Drugs causing such reactions should not be used in children.

Mild Tranquilizers and Sedatives

The mild tranquilizers and sedatives represent another category. In general they are less toxic than the phenothiazine group but they are also less potent. These drugs are usually diphenylmethane derivatives including some drugs that resemble antihistamines. Some of these drugs, such as meprobamate, are useful as mild sedatives and muscle relaxants, but habituation and addiction to meprobamate has been observed in adults.

Central Nervous System Stimulants

The central nervous system stimulants include amphetamine, dextroamphetamine, and methylphenidate. They have greatest usefulness in the treatment of the hyperactive, excessively distractible patients—often described as being organically brain damaged. However, they may cause excessive central nervous system stimulation and also appetite suppression.

Anticonvulsant Agents

The family of anticonvulsant agents includes barbiturates and hydantoin compounds and others. They are basically used to prevent various kinds of seizures or epilepsy. On occasion some youngsters with behavioral disorders have electroencephalographic abnormalities and may respond to anticonvulsant medication. It is in this small and limited group that a trial of medication can be helpful.

Antidepressant Drugs

Most of the antidepressant drugs are in the category of monoaminoxidase inhibitors. These drugs have certain toxic effects, and their use in children is rarely indicated.

From time to time drugs emerge and are lauded as valuable adjuncts to enhance learning abilities. The most recent of these compounds was diethyl-amino-ethanol (Deanol). Early published results of very poorly controlled studies indicated that this drug was of value in enhancing the ability to learn in children with difficulties in school. Subsequent studies, more carefully done, have negated this observation.

Hallucinogenic Drugs

The hallucinogenic drugs are powerful compounds that produce distinctive changes in perception. These changes are sometimes referred to as hallucinations, although the individual under the effect of the drug can distinguish his visions from reality. Another name for this group of drugs is "psychotomimetic," because in some cases the effects seem to mimic psychoses. These drugs have stimulated rapidly increasing interest among professional and lay groups. They have many interesting pharmacologic actions as well as toxic properties. At present these compounds are only tools for research in investigating mental illness. They have no therapeutic role in behavioral disorders of children that is known at the present time.

SUMMARY

Psychopharmacological agents are useful adjuncts in the management of selected cases of behavioral disorders in children. In neurotic disorders they are rarely effective, and in personality disorders they are of limited value. With the anxious child, or the chronically aggressive child, tranquilizers may help to alleviate the current crisis, although the drugs will not affect the underlying causations.

In psychotic or prepsychotic children, the major tranquilizers may be effective in opening the path for psychiatric management.

It is difficult to predict, before therapeutic trials, which drugs, if any, will be effective in dealing with hyperactivity. A series of trials with major and minor tranquilizers as well as stimulants may be necessary in order to find an effective one.

It is well known that almost any treatment for emotional disturbance in children can be effective, if only for a while. Individual cases have been considerably improved, but there is no conclusive evidence that emotionally disturbed children generally have benefited from drug therapy.

Drugs, especially the amphetamines, have a definite but limited role in the treatment of disturbed behavior. They do not substitute for identifying and eliminating factors that cause or accentuate the behavioral disorder. Certain stimulants are sometimes helpful in calming the child with organic brain damage. In dealing with the "brain-injured" child, however, it is important to remember that this is but one aspect of a complex problem. The brain-injured child does not present a stereotyped pattern. Diagnosis is often very difficult and requires the efforts of many disciplines. Management is equally complex. Unfortunately, the psychopharmacologic agents have not resolved all of these complexities.

Eisenberg (1964) has stated, "Drugs are neither the passport to a brave new world nor the gateway to hell." Used carefully they can add a significant element to a total plan of management.

SELECTED REFERENCES

Barron, F., Jarrik, M., and Bunnell, S., Jr. "The hallucinogenic drugs," *Scientific American*, 1964, 210, 29.

Bradley, C. "Characteristics and management of children with behavior problems associated with organic brain damage," *Pediatric Clinics of North America,* 1957, 4, 1049.

Eisenberg, L. "Role of drugs in treating disturbed children," *Children,* 1964, 11, 167–173.

Fisher, S. (ed.). *Child Research in Psychopharmacology,* Springfield, Ill., Charles C Thomas, 1959.

Freed, H. *The Chemistry and Therapy of Behavior Disorders in Children.* Springfield, Ill., Charles C Thomas, 1962.

Grant, Q. "Psychopharmacology in childhood emotional and mental disorders," *Journal of Pediatrics,* 1962, 61, 626–637.

Himwich, H. "The new psychiatric drugs," *Scientific American,* 1955, 195, 80–86.

Lourie, R. "Psychoactive drugs in pediatrics," *Pediatrics,* 1964, 34, 691–93.

Miller, J. G., and Uhr, L. *Drugs and Behavior.* New York: John Wiley, 1960.

Tarjan, G., Lowery, V., and Wright, S. "The use of Chlorpromazine in 278 mentally deficient patients," *American Medical Association Journal of Diseases in Children,* 1957, 94, 274.

Chapter 17

Standards for the Preparation of Teachers of Brain-Injured Children: Emotional Problems

WILLIAM C. MORSE, Ph.D.

EDITORIAL NOTE.—Dr. Rappaport states in Chapter 3, "Neurological impairment affects the child's total development." Too often the educator of brain-injured children is concerned primarily with the impact of neurological impairment on learning and achievement. Infrequently is the brain-injured child seen as a child with ego deficit and concomitant emotional problems. Dr. Morse elaborates the need for the competent teacher of brain-injured children to understand fully the nature of the emotional component and to be prepared to function as a significant resource to the child in this area of human development.

Dr. William C. Morse, Professor of Educational Psychology and Psychology at the University of Michigan, Ann Arbor, Michigan, received his Ph.D. degree from the University of Michigan in 1947. He has worked with disturbed children as director of a group therapy camp and has been responsible for preparation of professional personnel from classroom teachers to doctoral candidates in this area for many years. He serves as educational consultant to public schools and institutional programs for the disturbed child.

His publications include the study of school programs for the emotionally disturbed, as well as work in the general area of school mental health and educational psychology.

Chapter 17

Standards for the Preparation of Teachers of Brain-Injured Children: Emotional Problems

WILLIAM C. MORSE, Ph.D.

INTRODUCTION

One proposes specialized information on emotional problems for the teacher of brain-injured children with certain trepidation. Possible implications of emotional disturbance are seldom overlooked in discussions of these impaired children; at the same time, such aspects are infrequently emphasized. It is sometimes implied that certain of these children are classified as emotionally disturbed, not exactly as a misnomer, but in a manner that introduces unnecessary and unproductive complications. Consequently, there are teachers who harbor a degree of suspiciousness regarding the emotional components. Since, by and large, teachers are sympathetic individuals, they still respond to the feeling domain in the child's nature with concern, although often in a lay rather than professionally appropriate fashion. Dependence upon untutored goodness or intuition would not suffice for other areas of the special teacher's training and should not suffice when it comes to understanding emotional problems.

If teacher training is to produce more emphasis on the emotional life, it is well to examine the factors which have produced the present state of affairs. One is a concentration on neurological aspects to the point which suggests a polarization to the neophyte student teacher. To be sure, there are those who ascribe all learning problems to physiological causes and others who see only the psychogenic, but most leaders recognize an unlimited number of combinations, although it may not be so presented to the student.

However, the basic source of the trouble lies in the process of teacher training itself. In fact, it lies in the actual teaching task and how the prospective teacher is introduced to practical classroom work. Teaching

257

has no Hippocratic Oath, but it demands a high level of responsibility. When the teacher faces the actual demands of caring for youngsters, it is comforting to have a simplified paradigm with all the answers. One becomes most anxious when transported from the certainty of intellectual concepts to the amorphous classroom reality. It is an endless multiple-choice situation with no time to ponder the cues, where each decision made can lead to further complexity. It is under just such stress as this that toleration for ambiguity is reduced and flexibility of approach eschewed. A method which solves the issue of the moment becomes fixated. Theory becomes the rationalization of a practice rather than the guide to possibilities. And at this point of confrontation the supervising teacher gives voice to his own ideas—what it is all about in the real world of the classroom—in contrast to books and college professors. Indeed, in the process of establishing a sense of professional adequacy the new teacher forgets much that he ever knew. The dominant physiological condition in the brain-injured pupil becomes the single cause factor in the mind of the student. Thus, it is not that the teacher of the brain-injured is always shortchanged regarding emotional components, but that this part of the training is most unwieldy and is first to be discarded in the interests of parsimony. The answer is not more courses in dynamic or abnormal psychology. Until the stress and resolution process at the confrontation stage is more fully appreciated, it will not be possible to deepen the way the teacher of the brain-injured responds to the emotional sphere. The training climate must, for each individual trainee, modulate the anxiety without prescribing educational bromides at the sign of tension.

A psychological orientation maintains that the brain-injured child is first of all a child and secondly a brain-injured child. He will suffer the sequence of normal and atypical growth as do all children. While the impact of disability will constitute a handicap, the consequences may or may not be critical to emotional well-being. With the disability the *average* risk will be higher. Certain brain-injured children will be handled in ways which induce trauma and others will not. Given adjustment levels are not an inevitable consequence of organicity (Birch, Thomas, and Chess, 1964). At any rate, mental hygiene prophylaxis is certainly a major involvement of the teacher.

In short, the teacher of the brain-injured child should be continuously exposed to the ideology which asserts that these children have individual developmental and emotional patterns as do all children. Also, the teacher's particular concentration will be on the way in which the special deficit can become a source of emotional difficulty, and what steps can be taken to reduce negative effects. Whether it is usually cause, result, or independent of other learning difficulties need not be the issue; the fact is that many children with perceptual motor dysfunction exhibit emotional problems (Rubin, 1964). The implication of this issue has been resisted in special education. Special pupils are usually multiple-handicapped youngsters, although categorization follows the dominant symptomatology.

It cannot be argued too strongly that the sensitivity to dynamic psychology represented in the training team is of utmost importance. If single-dimension diagnoses are not accepted without question, the trainee will become aware of the heterogeneity of the individuals with the particular designation of brain-injured. This diversity is still more impressive than the identical segments. The student is encouraged to search out emotional, social, and organic factors with equal vigor. Children are not reduced to examples of an abstraction, "the brain-injured child." One cannot settle for less than such an attitude permeating the total training. While a student seldom identifies with the content of an abstract course, he does with the approach embodied in the practices of his clinical teachers. If one supposes this to be accomplished, and the confrontation experience to be managed with care, one can turn next to two considerations: teacher concepts and teacher skills which are concerned with the emotional area. One consists of organized conceptual subject matter, and the latter is the reworking and adapting of these concepts in skills applicable to the work of the teacher.

CONCEPTS

The capability of teacher candidates to understand relevant scientific information has been underestimated. Zeal to be practical can result in a nonintellectual profession. The content concerning the emotional life of children will seldom be usable in the form in which it is acquired: the purpose of this systematic knowledge is erudition rather than immediate utility. The psychological "pap" taught to teachers avoids basic psychological contention. The student is seldom even challenged to evaluate his own naive beliefs about human nature, inconsistent though they may be.

The teacher is expected to master the conceptual systems of developmental psychology, personality formulation, deviant behavior, and behavior alteration. Since the interest is primarily on emotional problems, the content relative to child neurosis, psychosis, the nature of the psychopath, and neglect would be emphasized. The very concept of mental health, being both philosophical and psychological, cannot be ignored.

While no satisfactory single list of required authorities could be drawn up, the thought behind this proposal should be clear. Teachers should master the basic psychological content, but interest lies more in the fundamental psychological issues than in abstract factual content alone. The essential stuff of human nature is not the same to Rogers, Maslow, or Freud. Neither are the concepts of development and influence. Erikson, Piaget, Havighurst, and Skinner hardly seem to be speaking of the same species, but they are representative of authoritative psychologists grappling with these problems, but concentrating on different modalities or interpretations. Or to look at it another way, the motivational psychologist sees one set of explanations, the phenomenological psychologist another, the field theory psychologist still a different set, and the behaviorist is willing to subsume all. Differences approach paranoia at points. The special teacher should not be taught a viewpoint about human nature. The special teacher is to earn the right to a viewpoint by knowing what is rejected as well as what is accepted.

This background knowledge can be gained through a study of the major explanations and issues regarding human nature, normal and pathological, but as a quest to understand children rather than abstract psychology. Yet, there is not to be an expectation of classroom application on first contact. Rather it is to be made real in psychological meaning and clear in terms of conceptual information employed. Since teachers work in group situations, the social aspects of behavior must be emphasized.

The psychological study delineated is not the predigested textbook approach, but fundamental theory with implications. Specialized work is needed on the theory and research related to brain damage as it tends to influence personality formulation. Here again there are authorities with various points of view, but the most complete dynamic presentation is found in the work of Rappaport (1961). At some point in the training, the student should master these concepts of the interrelationship of the disability and personality formation.

With these concepts and understandings the teacher will be in a position to evolve his own practical synthesis, as will be pointed out. All teachers do this anyway, at some level; the hope is for a sophisticated level of theory.

A second major area of content competency, personality assessment, is also one of indirect utilization. The essential problem is: How do psychologists collect data about personality and adjustment? While the goal is not to make a quasi-clinician teacher, the teaching method may well incorporate some direct experience with techniques. There is to be no special psychological test magic kept secret from teachers (Long, Morse, and Newman, 1965).

How does one accumulate information used in making inferences about a child or for that matter a teacher in training? What are the methods of "objective" observation each with attendant difficulties? Matters of rating, scaling, categorizing, and bias all become important. Case-history technique is most frequently employed but seldom studied as a procedure. More time is spent talking to children than any other thing; the probing, evaluative interview is an art in itself. Group discussions are seldom appreciated as data-producing situations.

Direct-questioning devices have been playing an increasing role of late. The teacher's familiarity with common scales and self-made devices leads to a critical view of simple decisions made on the basis of these data. The many projective devices which psychologists employ must be more than names to the teacher, particularly since many have close parallels in classroom activity. The fact that these instruments attempt to enter personality dynamics at different levels is a matter for consideration. This second area of competency is understanding the assessment of personality and adjustment, including the devices of the profession.

The third major area of psychological content, although still without the assumption of direct application, is behavior modification. Here again is a wide-open, controversial field at the present time, but teachers have in general been given a passed-on prejudice rather than an intellectual challenge. Teachers can assimilate the fact of many therapies—all with avid devotees and most with extensions relevant to school practice. Classical therapy is by no means in disuse, although some would imply that their flaying has left it lifeless. The teacher should be exposed to the theory and observation of individual psychotherapy in order to appreciate the possible effects of this process on the child in school. Play therapy and group therapy are long-standing treatment procedures. Total milieu design and social psychiatry offer new emphases. There are nondirective exponents to be contrasted with the didactic and rational therapists. With operant behavior therapy receiving tremendous attention, a teacher must certainly know what its proponents claim and critics indicate. The teacher's interest is in understanding how each system purports to cause changes in behavior and in what is intrinsically implied concerning human nature. Described effectiveness and research evaluations are to be examined dispassionately. Ignorant as teachers in general have been about these fields, they have become the prey of charismatic, simple-solution advocates.

It may be argued that the three conceptual content areas outlined do have direct relevance to work with pupils who are disturbed, and such may well be the case eventually. However, here the goal is understanding emotional disturbance in children. As co-workers with psychologists, social workers, and psychiatrists, educators cannot develop adequate role and status without knowledge. The present lopsided nature of work with disturbed youngsters is partly the consequence of educators not being able to comprehend the related disciplines. Some teachers develop an awe for that which they do not understand. Others degrade what is foreign. In either case, the proper teacher role is unfulfilled.

SKILLS

So far the argument has run as follows: many organically handicapped children are actually multiply handicapped. Hence, the first competency is a thorough understanding of normal and aberrant personality development, personality assessment, and the modes of behavior change. But these are not studied with the expectation of direct application.

The next series of competencies are of a different order. While they are not derived directly from the knowledge above, they could not be developed without such prior knowledge. However, beyond that, the teacher needs to know techniques to employ in the classroom to help the disturbed child cope with his difficulties. These are skills embedded in unique conceptional understanding. While one can read about such skills, their accomplishment rests on learning through supervised practice. What to do can be explained but knowing how and when to apply a technique comes only through supervision during confrontation. The artificial demarcation between sacred and profane therapeutic intervention disappears. The teacher knows that much of what can be done to help the disturbed child can be done in the classroom milieu and is based upon well-recognized principles. The problem now becomes the special ways one modulates the educational experience to meet the emotional difficulties of the child while still functioning as a teacher. Casebook-type pupils are few; there are endless constellations of behavior for which there is no book description. The teacher must learn through actual case-finding examples what each of the several disciplines can contribute both to the understanding of each case as a unique entity and to the possibilities of classroom help.

Two conditions are soon apparent to the trainee. First, once the available information on a child is collated, there are still questions which do not easily evolve into action steps. This is because the child in the classroom is only partly the child in the clinic. The teacher may not be confronted with his basic underlying difficulty. While his deep sense of inadequacy may be at the root, he seldom makes this accessible. What he does present is a hostile, belligerent manner which upsets the classroom. This is the first lesson of confrontation. A teacher must deal with the behavior which, while it stems from the acknowledged source, does not have a direct connecting link. In other words, one cannot reduce the child's underlying sense of inadequacy by allowing him too much omnipotence in the group even though it is clear that he needs to feel his importance as a person. While the general consensus is that these pupils should not be given a permissive environment, some school authorities have found there are instances where restriction and control are not the primary mode. Even with pressure for control, more may be tolerated here than in a regular class; still the group cannot be sacrificed. Such a pupil is not about to have his "real nature" explained either. Experiences of this type help the teacher see the complexity in dealing with emotional components and the necessity of evolving a practice generic to the educational scene. Unless this confrontation is used in the educational process through seminar discussion and supervisory sessions, something less than a methodology for working with disturbance in the classroom will result. It becomes clear that more insight relevant to the classroom will be needed, because this is the setting where behavior must be handled.

The first area of practical competency for the teacher will be in classroom behavior appraisal which is an outgrowth of the previous theoretical knowledge. The important aspect is the use of behavior appraisal, that is, what brings on misbehavior and how the pupil can be taught to cope with instigating pressures. These are the teacher's interests in studying behavior.

The teacher learns to use consultation and to practice team efforts by balancing his own contribution with those of the related disciplines. However, it is diagnosis for prognosis and handling rather than for historical or even contemporary analysis in its own right (Morse, 1965). As information from various sources is compiled, the teacher learns to focus on solving the problem of what can be done to help the child in the educational setting under the given limitations. This moves from the general to the specific. Rather than "he needs love," it becomes "what to do when he does thus and so." The skill of using other data sources and personnel to evolve educational methodology is most important. It is accomplished by converting case-finding conferences to problem-solving sessions, and is possible only when the teacher has the security given of psychological understanding.

Secondly, the teacher needs to learn how to adapt and construct assessment devices particular to the needs of the classroom setting. For example, there are check sheets, behavior lists, and rating devices which quantify behavior the teacher sees in the school setting. The classroom teacher can be assisted by devices which cover topics of direct interest to the school setting, i.e., attitude toward teachers, peers, subject matter, and so forth. Dimensions pertinent to the school are explored rather than the areas of study of other professions emulated.

Thirdly, the pupil's self-concept, especially the matter of school self-esteem, is a particular area teachers can learn to study both by indirect and direct means. Learning problems, be they from neurotic, lower-class, or neurological genesis, limit normal responses. Sarvis (1965) has found that conscious or unconscious self-depreciation with lowered self-esteem or self-hatred predominates in many of these children. While lower-class youngsters act out and middle-class youngsters tend to be passive with covert negativism, brain-damaged youngsters tend to identify either with aggressive behavior, and consider themselves bad, or with the mother on an effeminate basis. While some have seen depression in many of these children, Rappaport suggests the basic process is typically passive obstinancy.

The underlying dynamic is a poor self-image as a consequence of failure. In one small class of young, minimally brain-damaged youngsters, the average over-all self-concept was at the fifteenth percentile, while the esteem in the social, home, and school areas hovered at about the seventh percentile. Such a grossly disheartened group seldom occurs with only emotionally disturbed children, because they developed more pronounced defenses. These brain-injured children were most discouraged and anxious, although anything but pliable. Many of these youngsters characterize themselves as self-perceived troublemakers, at odds with the teacher, the task, and the peers. Cover-ups for discouragement typically include the motoric surge of the hyperactive or a compliant depression with apparent eagerness to learn belied by a lack of any real investment of energy in the process.

For the teacher the essential fact is that failure to learn both in school and in general social living leaves the brain-injured child wanting in the substance of ego and self-esteem. He does not believe in himself. How he has learned of his limitations, how it has been emphasized, and what has been tried to help him are all important to the educational dynamics. The study of the pupil's self-concept will comprise a working synthesis of psychological theory for the teacher.

An essential aspect of data collection is usually overlooked. There are dividends in excess of the information itself. One is that primary knowledge changes the person who gains it. That is, teachers need to be able to administer simple scales and devices and interpret them, because they change the beholder much more deeply than will another's words. When the child puts himself low on the teacher's scale of self-esteem, that teacher is moved by this direct communication. It is not a mere score in the records. Secondly, any productive interchange between the teacher and pupil has opened up a privileged communication system. The adult who knows is not the same adult as he was when ignorant. This is the real importance of data collection and communication. Productive relationships are not born in a psychological vacuum.

The fourth essential is that the teacher develop skill in interviewing. Since there is such a volume of verbal interplay between teacher and pupil, the teacher must learn how to talk productively with youngsters in a manner appropriate to the school setting. Alternatives are to moralize or repress. While interviews will have many purposes, basically the purpose is to understand the world and events as the child perceives them in order to know his inner nature better. This leads to appropriate interventions. Talking *at* children is universal adult practice; talking effectively *with* children is a teacher competency of major significance. The flexible reality-focused schema embodied in "life space interviewing" (Redl, 1959) is preferred over derivations of psychiatric or nondirective practice.

Interviewing moves one from diagnosing to intervening since it serves both purposes. To deal with the disturbed child, the teacher must have a method of hygienic management in a style which not only encourages open discussion and certain ventilation, but moves toward closure and the imposition of sanctions as necessary. The purpose of such interviewing is to open up communication about the anger, frustration, depression, or so forth, which is already amply displayed in the classroom behavior shared by both adult and child. It is through such explanations and assistance that the child is taught coping patterns to meet his difficulties. Since there are many known methods of behavior change, the plans developed to help the child may in one instance be behavioristic and in another dynamic in approach.

Further teacher skills are as follows:

The teacher becomes competent in evaluating the social-milieu aspects of the classroom. Group dynamics and field theory give an analysis of environmental forces and roles which induce behavior. The teacher puts this to work by designing a milieu specific to the support needs of the pupils. For example, children like these who are easily distracted are not saturated with social stimulation; in fact, reduction of normal peer contact may be required. Group processes are watched. Role interactions are a common source of difficulty and a possible resource for treatment. Space is provided for private discussion beyond sound range. Retreat spaces are available when the child needs one. The geographical potentials are exploited.

The teacher becomes competent in utilizing the psychological components of activities for therapeutic purposes (Morse, 1963). Both work and play are recognized as having potential. Games have implicit meanings. Identical or dissimilar lessons for all pupils induce given competitive tensions. It is well known that success is a major road to ego substantiation with children. The special teacher sees how a carefully designed educational experience enabling the child to learn may do more for his self-esteem than other therapeutic approaches. Self-expression through motor activity, creative arts, and music offers gratifications which are reflected in personality development.

The special teacher becomes competent in desensitizing the emotional threat of past failure experience. Keeping overloaded demands from the scene is a major skill accomplished through curriculum alteration and special planning for each individual. Small tasks, easy tasks, disguised tasks, and escalating tasks are examples. Support at time of acute tension is another. Recognizing the power of emotions, the teacher reduces the potential to a manageable level, regardless of how far this reduction must go.

Finally, the teacher learns to use personal relationship for its corrective and identification-building potentials. A relationship with a teacher has as much possibility as one with other helping persons. Relationship is enhanced by treating the pupil with absolute respect, by being genuinely concerned for his welfare, and by helping him with his problems. The type of acceptance of another human being that is anticipated is built upon a high level of teacher understanding, so that covert rejections, countertransferences, or overidentifications are not the order of the day. To be free to help another, one cannot be encumbered with too much unfinished business. Consultation, test data, and frank discussion are ways to expand the teacher's self-awareness.

CONCLUSION

The sequence presented is simple. Many brain-injured children are emotionally handicapped. It will be difficult to obtain the investment this area requires in teacher training, and it will be a consequence of the training *process* as well as academic *content*. Teachers are to be given the relevant conceptual material from psychology without apology. With this background, as the teacher is confronted with the actual situation, the special competencies needed in therapeutic teaching can be developed.

SELECTED REFERENCES

Birch, Herbert G., Thomas, Alexander, and Chess, Stella. "Behavioral development in brain-injured children," *Archives of General Psychiatry*, 1964, pp. 593–603.
Long, Nicholas, Morse, William C., and Newman, Ruth. *Conflict in the classroom.* Belmont, Calif.: Wadsworth, 1965.

Miller, Nadine. "Teaching an emotionally disturbed brain-injured child," *Reading Teacher*, 1964, 17, 460–465.

Morse, William C. "Intervention techniques for the classroom teachers of the emotionally disturbed" in *Educational programming for emotionally disturbed children: The decade ahead.* Peter Knoblock (ed.). Syracuse: Division of Special Education and Rehabilitation, Syracuse University, 1965.

———. "The mental hygiene viewpoint on school discipline," *High School Journal*, 1965, 47, 396–401.

———, "Working paper: Training teachers in life space interviewing," *American Journal of Orthopsychiatry*, 1963, 33(4), 727–730.

Rappaport, S. R. "Behavior disorder and ego development in a brain-injured child," *The Psychoanalytic Study of the Child*, 1961, 16, 423–450.

Redl, Fritz. "Strategy and technique of life space interview," *American Journal of Orthopsychiatry*, 1959, 29, 1–18.

Rubin, Eli. "Secondary emotional disorders in children with perceptual motor dysfunction," *American Journal of Orthopsychiatry*, 1964, 34, 296–297.

Sarvis, Mary A. "Evil self image: A common denominator in learning problems," *Mental Hygiene*, 1965, 49, 308–310.

Chapter 18

The Needs of Teachers for Specialized Information in the Area of Pediatric Psychiatry

WILLIAM C. ADAMSON, M.D.

EDITORIAL NOTE.—Too infrequently is the educator of brain-injured children exposed to psychiatric orientation or ego psychology in a consistent and organized manner. In an interdisciplinary structure, as is being advocated in this discussion of competencies, the role of pediatric psychiatry and the educator's understanding, responsibility, and involvement in it is essential to effective work with brain-injured children. Dr. Adamson clearly delineates the educational competency in this phase of professional preparation.

Dr. William C. Adamson, Chief Child Psychiatrist of The Pathway School in Jeffersonville, Pennsylvania, has worked as a member of the educational-clinical team model in several school settings. He received the B.A. degree from Swarthmore College in 1940; the M.D. degree from the University of Pennsylvania in 1943; and specialized in adult and child psychiatry at the Institute of the Pennsylvania Hospital and the Philadelphia Child Guidance Clinic. As Director of the Community Guidance Center of Austin, Texas, 1951–56, and Director of the Child Study, Treatment and Research Center of The Woods Schools, 1956–63, he worked in both public and residential schools. He was Mental Health Consultant to the School District of Cheltenham Township, Pennsylvania, from 1960 to 1964.

His publications include "Some Psychological Aspects of the Management of the Brain-Damaged Adolescent in a Residential Setting" and "Development and Design of Mental Health Programs for Public Schools."

Chapter 18

The Needs of Teachers for Specialized Information in the Area of Pediatric Psychiatry

WILLIAM C. ADAMSON, M.D.

INTRODUCTION

Pediatric psychiatry was still in its infancy when it first became concerned with the complex problems of brain-injured children. The period of nineteenth-century optimistic enthusiasm in the treatment and training of the mentally retarded by Itard, Seguin, Guggenbühl, and others, had come and gone. Binet and Simon had developed a standardized instrument for measuring certain aspects of mental functioning in children which led to an era of realism and objectivity during the early part of the twentieth century.

Among clinicians interested in pediatric psychiatry in the period from 1920 to 1950, the following have made significant contributions to understanding of the social, educational, and emotional problems of brain-injured children: Allen and Pearson (1928), Schilder (1931, 1935, 1937, 1951), Clark (1933), Bender (1938, 1940, 1946, 1949, 1951, 1956), Strauss and Werner (1942, 1943), and Strauss and Lehtinen (1947).

MILESTONES

In 1956 Bender published the observations, formulations, interpretations and theorizations covering nearly thirty years' clinical work with brain-injured children. This book, *Psychopathology of Children with Organic Brain Disorders,* was one of the milestones in the literature on this subject in the last decade. Bender emphasized that children "with various biological problems have a number of common psychological problems. These common problems may include: (1) difficulties in pattern behavior in impulse, motor, perceptual and integrative areas with a tendency to disorganization and regressed or retarded maturation, (2) a severe anxiety also poorly patterned with associated body-image

271

and identification problems, (3) a greatly increased need for human support in all these areas." Bender also highlighted the importance of the problem of anxiety, indicating that it was "inadequately understood before the work of Greenacre (1941)."

> Greenacre had postulated a normal pattern of predisposition to anxiety as a physiological tendency in all newborn infants during the perinatal experience and a secondary anxiety arising from experiences of frustration and certain inadequacies in the mechanisms of defense by which the developing child attempts to meet the normal and excessive vicissitudes of growing up emotionally (Bender, 1956, p. 135).

Bender emphasized that this heightened anxiety often seen in brain-injured children

> is best met by a close and continuous stream of well-patterned support in the earliest years with a prolongation of the infantile period. It should be realized, however, that the security gained for the child in support of posture and motility and perceptual experiences and relationship with the environment is not an end in itself but is only a means for subsequent independent action. The impulse for action is as basic as the need for security. There are many remarkable things about the brain-damaged child which also remind us of the miraculous capacity of all children to grow up, to mature and to be as normal as they are. The drive for normality and for living through a regular maturation pattern as a global response of the biological unit is much stronger than the disorganization resulting from either focal or diffuse structural pathology or destructive and depriving environmental influences (Bender, 1956, pp. 135–136).

In planning the management of these brain-injured children, Bender put particular emphasis on "a closely supporting, warm, mothering relationship throughout the period of dependency, with an extension of the period of dependency as long as necessary to meet the child's needs." She also suggested that special teachers could serve "as parent substitutes to further promote inter-human relationships and to relieve the excessive demands on the mother, but not by means of extended separation from the mother or mother figure. There should be a free use of siblings or sibling equivalents as in nursery schools, to promote identification and afford opportunities for imitation or mirroring behavior. It is especially helpful in this regard to bring together children with similar and also dissimilar disabilities. Animal pets and doll play may be used also." Bender makes a final observation:

A program should be planned which will help in the patterning of impulses even at the expense of producing obsessional compulsive patterns and personality characteristics provided that the patterns can be used by the child constructively and independently for adaptation. Motility games, dance, music, plastic and graphic art, hobbies, are all useful. They should be developed at a slower pace than for the normal child and with infinite repetitions. The mothering relationship to the adult and the sibling relationship to other children in the group should be emphasized. . . . The treatment program should include the mother and other adults that care for the child by sharing with them all the knowledge that we have concerning the child's problems and needs and methods of meeting them, and giving support to the parents and parent substitutes in their difficult but rewarding task. This can often be done in parent groups (Bender, 1956, pp. 137–138).

The *rapprochement* between education and pediatric psychiatry reached its height in the outstanding work of Strauss and his co-workers which was begun in 1937. It would be difficult to highlight the many contributions coming from this group of co-workers in education, psychology, and clinical psychiatry. Undoubtedly, every paper in this symposium has been influenced in some way by the work of Strauss, Werner, Lehtinen, Kephart, and others associated with them.

From the point of view of pediatric psychiatry, as it relates to this study, the following observations seem most pertinent:

Strauss and Lehtinen (1947) were among the first investigators to describe the therapeutic educational environment for the brain-injured child, wherein the teacher is viewed as a therapist, in the broadest sense of the word, since the aim is one of habilitation. The teacher is not expected to function as a psychotherapist, who seeks to help a child help himself to work through individual intrapsychic conflicts or neurotic problems related to growing up as a brain-injured child in a family, in a social community. Rather, Strauss and Lehtinen emphasize that in the role as teacher-therapist, one must be skilled in the observation of behavior, must be well acquainted with each child, not only from a personality standpoint but from the point of view of particular organic disturbances, and must have the ability to analyze a failure and to devise a correction for it. In seeking to analyze the child's failure in a task given to him, the teacher-therapist is instructed to ask the relevant questions:

Were too many elements presented at once? Was the material too distracting? Did the activity lack structure, so that foreground could be confused with background? Was the child's [visual and auditory] perception fragmented? Did he lose sight of the whole by fixation on details? Did he seem to understand but fail because of perseveration? Through such analysis the source of the failure can usually be discovered and a plan devised which will prevent it. In a similar way an analysis should be made of a child's behavior disturbances. Outbursts, explosions, refusals . . . deviations from established behavior . . . can usually be traced to injudicious handling or to demands in excess of the child's ability or emotional reserve (Strauss and Lehtinen, 1947, pp. 141–142).

Strauss was one of the first clinicians to emphasize that "the perceptually disturbed child may not receive the same image as a normal child does from the same set of stimuli. . . . Such a disability results in an endless sequence of perceptual errors or misconceptions of reality. . . . This deficiency applies to social perceptions as well as to sensory stimuli" (Lewis and Strauss, 1961, p. 17).

In seeking to describe the neurophysiologic mechanism of underlying behavioral patterns in brain-injured children, Strauss and Kephart (1955) cited the observations of Lorenz (1950) and Tinbergen (1950):

From observations of animal behavior Lorenz postulated the innate or endogenous production of what he called "action-specific energy." (Comparable innate behavior patterns in humans might be the sucking reflex and the gross motor reflex movements of infancy.) Tinbergen postulated "an innate (neurosensory) releasing mechanism" that releases the action-specific energy and "is responsible for its selective sensibility to such special combinations of sign stimuli. . . . It is as though a backlog of energy is built up which is concerned with the operation of the endogenous movements. When this energy is triggered by the innate releasing mechanism, it is released and the pattern of movements characteristic of the mechanism occurs (p. 129).

The hypothesis is made that brain injury deprives the individual of "highly coordinated series of perceptions" which would normally "drain off" or sublimate the action-specific energy in the developing individual. This failure to drain off such energy would result in a higher action-specific energy level which could then override the inhibitory functions of the cortex, allowing discharge in response to a less adequate stimulus pattern, as well as creating a more violent and/or primitive behavioral pattern of activity. A very clear description of this hypothesis and its possible relationship to the "explosive" behavior sometimes seen in brain-injured children is found in the book for parents and laymen written by Lewis, Strauss, and Lehtinen (1960).

In their view the explosion characterized by the sudden, violent eruption of physical activity, the wild shriek, the running about or jumping up and down, stamping of feet, waving of arms, pushing out at other children, the kicking out or throwing a toy across the room, appear "analogous to the breaking of a dam, with the quick, uncontrolled release of stored energy." The authors indicate that the action-specific energy usually drained off in the normal process of development has not been so drained because the brain-injured child was not able to make as many perceptual and conceptual responses as the normal child and was less able to use up his energy in purposive motor activity. They also indicated that because of the limitation in his mental activities, the brain-injured child, "if he is in a situation requiring restraint and inhibition, tends to accumulate action-specific energy to a greater degree than the normal child. As the energy level rises, the strength of stimulus required to release it becomes less." For the teacher of brain-injured children, it becomes significant to note that "stimuli which are tolerated adaptively in the forenoon of a school day may not be successfully handled in the afternoon. Unable to control the intensity of his response because of the energy accumulation, the child just lets go. . . . Hyper-response, from our observation, is most effectively reduced, first, by protecting the child from overstimulation and, second, by enabling the child, through a program of education, to increase the number of responses he makes in all situations so that the reservoir of action-specific energy is maintained at a controllable level" (pp. 75–77).

Strauss and Kephart make it clear in their text that they do not view all behavior "as the result of innate behavior patterns," but they do feel "that many of the behavior episodes so frequently observed in brain-injured children might well be explained by such a hypothesis" (1955, p. 133).

In writing their book for parents and laymen, Lewis, Strauss, and Lehtinen (1960) eloquently stated their point of view when they wrote, "The brain is the architect of the human personality. If it is damaged, it functions irregularly. In consequence, the performance, the personality and the behavior become irregular." They emphasized certain behavioral difficulties and characteristics which they feel are related to brain injury and which distinguish these children as "otherwise," or being other than normal children. They indicate that they view "these behavior manifestations as physiologic rather than emotional in origin in so far as they appear to be the consequence of *neuromental malfunctioning*. . . . The most conspicuous of these difficulties are hyperkinesis (hyperactivity), distractibility (short attention span), disinhibition (impulsivity), inflexibility (including perseveration), and emotional instability. . . . The brain-injured child's physiologically based behavior anomalies may result in emotional disturbance inasmuch as they increase his environmental difficulties and influence the attitude of others toward him. Since his behavior is more difficult than that of other children in the family, he is corrected more often and more vehemently; it is not surprising if he begins to feel unfairly treated and resentful because of these feelings" (pp. 61–62).

A third milestone in the contribution of pediatric psychiatry to the understanding of brain-injured children was made by Eisenberg (1957). This paper is outstanding for its clarity of content and its attempt to correlate relevant neurophysiologic concepts with the understanding of patterns of behavior in the brain-injured population. Eisenberg views brain injury as a psychobiological disorder affecting the child on three levels, namely: (1) on the level of quantitative and qualitative alterations in brain function produced by damage to its structures, (2) on the level of behavior influenced by the reorganization of the previous personality of the patient in the face of his functional deficit, and (3) on the level of the social environment which has a profound influence on the patient's performance and, under certain conditions, might be considered the decisive influence.

Eisenberg was one of the first pediatric psychiatrists to attempt to correlate the emerging neurophysiologic observations with aspects of learning and behavior in brain-injured children. He postulated that interference with inhibitory response systems which are found in the brain stem and cortex might be the basis for attention defects in these children. Signals arriving at a primary receptive zone in the cortex can no longer initiate the same quality of depression of response—i.e., "surround inhibition" (Mountcastle and Powell, 1959)—in other cortical zones (Eisenberg, 1964, p. 65).

Eisenberg suggested that the figure-ground discrimination problem in these children might be, in part, related to this dysfunction in the attention-focusing process and perhaps, in part, due to their failure to learn the conditioned responses necessary for such selective cortical inhibition. Eisenberg cited the work of Morrell and Ross (1953) and Reese, Doss, and Gantt (1953) as a basis for these suppositions. Reese et al. have shown that patients with cerebral lesions have considerable difficulty learning conditioned responses which normal subjects learn regularly and promptly.

Hyperkinesis as a behavior syndrome was reviewed in 1957 and in Eisenberg's later paper (1964):

In a discussion edited by Birch (1964, p. 74) "it was generally agreed that our present knowledge cannot provide a definitive set of answers for questions that have been raised in connection with hyperkinetic behavior." The need for detailed behavioral observations, the determination of conditions necessary for and the periodicity of hyperkinetic behaviors, and an analysis of those environments which promote non-hyperkinetic functioning was emphasized. The question was posed as to whether "the problem we must deal with is that of overactivity, per se, deriving spontaneously as a behavioral projection from patterns of neural dysfunction . . . or whether we are dealing with another manifestation of undirectedness [lack of attending] and inappropriateness of focus in behavior which, because of its incongruity to the demands of the social situation, is interpreted as hyperkinesis."

Finally, Eisenberg noted the marked responsiveness of the reticular formation to drugs (phenothiazines depress its function, epinephrine activates the upper part at a midbrain level, and propanediols may slightly stimulate it).

Many clinicians, teachers, and physicians interested in the use of, and the theory of, drug action on the central nervous system, particularly as it relates to the problems of brain-injured children, would find the small textbook by Freed (1962) both interesting and readily understandable.

There are at least three reasons why the fourth milestone, the isolation of the ascending reticular activating system (ARAS) by Moruzzi, Magoun, and their co-workers (1949, 1952, 1963), should be of special interest to teachers of brain-injured children: (1) We can now describe a biologic basis for the sensory modality (VAKT) theory of reinforcement. (2) We can now give a partial explanation for the long-standing hypothesis that habilitation of brain-injured children is made possible by finding "other pathways" to do the work of damaged pathways. Experimentation shows that when the traditional sensory pathway to the brain has been interrupted at any level, the central, nonspecific ascending reticular activating system can continue to carry sensory impulses sufficient to activate all functions of the cortex. (3) We can now point to one neurophysiologic mechanism by which classroom conditioning may be facilitated. Carefully structuring the learning environment in the classroom while creating a positive teacher-student relationship serves to reinforce the self-regulating process which has been described as part of this ascending reticular activating system.

A fifth and final milestone was the significant paper by Rappaport

(1961) on ego development in a brain-injured child. He emphasized that it was important to avoid "the assumption that damage to neural tissue plays the paramount role in [the brain-injured child's] behavior and thought disturbances." Instead he put forth the thesis that: "Behavioral disturbance [in these cases] (1) is not due solely to damaged brain tissue per se and therefore is not necessarily irreversible: (2) but is due to a considerable degree to the disturbance which that damage causes in the epigenesis [development after birth] of the ego: (3) the deviant ego maturation fostering a disturbed parent-child relationship that in turn inhibits proper ego development; and (4) the disturbance both in ego development and in the parent-child relationship can be alleviated by psychotherapy and adjunctive therapies" (p. 425).

Recognizing that the study of the nature of ego functions in brain-injured children had been neglected, Rappaport suggested that "to approach the brain-damaged child from the standpoint of ego functioning permits us to study the interaction of neurologic and psychologic factors and provides the opportunity for treating him more efficaciously, as a whole person" (p. 425).

Material from a case history was cited to illustrate this point. Rappaport observed that lack of intactness in the child's central nervous system fostered an equivalent lack of intactness in his primary self-organizing ego functions of motility, perception, language, and intention. The result was an unconscious lack of responsiveness in the child's mother which, in turn, interfered with what Erikson (1950, 1953) referred to as the mutuality phase (or first stage) of ego development.

Subsequently, in the case presented, Rappaport described how inadequate motor and perceptual functions interfered with the process of social differentiation. Whereas the normal developing child of three to five years of age is able to separate himself emotionally from other persons in his environment (the awareness of the difference between the "I" and the "you"), Rappaport noted that his patient had not achieved an adequately differentiated self-image at the age of eight to nine years.

Teachers of preschool and elementary age brain-injured children will need to be aware of the consequences of this kind of delay in the process of social differentiation. For until the child is aware of himself as a separate person, he may continually confuse the boundaries of his inner world with those of the outer world. The feelings of failure, of inability to do a task, and the hurt pride which accompanies these experiences of failure may be attributed by the child to the teacher and to his faulty perception of what she is attempting to do to and for him. This is very much like the child who will blame the chair for hurting him when he himself has run into the chair. He will in turn kick or spank the chair for hurting him. All have seen older brain-injured children who will kick or strike out at a classmate without apparent provocation. Actually he is attributing his own failure, and the resultant feelings of frustration, to his nearest classmate from whom he has not fully differentiated himself.

Suggesting a problem for future research, Rappaport observed that the libidinal development in many brain-injured children seemed to be delayed along with ego development and subsequently to progress with it. He noted that this was in contrast to psychogenically ego-disturbed children whose libido seemed to show evidence of continuous psychosexual development in spite of fragmented or disturbed ego development.

The writer's experience has been similar. In a residential school population of brain-injured adolescents, a syndrome of prolonged emotional dependency, ego constriction, and a delay in psychosexual and psychosocial maturation was observed (Adamson, Hersh, and Creasy, 1960).

The significant paper by Rappaport, stressing the need to view brain-damaged children from the point of view of their ego development and the ego's continuous attempts to cope with and master degrees of central nervous system dysfunction, leads to the main thesis of this study, namely, the concept of "total-life-relationship structure" for brain-injured children.

CONCEPT OF "TOTAL-LIFE-RELATIONSHIP STRUCTURE"

During the past two years, the staff of the Pathway School in Jeffersonville, Pennsylvania, has been developing an educational and therapeutic approach to meet the needs of brain-injured children. This program has centered around the establishment of a "total-life-relationship structure" model which enables the developing student to cope with his own inner needs and the dysfunctions in his central nervous system, as well as with the demands and stimulations of the outside world.

The remediation or habilitation team consists of teachers, psychologists, parent counselors (social workers), psychotherapists (including one or more child psychiatrists), special subject teachers, teacher aides, and a receptionist-secretary.

All of the participants in this model are well known today. The new discipline which has been emerging over the past two decades has been that of the parent counselor. Historically, either the teacher or the psychotherapist carried the parent counselor role. This was usually unsatisfactory because both disciplines were generically geared to teaching or treating the child. Therefore, they usually overidentified with the child and failed to see and support the nature of the parents' psychological problem in having a brain-injured child, however handicapped or deviant. The addition of counseling for parents by trained social case workers on the staff of schools attempting to habilitate children with brain dysfunction strengthens the effectiveness of this "total-life-relationship structure" model.

Within the school setting several conditions are essential to mobilize and sustain such a model. These include: (1) a climate of mutual trust; (2) willingness and readiness to communicate; (3) regularly scheduled interviews and conference time to facilitate communication; (4) regularly scheduled in-service training to allow the staff to discuss, in depth, the contributions which each professional discipline can make to the model as it applies to each individual child in the school's population; (5) clinical staff availability to teachers, child, and parents; (6) multilateral rather than unilateral decision in planning for the child so that all the participants in the model are included in the process of decision-making; (7) skillful timing in setting in motion any of the transactions which involve participants, especially the child and his parents; (8) mutual collaboration between interdisciplinary staff members rather than attempts at "alien" supervision; (9) parent-teacher-psychotherapist–parent counselor support system which allows verbalizations of conscious emotions and defines socially acceptable patterns of self-expression; (10) recognition that brain-injured children are struggling to master many complex psychological problems; and (11) total staff willingness to undertake the skillful "working through" of these complex psychological problems over a period of time, usually years rather than months.

The importance of some of these conditions might be briefly illustrated by discussion and examples of the experiences of the Pathway School staff.

Climate of Mutual Trust

Whether one is willing to admit it or not, conscious and unconscious prestige struggles among the multidisciplines working within this total-life-relationship structure model continued to dilute our effort. In-service training and continuous interstaff communication will attenuate but can never completely offset this problem. Able leadership at the administrative level is also an important factor in creating a climate of mutual trust and facilitating an amalgamation of different professional disciplines and individual personalities.

Staff Availability

Many times during the past two years staff availability was found to be an essential condition to the smooth operation of the therapeutic-educational model. This was especially true when rapidly developing family crises (sickness of a sibling, hospitalization of one of the parents, death of a relative, conflict over homework, acting-out behavior, or a will struggle with the parents) would upset the students the night or the morning before coming to school. Invariably, when parents called the parent counselor or advised the school staff by note of such a crisis, the staff was able to help the teacher anticipate the child's reaction. At the same time, the psychotherapist was able to see the student to help him through the implications of the emotional crisis so that the backwash of feelings did not spill over so totally into the classroom as it might have otherwise.

On other occasions where the school was not forewarned or where the child overreacted to school-centered situations, the psychotherapist was able to see the child in what Redl has called a "life-space interview." This separation of the child from the classroom and the on-the-spot assistance not only prevented further classroom contagion and group disruption but also met the child at the moment of greatest need. It was in moments such as this that it was possible for the psychotherapist to help the child see more clearly the nature of his emotional problem and help him find constructive (ego-syntonic) ways of dealing with it. Kurlander and Colodny (1965) referred to this therapeutic approach. They found specific instruction in human relations, explaining the most basic facts and rules of human conduct to the child, along with pointing out old patterns of behavior and building toward new ones, to be very effective in their treatment of brain-injured children. They recognized that this treatment approach was different from psychotherapy with neurotic children, which utilized greater permissiveness, encouragement of abreaction and release of emotions, and the uncovering and inter-pretation of resistances to treatment and emotional growth. In elaborat-ing on this difference in psychotherapeutic work with brain-injured as compared to neurotic children, Doris and Solnit (1963) point out that verbal communication for clarification and interpretation is used in the treatment of brain-injured children, but that it plays a less dominant role. "Children with a central nervous system deficit often are unable to use thought, memory, and language with as much cathexis and dis-charge as neurotic children without organic deficits. . . . Thus, the treatment situation also serves to make clear what advice can be given to promote a more effective social and academic adaptation."

Timing of Planned Moves or Changes

Another observation made was the importance of skillful timing in planned moves or changes of students from one classroom to another.

As a student becomes educationally ready for a higher level of individual academic performance or for the next level of group learning, such a promotion will necessitate a move to a new teacher and a new classroom setting. Several instances have been noted where students have been ready educationally but not emotionally for such a move. In fact, these students have been able to verbalize their overwhelming sense of anxiety of being promoted, have often recapitulated aspects of their psychopathology as such a move was discussed with them, and have made substantial gains educationally and emotionally when the planned move has been delayed for one to six months, until they were emotionally ready to cope with the new classroom situation. This experience suggests that unilateral decisions to promote or move a child from one learning milieu to another, without including the child and the other supporting adults in this decision, can be very disruptive to the total (ego-developmental) needs of the child.

We have been equally impressed by the opposite aspect of this "promotion." We have seen some students who have appeared to be emotionally ready for promotion, or even a transfer to a new school, but whose academic work has continued to be spotty and uneven. In these cases a different decision proved effective. Students who had made a maximum use of our school program in building up adequate primary ego-adaptive apparatuses (i.e., motility, language, perception, and intention skills), but who showed a lag of two to three years in one subject while working near grade level for their age in all other subjects were encouraged to graduate to a new school program. In these cases we felt it was important to continue with tutoring in the academically weak subject and with the psychotherapy throughout the period of transition. In every case such transfers were successfully made.

Distinction Between Collaboration and Supervision

In coordinating the team effort necessary to make the "life-relationship" model a truly working one, we found that the quality of interstaff communication became one of the keys to success or failure. The psychotherapist had made many observations about the child from seeing him in the therapy hours twice a week. The parent counselor was in continuous communication with the parents about the child's emerging behavior and learning patterns in the home and social community. The teacher was observing and teaching the child daily in both individual- and group-structured learning situations. How did each of these separate but related disciplines share with one another their multiple observations, which would then become guidelines to structuring the child's relationships in the present and in his emerging future? How would one discipline transpose the observations of another into their own system of values and usefulness? We hope to find more detailed answers to these questions in our in-service training seminar during 1966.

Experience thus far suggests that several principles are essential for such coordination of effort. First, the observations shared by psychotherapist with teacher must be done without expecting the teacher to function as a psychotherapist. We can support teachers in their role as teacher-therapist as defined by Strauss and Lehtinen (1947) without diluting their function as teachers of a group of six, eight, or twelve individual students. In practice, this means that psychological interpretation of the child's behavior does not imply either special favors or immunity from classroom discipline. Such interpretations should be jargon-free and, hopefully, sufficiently relevant to the "here and now" of the child's classroom behavior that the teacher has been given a constructive psychological tool to assist the child in his efforts toward mastery of all dimensions of his growth.

Secondly, such transposing from the language of the psychotherapist to the application of educational principles must be done in the spirit of co-laboring (process of collaboration) rather than in an unwelcomed climate which might suggest that the psychotherapist is supervising the teacher in methods of handling children in the classroom setting.

Thirdly, the teacher should not have an excessively high level of expectation as to "the pearls of wisdom on behavioral management" which will be coming from the psychotherapist. Growing up socially and emotionally is, for brain-injured children, a slow and arduous process. There are no short cuts or magic words which will hasten the process. Nevertheless, such emotional growth can and will take place in the life-relationship structure set up for these children provided each participant is in harmony with the total effort being made at any one time.

Teachers need to know that many of the observations made and shared by the psychotherapist are often harbingers of things to come. The child in therapy is trying out, in this one-to-one relationship, many shades and kinds of feelings and many patterns of behavior, before venturing either increasing assertiveness or increasing adaptability as part of his life experience in the larger community of his home and classroom.

Fourthly, skillful parent counseling can serve as an effective tranquilizer in the operation of the life-space model. Many of the frustrations, aggravations, apprehensions, and pathological defenses stirred up in the parents of brain-injured children, and subsequently displaced on these children or their teachers, can be successfully "drained off" in the parent counselor's office. If psychotherapists and teachers can support the development of a strong, healthy counseling relationship between parents and parent counselor, they will find the inclusion of this third professional discipline in the life-relationship structure model a great aid to their own professional efforts. It takes several years of collaborative effort to understand truly the contribution to be made to the team effort by the skilled social case worker in the role of parent counselor. It takes several more years to know how to support and augment social case workers in their work with parents. For the team members, this skill lies in knowing when to see parents, what to say to them, and when to refer them to the parent counselor. In most instances, we have had greatest success when we delegated the primary responsibility for working with parents to one of the parent counselors and have kept that counselor well informed as to the shifts and changes in the child in psychotherapy and in the classroom.

We have also found that individual parent counseling can be effectively augmented by group sessions for parents, once or twice a month, somewhat along the lines described by Barsch (1961).

Verbalization of Conscious Emotions

One common denominator found to be important for brain-injured children has been to encourage and to allow them to verbalize their conscious emotions in all their life-relationships.

This does not imply an indiscriminate or totally permissive verbal outburst. Rather, we encourage parents, teachers, and psychotherapists to allow the feelings to be expressed but to define for these children socially acceptable patterns of verbal and self-expression.

From therapeutic experience, we feel that it is important that parents and teachers be helped by parent counselors and psychotherapists to support healthy verbalizations in their children. By encouraging verbalization, we are helping the children become more aware of their thoughts and feelings. At the same time, such an attitude on the part of parents and teachers serves to create in the total-life-relationship structure a spiral effect which helps the children become increasingly willing to verbalize their conscious emotions. As a result, brain-injured children benefit in several ways: (1) Parents and teachers know more adequately where they stand with their children. Hence, their uncertainty gives way to greater certainty in parental child-rearing practices and in classroom teaching efforts. (2) Antagonism in parents and teachers over puzzling aspects of a child's behavior will give way to greater understanding and sympathy. As children become more articulate about the feelings which are the source of their behavior, adults no longer feel they are fighting shadows of behavior which they do not understand. (3) These children learn to handle in a more open and healthy way the everyday verbal barbs often thrust at them for many reasons by groups of their peers or by their own siblings.

Complex Psychological Problems

Strauss and his co-workers have attempted to describe certain behavior patterns which they feel may be the result of brain injury (e.g., hyperkinesis, disinhibition, poor impulse control, and emotional lability). Birch (1959, 1964), Eisenberg (1964), and Graham *et al.* (1963), among others, have suggested that the evidence for such a relation between personality characteristics and brain injury is meager. In fact, Ernhart *et al.* (1963) found in a group of brain-injured, preschool children, with heterogeneous etiology occurring at different ages between birth and five and a half years, that the hyperkinetic personality syndrome is not a typical picture.

Using ego development as a frame of reference (Rappaport, 1961, p. 447), the central core of the emotional problem of brain-injured children could be designated as an *ego insufficiency*. We have carefully chosen the designation *insufficiency* in preference to other terms in the literature, such as ego defect (Clark, 1963; Pearson, 1942), ego deficit (Doris and Solnit, 1963), and ego weakness.

The word insufficiency means "the inability to fulfill requirements" or the "inability of a bodily organ to do its work" (Oxford Dictionary, 1955). Just as the clinical description "myocardial insufficiency" designates heart disease which can be organic and/or functional, we recognize that the psychopathology of brain-injured children can be the result of the inextricable combination of neurologic and psychologic determinants.

The problems in psychosocial adaptation which result from ego insufficiency are psychological problems which may be present for a variety of reasons. Their appearance in a child's life is not pathognomonic of brain injury. Brain-injured children, however, usually experience these problems to a greater degree and over a longer period of time than do children without brain dysfunction.

The analogy might be drawn of a train track running from the town of Infancy to a town called Adulthood. Along the track there are many stations. A child without brain dysfunction is like the express train. It runs fast, usually on schedule, and stops only at the major stations.

Brain-injured children are like the local trains. They run at different speeds, are often held up by obstacles in their path, stop many times along the way, pulling into sidings or deviating from the main line. Not all the local trains stop at the same station. Nor do they all travel at the same speed. So it is with brain-injured children. At some time in their lives they will stop at or will pass by some of these stations (psychological problems) listed below.

It would be helpful for teachers to recognize these "station stops" when they see them in children in their classroom. Perhaps with the help of the psychotherapist, the parent counselor, and the parents, teachers can help these children leave these stations behind in their journey toward self-realization and adulthood. Some of the "stations" or psychological problems arising from ego *insufficiency* include the following (see also Doris and Solnit, 1963, p. 633): perceptual impairment; poor motility control; defective speech development; relative inability to postpone discharge of impulse into action or to accept substitute gratification; the quest for self-identity and adequacy; the hurt pride or narcissistic hypersensitivity; the need for external impulse controls; the feelings of body mutilation and disorganization of body image; the fear of being different which is often equated with "being bad and inferior"; diffuse difficulty in the use of the symbolic process; relative inability to transform impulses, i.e., to sublimate them and to have available the psychic energies necessary for trial-action functions such as speech, thought, or memory; inability to cope simultaneously with outer stimulation and inner needs; and the pattern of persistent denial as a defense against anxiety.

Space does not permit citing case histories to illustrate each of these psychological problems in ego maturation and adaptation. Teachers of brain-injured children are familiar with them in one form or another.

The following excerpts of a series of psychotherapy hours which were used to help a student work through her feelings of hurt pride and narcissistic hypersensitivity, which seems to be the most ubiquitous problem in brain-injured children and yet the least understood by parents and teachers, will serve as one illustration:

At the beginning of therapy this eleven-year-old girl indicated that coming to Pathway School, after attending another special school for several years, had really been most upsetting to her. She said it made her feel all alone, like everyone was against her—"the doctors, the teachers, and my parents." This opened up some discussion as to how she might have received the brain injury which necessitated her coming to the Pathway School. I let her know that we didn't always know just how our brains were hurt or injured, but the important thing was that we could do everything possible to help us get the pathways in the brain straightened out so she could go ahead and do her reading, arithmetic, spelling, and other school work. That was half of it. The other half was to help her with all the loaded feelings which were now dammed up inside her like a great reservoir. She acknowledged that that was right. She said she felt like she was constantly under pressure—feeling pressure from her family and from the teachers.

In subsequent hours I had a chance to open up with her more directly the kinds of things with which she had been struggling over the years. Our parent counselor had been working with the parents to help them see the nature of their daughter's problem in terms of her brain dysfunctioning pattern. Both parents had seemed ready to support this notion even though it was difficult for them. When I talked with her about the fact that it did appear that she had had a bruise or an injury to her brain sometime in the past, she said that no one had ever really told her this, but she knew something wasn't quite right. She said she knew that if her brain was bruised, it meant that some of it, or perhaps most of it, had healed up just like the bruise she might have on her arm. I agreed, but pointed out that during all the period of time that she had had the bruise, she had had a great deal of trouble learning to read. Her poor reading had led to certain other problems. She said she knew this. The biggest problem it led to was the fact that "everybody was disappointed in me." It just felt to her as if everyone was saying, "It's her fault she can't read." When I recognized with her that it must have stirred up an awful lot of feeling for them to go around saying it was all her fault, she could reply that it certainly did make her feel very badly. And I wondered if there were any other kinds of feelings besides feeling badly. With some help from me she could agree that it also made her feel pretty mad. "Sometimes I felt like I wanted to kill the world. I wanted to fight my teachers." When I wondered how far she got with all of this, she said that she usually "got disgusted and finally gave up in everything." I helped her move to the end of the hour by suggesting that perhaps in the hours we had together, I could help her drain off some of the strong, angry, hurt feelings so she might put more of that energy into the business of learning to read through some of the special methods we had at the Pathway School.

It was very interesting to see how in the following hours there was a gradual shift in this girl from her focus on global anger and global hostility, a kind of "kill the world" approach, to focusing more and more anger on her teacher at Pathway School. There were many hours with a great deal of blasting away at her teacher, both verbally as well as in some play acting-out. However, over the period of weeks and months this extreme narcissistic hypersensitivity and hurt pride gradually gave way to increased determination. Along with determination, considerable patience on the part of the teacher, as well as a well-structured curriculum specifically designed to meet the needs of a brain-injured preadolescent, this young lady began to travel toward young adulthood. Within a period of two years she was able to move from the pace of a "local train," stopping at nearly all of the "stations" listed above, to the efficiency of an express, approximately two years behind her age group in all subjects, but rapidly making up for lost time.

SUMMARY

This paper has been an attempt to share with teachers of brain-injured children some of the specialized information from the area of pediatric psychiatry. Five of the milestones which have been significant in the way pediatric psychiatry views the problems of children with central nervous system dysfunction have been reviewed. The work of Bender (1956), Strauss and his co-workers (1947, 1954), the paper by Eisenberg (1957), the significant contribution to neurophysiology by Moruzzi and Magoun (1949), and an important paper on "Ego Development in a Brain-Injured Child" by Rappaport (1961) were discussed in some detail as background material.

The concept of "total-life-relationship structure" was presented as an established educational and therapeutic approach to meet the needs of brain-injured children. Several of the conditions essential to mobilize and sustain such a "total-life-relationship structure" model within a school setting were described in some detail. Experience derived from the past two years at the Pathway School in Jeffersonville, Pennsylvania, was used as a source for material in the paper.

A short section described some of the complex psychological problems which arise from an ego insufficiency, which we have found to be the core emotional problem of brain-injured children, and a short case study illustrated the problem of narcissistic hypersensitivity or hurt pride so frequently seen in brain-injured children and often difficult to cope with in the home and classroom.

SELECTED REFERENCES

Adamson, W. C., Hersh, A., and Creasy, W. T. "Some psychological aspects of the management of the brain-damaged adolescent in a residential setting," *Journal of Child Psychology and Psychiatry*, 1961, 2, 156–164.

Allen, F. H., and Pearson, G. H. "The emotional problems of the physically handicapped child," *British Journal of Medicine*, 1928, 8, 212–225.

Barsch, R. H. "Counseling the parents of brain-damaged children," *Journal of Rehabilitation*, 1961, 27, 26.

Bender, L. "Organic brain disorders producing behavior disorders in children," *Recent trends in child psychiatry*. N. D. C. Lewis and B. Pacella (eds.). New York: Grune & Stratton, 1946.

———. "The psychological problems of children with organic brain disorders," *American Journal of Orthopsychiatry*, 1949, 19, 404–415.

————. "The psychological treatment of the brain damaged child," *Quarterly Journal of Child Behavior*, 1951, 3, 123–132.

————. "The psychology of children suffering from organic disturbances of the cerebellum," *American Journal of Orthopsychiatry*, 1940, 10, 287–293.

————. Psychopathology of children with organic brain disorders. Springfield, Ill.: Charles C Thomas, 1956.

————. *The visual motor Gestalt test and its clinical use.* Research Monograph No. 3. New York: American Orthopsychiatry Association, 1938.

Birch, H. G. "The problem of 'brain damage' in children," in *Brain Damage in children: The biological and social aspects.* H. G. Birch (ed.). Baltimore: Williams & Wilkins, 1964.

Birch, H. G., and Diller, L. "Rorschach signs of 'organicity': A physiological basis for perceptual disturbances," *Journal of Projective Techniques*, 1959, 23, 184–197.

Clark, L. P. *The nature and treatment of amentia.* London: Bailliere, Tindall and Cox, 1933.

Doris, J., and Solnit, A. J. "Treatment of children with brain damage and associated school problems," *Journal of the American Academy of Child Psychiatry*, 1963, 2, 618–635.

Eisenberg, L. "Behavioral manifestations of cerebral damage in childhood," in *Brain damage in children: The biological and social aspects.* H. G. Birch (ed.). Baltimore: Williams & Wilkins, 1964.

————. "Psychiatric implications of brain damage in children," *Psychiatric Quarterly*, 1957, 31, 72–92.

Erikson, E. H. *Childhood and society.* New York: Norton, 1950.

————. "Growth and crisis of the healthy personality." *Personality in nature, society and culture.* C. Kluckhohn and H. A. Murray (eds.). New York: Knopf, 1953.

Ernhart, C. B., Graham, F. K., Eichman, P. L., Marshall, J. M., and Thurston, D. "Brain injury in the pre-school child: Some developmental considerations: II. Comparison of brain-injured and normal children," *Psychological Monographs: Genetic and Applied*, 1963, 77, 16–33.

Freed, H. *The chemistry and therapy of behavior disorders in children.* Springfield, Ill.: Charles C Thomas, 1962.

Graham, F. K., Ernhart, C. B., Craft, M., and Berman, P. W. "Brain injury in the pre-school child: Some developmental considerations: I. Performance of normal children," *Psychological Monographs: Genetic and Applied*, 1963, 77, 1–16.

Greenacre, P. "Predisposition to anxiety," *Psychoanalytic Quarterly*, 1941, 4, 610–639.

Kurlander, L. F., and Colodny, D. " 'Pseudoneurosis' in the neurologically handicapped child," *American Journal of Orthopsychiatry*, 1965, 35, 733–738.

Lewis, R. S., Strauss, A. A., and Lehtinen, L. E. *The other child.* New York: Grune & Stratton, 1960.

Lorenz, K. Z. "The comparative method in studying innate behavior patterns," in *Physiological mechanisms in animal behavior.* Symposia of the Society for Experimental Biology, No. IV. New York: Academic Press, 1950.

Magoun, H. W. *The waking brain.* Springfield, Ill.: Charles C Thomas, 1963.

Morrell, F., and Ross, M. A. "Central inhibition in cortical conditioned reflexes," *Archives of Neurology and Psychiatry*, 1953, 70, 611–616.

Moruzzi, G., and Magoun, H. W. "Brain stem reticular formation and activation of the EEG," *Electroencephalographic and Clinical Neurophysiology*, 1949, 1, 455–473.

Mountcastle, V. B., and Powell, T. P. S. "Neural mechanisms subserving cutaneous sensibility," *Bulletin of the Johns Hopkins Hospital*, 1959, 105, 201–222.

Pearson, G. H. J. *Emotional disorders of children*. New York: Norton, 1949.

Rappaport, S. R. "Behavior disorder and ego development in a brain-injured child," *The Psychoanalytic Study of the Child*, 1961, 16, 423–450.

Reese, W. G., Doss, R., and Gantt, W. H. "Autonomic responses in differential diagnosis of organic and psychogenic psychosis," *Archives of Neurology and Psychiatry*, 1953, 70, 778–793.

Schilder, P. *Image and appearance of the human body*. New York: International University Press, 1951.

———. "Organic problems in child guidance," *Mental Hygiene*, 1931, 15, 480–486.

———. "The psychological implication of motor development in children," *Proceedings of the Fourth Institute on the Exceptional Child*, Child's Research Clinic of Woods Schools, 1937, 4, 38–59.

———. "Reaction types resembling functional psychoses in childhood on the basis of an organic inferiority of the brain," *Mental Hygiene*, 1935, 19, 439–446.

Strauss, A. A,. and Lehtinen, L. E. *Psychopathology and education of the brain-injured child*. New York: Grune & Stratton, 1947.

Strauss, A. A., and Werner, H. "Experimental analysis of the clinical symptom 'perseveration' in mentally retarded children," *American Journal of Mental Deficiency*, 1942, 27, 185–187.

———. "Impairment in thought processes of brain-injured children," *American Journal of Mental Deficiency*, 1943, 47, 291–295.

Tinbergen, N. "The hierarchical organization of nervous mechanisms underlying instinctive behavior," in *Physiological mechanisms in animal behavior*. Symposia of the Society for Experimental Biology. No. IV. New York: Academic Press, 1950.

PART V
INTERDISCIPLINARY COMPETENCIES

Chapter 19

The Needs of Teachers for Specialized Information Regarding Their Role in Interdisciplinary Teams

PETER KNOBLOCK, Ph.D.

EDITORIAL NOTE.—The "team approach" is almost a myth, if one bases an appraisal of the team in terms of demonstrations of effective team operation. The major cause of ineffective team work is the lack of a clear-cut point of view regarding the team concept itself, the role of the participants, and practice in effectively serving in a team situation. The interdisciplinary concept is basic to effective work with brain-injured children, and without it children are not adequately served. Dr. Knoblock's paper goes far to define the educator's role in team function and to isolate for the reader the specialized competencies which educators must have for effective membership in this type of professional activity.

DR. PETER KNOBLOCK is currently program director for the training of teachers of emotionally disturbed children in the Division of Special Education and Rehabilitation at Syracuse University, Syracuse, New York. He received his Ph.D. degree in education and psychology from the University of Michigan in 1962. His experience includes positions at Hawthorn Center, Northville, Michigan; University of Michigan Fresh Air Camp; and the California Youth Authority.

He has recently edited *Educational Programming for Emotionally Disturbed Children: The Decade Ahead.*

Chapter 19

The Needs of Teachers for Specialized Information Regarding Their Role in Interdisciplinary Teams

PETER KNOBLOCK, Ph.D.

PETER KNOBLOCK, Ph.D.

INTERDISCIPLINARY TEAM FUNCTIONING IN HISTORICAL PERSPECTIVE

In retrospect, there would seem to be three closely parallel developments which account for present interest in team functioning. First, medical hospital treatment of patients, both children and adults, has evolved largely around the advantages accruing to such patients from the bringing together of highly trained practitioners. At any given moment, depending upon the decision of the physician responsible for a particular case, the entire machinery or relevant parts thereof can be mobilized and brought to bear on the problem confronting patient and physician. Specific advances and changes in medical care and treatment stem from this focusing on the advantages of the total treatment possibilities found in team functioning. The downward trend in infant mortality rates, in certain segments of the population, is one good example of this society's reliance upon well-equipped and staffed hospitals and clinics which provide multiservice programs. It can be seen that the concept of team functioning meets the physical and emotional needs of both physicians and patients. Medical personnel insisted that care and treatment of the highest caliber could only be offered the public within such medical centers. Patients, in a similar fashion, began to recognize the benefits to be gained from such comprehensive centers "in case of an emergency." It is not unusual to find communities of moderate size and resources with large, well-equipped medical centers serving regional areas. The trend toward comprehensive care is now generally accepted and looked upon as not only desirable, but necessary. This is also the case, as can now be seen, in the designing of mental health centers.

Some might wish to make a distinction between team functioning and interdisciplinary team functioning. Such a distinction would seem legitimate, and the paradigm for this can be found in the development

293

of the child guidance movement in this country. This was a planned endeavor to utilize the competencies of several different professional disciplines such as psychiatric social work, clinical psychology, and child psychiatry in an effort to design preventive services for children. In all probability, this was the first large-scale attempt to implement a mental health intervention approach based on the utilization and cooperation of diverse professions. Closely parallel to the above design has been the rise of rehabilitation units which attempt to view the entire problem of the individual, which may encompass social and emotional, as well as physical, aspects. Such rehabilitation units may operate with many professionally trained workers from diverse disciplines, such as physical therapists, recreation personnel, occupational therapists, vocational rehabilitation counselors, counseling psychologists, as well as medical personnel.

Finally, the tremendous expansion of technical knowledge along with the specialized nature of much of this information has greatly fostered the desirability of bringing practitioners together from many related disciplines. It is believed that the greatest good comes out of the focusing on one problem by individuals with diverse yet relevant points of view.

THE TEACHER'S FUNCTIONING ROLE WITHIN THE INTERDISCIPLINARY TEAM

There may be as many operational and functional roles of teachers within team functioning as there are teams. It would seem of some benefit, however, to sketch the more prevalent roles in which teachers operate. A word of further caution is needed at this juncture: the roles ascribed to and acquired by teachers functioning as team members can never be discussed in static terms. It is not likely that a teacher inherits a position on a team, and if such is the case, the personality and/or professional merits of the teacher and his colleagues, as well as the organizational structure, ultimately determine the role a teacher will play.

In describing the following roles, no value judgments will be implied. It is equally difficult to assign numerical weights to these role descriptions in terms of their prevalence and/or acceptability by members of the teaching profession.

The Teacher as a Supplier of Information

It is logical to conclude that a team of professional workers sustains itself through and is dependent upon the steady input of information. Naturally, the quality and content of this information are important variables. While there does not seem to be a definite correlation between the composition of the team in terms of the disciplines represented and the degree to which they rely upon teachers as suppliers of information, there is often a tendency for school-related personnel to request this role from other colleagues. This is essentially a nonjudgmental team task in which the teacher is asked to contribute specific bits of information which can be integrated with the larger body of material being accumulated. Most often, teachers in this role find themselves in a close-ended situation which essentially demands responses to specific and often predetermined questions.

The receptivity of the other team members to the information contributed by the teacher may be higher in instances of within- (or intra-) profession team functioning as opposed to interdisciplinary team functioning. It has been the writer's experience that the degree of receptivity is not necessarily dependent upon the quality of the information supplied by the teacher. Ultimately, the question of the relationship between the value of the material contributed by the teacher and the usefulness of such material to the team needs to be explored.

The Teacher as a Validator of Hypotheses

Teachers employed in hospital and residential programs for brain-injured and other types of exceptional children are frequently found to be functioning on interdisciplinary teams as validators of hypotheses. There would seem to be several factors inherent in the environmental setting which could account for teachers functioning in this manner. In the first place, there is a longer history of teachers functioning as members of interdisciplinary teams within such hospital and residential programs. As opposed to the over-all staffing pattern of public schools, residential programs are specifically designed to incorporate and utilize members of various professions. Related to this point is the interdependency one activity within the setting has upon another. Generally, residential programs consider one of their greatest assets to be their ability to program a child's entire day within some meaningful framework which reflects the emotional and physical needs of the child. In order to maximize such a program it is necessary for staff members, including teachers, to maintain their lines of communication and to function as "validators." What this means is that teachers, along with other personnel, are called upon to aid in the verification process in terms of the behavioral and/or academic hypotheses other team members may have regarding a child's development. "Is the behavior evidenced in the classroom?" "In my therapy sessions with this child, I find I have to couch my remarks in very concrete terms. Is this also true in his classroom work?" In the never-ending search for normative behavior regarding the acceptability or deviancy of certain behaviors, many interdisciplinary teams will look toward the teacher as one who can aid in such a data-gathering process and, in so doing, contribute materially to reducing the uncertainty surrounding much symptomatic behavior.

The Teacher as a Decision-Maker

To some it would appear a paradoxical situation when teachers function as decision-makers in their classroom and not in their contacts with other professions. Thus, many practitioners, for the reasons stated above and for others which will be discussed in other sections of this paper, maintain that a role equilibrium is established when teachers are cast as decision-makers. As opposed to teachers as validators of hypotheses, information for which is usually obtained on an after-the-fact basis, those looked to as decision-makers are asked to aid in specifying certain outcomes to be anticipated as the result of following certain prescribed interventions or choices. It is of interest to note that when teachers are asked to function in this capacity they are often asked to make decisions regarding events and behavior which may be only remotely related to their sphere of competency. The assumption on the part of other team members is that if one can be looked upon as a decision-maker, the skills possessed by this person can be generalized. Thus, teachers looked upon as decision-makers are asked to function as generalists as opposed to the somewhat more specific task requirements and demands made by the other roles. If this is true, then it could be argued that this role resembles more closely the roles other team members may play, and implications for status rankings may be inherent in this view of the teacher.

THE MAJOR ISSUE

While many issues may be directly related to and dependent upon roles played by teachers of brain-injured children, there is one large issue which requires some discussion; that is, whether the concept or vehicle of the interdisciplinary team is a myth or reality. So much positive affect has been expressed regarding the necessity and value of team functioning that its place in professional settings has often been uncritically accepted. Quite recently, several attempts have been made to conceptualize interdisciplinary team functioning as it relates to the operations of various disciplines. In a sense, these have been pioneering efforts, since they are part of a growing body of literature which is attempting to answer the broad question of whether such functioning does in fact exist, and, if it is a reality, what are the environmental and personal conditions which foster or impede team interactions.

In a recent study of special class programs for emotionally handicapped children, Morse, Cutler, and Fink (1964) investigated the utilization of various school workers as back-up or support personnel for the classroom teacher. Perhaps of greatest significance was their observation that no single or predominant pattern of team functioning existed. They found that diverse role relationships contributed to the establishment of several different patterns of communications. In general, it was found that teachers were looked upon as the ones most competent to handle classroom problems, and related to this was the correlation between the perception of teacher competency and his degree of autonomy or perhaps of decision-making.

In those instances when it became necessary to request assistance from other school personnel, the pattern of communication was predominantly between teacher and principal. It would seem from the information supplied in this publication that, as the teacher's ability to cope with the classroom situation diminished, other school workers were utilized. Also of significance, according to the charts and tables presented, was the teacher's rather limited accessibility to other personnel in contrast to the principal's ability for calling forth a far greater range of disciplines operating within the school. In contrast to the prevalent notion that the more professionals you have focusing on a problem the better it is, the authors make the following statement:

> While the teacher was most often on his own in control matters, when things went wrong a simple dyad was enough, or on occasion a whole series of contacts were called forth. This welter of involved people accounted for some of the difficulties in operating these programs. Who was to do what and when he was to do it required a lot of clearance. The teacher may have felt, in many instances, that all help was too little and too late (p. 84).

A study (Cumming and Ise, 1965) dealing with the attitudes of family doctors toward the utilization of other medical personnel and outside resources points up many of the same findings mentioned above. In this study thirty-two family physicians were interviewed and, in general, the physicians reported little knowledge of, or satisfaction with, community agencies. Their referral pattern was directed primarily at other medical personnel, to the exclusion of psychiatric services. The authors hypothesize that the more competent the physician becomes, the greater his felt need is to utilize other medical and community services. What serves to get in his way, however, is the *role* he has developed for himself, namely that of treating the *whole man*. Again one can see the issue and importance of role definition as it relates not only to teachers but to other professional workers.

If the actual existence and operations of interdisciplinary teams is open to as many questions and variables as outlined above, then it is of crucial importance to conceptualize the specific needs teachers may have for specialized information and skills in order to function as contributing members of an interdisciplinary team.

THE NEEDS OF TEACHERS FOR SPECIALIZED INFORMATION

The writer feels that the teacher's participation as a member of a team is dependent upon certain historical factors, role definitions, and estimates of competency. While all of this would seem to argue in favor of specific skills and needs, an equal case could be made for the development of a range of *generic* skills which would then place teachers in a position to handle better the issues of role definition and competency.

What one decides upon as the generically important skills and information which teachers should possess depends to a degree upon the value placed upon such team functioning. There are those who maintain, with some degree of validity, that effective interdisciplinary team functioning as traditionally defined is not a workable concept. As a direct result of such thinking, proponents of this view would tend to equip teachers with all the "necessary" skills and techniques in order for them to be able to function autonomously without the aid of other disciplines except when absolutely necessary. Others, however, view interdisciplinary team functioning in a more positive fashion and would want to equip teachers with the necessary information which would materially aid them in contributing to and being accepted by other participating members of a team. It would seem to be of no inherent value at this stage of knowledge to conclude that one or the other of these views is correct. In all probability, an effective teacher desiring to maneuver in an interdisciplinary setting would need independent as well as interdependent skills.

Knowledge of the Process and Operations of Team Functioning

Again, depending on the setting, the staffing pattern, and the nature of the goals of the members, the actual operations of an interdisciplinary team may vary. In the final analysis, however, there seem to be certain characteristics of small group, interdisciplinary team functioning which serve to contrast such a group with the practices of individual teachers.

For example, one of the most significant distinguishing features of team versus individual teacher functioning has to do with the procedural nature of team interaction and decision-making. In contrast to the crisis reactions involved in such individual teacher behavior, teams most often operate with either explicitly or implicitly determined procedures. Frequently these are in a "step-like" progression that takes the participants through certain data-gathering procedures which eventually lead to disposition of the problem under consideration. This aspect of the team being in a more advantageous position to engage in a detailed data-gathering and -analysis scheme is also in direct contrast to the position many teachers face when, by reason of limited time and access to support personnel, they accept incomplete evidence regarding a child and his problem and base their techniques and recommendation on such incomplete information.

In the process of determining choices or courses of action, interdisciplinary teams may, in one sense, be a disadvantage in that the number and type of decisions may be limited by the need for consensus. On the other hand, the alternatives available to individual teachers are limited only by their repertoire of skills. Earlier in this paper, the focus was on several different roles teachers may play while functioning as a member of a team. In keeping with that discussion, there are many who maintain that one of the primary functions of such teams revolves around their unique ability to validate hypotheses. If this conceptualization is correct, then perhaps those teachers who are viewed by their colleagues as validators of hypotheses may have easier access to such teams and in fact function in a more effective manner, that is, in a way which is compatible with the group's goals.

In closing this section, it should be reiterated that a teacher's opportunities to participate effectively as a contributing member of a team appear to be enhanced when he has a sound grasp of the range of assets and limitations inherent in such groups.

Knowledge of the Roles of the Helping Professions

Related to the above discussion dealing with an awareness of the goals and operations of interdisciplinary teams is a heightened sensitivity and possession of "hard" information regarding the roles of the various helping professions. Konopka (1963) points out in a discussion of the functioning of social group workers:

A combination of an innate capacity for empathy with heightened awareness of oneself and one's value system, and constant patient exercise in sharpening the powers of observation and listening are needed for the particular "fact-finding" process of social group work. The knowledge of individual and group dynamics then contributes to the ordering of the facts and their proper assessment. The group worker's fact-finding tools are not always sufficient for all the group situations he encounters. His professional integrity then demands consultation and help from others in such related professions as psychology, psychiatry, education, and so forth (p. 94).

Undoubtedly, many professionals find themselves in the same predicament. Critics of teachers' functioning within team settings have long pointed to the need for teachers to "prove" themselves. While the need remains for teachers to serve as contributing members, the need may be equally as pressing for teachers to comprehend adequately what it is that other professional disciplines are striving to achieve. There is every reason to believe, just as is true with the statement quoted above, that the degree of overlapping goals and motives between professions is great, and, ultimately, relations between professional groups can be enhanced by such understandings.

From the field of social group work, the following statement of function has direct applicability to much of what teachers strive to accomplish:

1. Social group work is a method of rendering service to persons, through providing experience in groups. Development of the person towards his individual potential, improvement of relationship and social functioning competencies, and social action are recognized as purposes of social group work. The worker functions within a framework of ethical and social values.
2. Social group work is a generic method which can be used in different settings.
3. The method includes conscious use of worker-member relationships, relationships among members, and of group activity. The worker simultaneously uses relationships with individual members and with the group as a whole. He works as an enabler with both, helping members and the group to use their capacities and strengths. He uses himself differently in accordance with specific objectives and his assessment of members' needs, interests and capacities (Murphy, 1959, p. 78).

Similarly, in a document titled *Psychology and its Relations with Other Professions* (American Psychological Association, 1954), there is a section dealing with "aspirations for the good profession of psychology." With only slight modification, such a statement would be applicable to many professional groups. The characteristics include:

1. A good profession guides its practices and policies by a sense of social responsibility.
2. A good profession will devote relatively little of its energy to "guild" functions, to the building of its own in-group strength, and relatively much of its energy to the serving of its social functions.

3. A good profession will not represent itself as able to render services outside its demonstrable competence.

4. A good profession has a code of ethics designed primarily to protect the client and only secondarily to protect the members of the profession.

5. A good profession will find its unique pattern of competence and focus its efforts on carrying out those functions for which it is best equipped.

6. A good profession will engage in rational and cooperative relations with other professions having related or overlapping competences and common purposes.

7. A good profession will be characterized by an adaptive balance among efforts devoted to research, to teaching, and to application.

8. A good profession will maintain good channels of communication among the "discoverers, the teachers, and the appliers of knowledge."

9. A good profession is free of nonfunctional entrance requirements.

10. A good profession is one in which preparatory training is validly related to the ultimate function of the members of the profession.

11. A good profession will guard against adopting any technique or theory as the final solution to its problems.

12. A good profession is one whose members are socially and financially accessible to the public.

13. A good profession is a free profession.

Only two professional groups have been discussed from the point of view of how they as professionals would like to present themselves to their colleagues. It would also be necessary, of course, for teachers to attempt to gain an understanding of other groups as they interact as members of a team. Most importantly, the perceptive teachers will strive to understand their role clearly, as discussed earlier, as it compares and contrasts with that of other team members.

The Need for Interdisciplinary Practicum Experience

The hope is that individuals in training to teach brain-injured children will be provided with an opportunity for supervised practice in a multidiscipline setting.

It is anticipated that such placement would serve two purposes. First, it would be an essential experience for those desiring a clearer notion of which professional attributes of a particular discipline are common to all or many members of that group and which seem to be idiosyncratic in nature. Secondly, the hope is that other disciplines will gain a more realistic concept of the type of training involved in a special education background and the potential contribution such a specially prepared individual may offer. This is the point at which many professionals differ. There are those who feel that if teachers are to participate as vital members of a team they must function as generalists and perhaps take on the characteristics of the other disciplines. This writer, on the other hand, agrees with Rabinow (1964) who says,

> The fear that emphasis on the teaching function of the teacher with disturbed children may undo the teacher's availability for participating in an integrated effort with other professional disciplines fails to take into account a necessary condition for such collaborative work, namely that each team member must have a clearly defined orbit of competence. The teacher of disturbed children without teaching skills has nothing to integrate. The full integration of the teacher in any team effort with other professions cannot be realized until the teacher has enough skill and security with her teaching abilities (p. 10).

The last point made by Rabinow deserves some elaboration. One of the problems teacher-educators have had to face and deal with has been the premature placement of a student in an interdisciplinary setting. Depending on the needs and personnel of such a setting, it would seem most advantageous as a general principle to effect such a placement toward the middle or latter part of training. This serves the purpose of enabling the student to develop skills and a role concept before placement into an interdisciplinary setting. Regardless of the placement strategy employed, there does seem to be a strong tendency on the part of many practicum agencies to view such students as participating members of the agency and equipped to perform in a service capacity. Such an agency attitude may be desirable and even necessary, but the implication is that university training programs will be obligated to maintain close liaison with cooperating agencies in order to represent realistically the needs and interests of the students to agency personnel.

The university's cooperative role with the practicum setting takes on added importance with those students who experience and express great amounts of anxiety and resistance at having to function in an interdisciplinary setting. In an article describing the staff anxieties caused by the conducting of research in a clinical setting, Mitchell and Mudd (1957) state, "For short-range cures agency administrators might do well to apply the same methods found effective in handling neurotic anxiety in their clients to staff members who resist unduly the integration of research techniques into the helping process" (p. 321). It may be necessary for training programs to utilize what Mitchell and Mudd refer to as "covering-up" therapeutic approaches. These imply constant interpretation to students of agency policy, staffing patterns, and goals as well as aiding the students in determining their sphere of responsibility by reassurance, persuasion, advice, and similar techniques. In other instances it may be necessary to approach student concerns on a somewhat deeper, more intense level through role-playing and group discussions, to cite just two possibilities.

Need for an Understanding of the Interpersonal Process

As this writer has pointed out in another publication (in press), the problems inherent in diagnosing and treating this broad group of exceptional children utilizing symptom clusters have served to immobilize professional workers. Definitional problems have plagued this field, and efforts have been directed primarily toward gaining a clearer understanding of the *type* of child under consideration. There are many educators, however, who are placing an increasing emphasis on an analysis of the relationship process as opposed to the use of intervention techniques on a crisis basis. This trend, if it is one, is in part due to a desensitization of the "teacher or therapist" controversy. Many special education training programs conceive of the role of their trainees as therapeutic educators insofar as they are able to provide a maximally effective learning environment which takes into consideration the self-concept of the learner, the group, and authority relationships, as well as an understanding of the nature of the task.

From many sources interest is now being shown in the focusing on stages and the breaking down of the teaching-learning relationship into a process analysis of the ingredients which go into such relationships. Devereux (1956), for example, discusses the essential ingredients of therapeutic education by breaking it down into its component parts. In essence, he attempts to translate psychoanalytic concepts into psycho-educationally relevant terms. His framework is divided into three stages referred to as the unlearning, neutral, and relearning phases.

In another context Cohen (1964) has described the stages through which a group of seriously withdrawn children must be helped in order for them to move from the periphery of the group to the center.

Several recent attempts at conceptualizing the relationship process have grown out of a direct need to aid trainees in developing both empathic and technical skills when dealing with exceptional children. For example, this writer, while involved with a group of trainees at a summer camp for emotionally disturbed children, developed a method for the analysis of the tutorial relationship based on narrative accounts and anecdotal records made by the trainees. Each aspect of the framework has been operationally defined and the method of scoring is currently undergoing reliability studies. In brief, what this method enables one to do is to chart the stages through which the tutorial relationship has passed to aid students in focusing on particular difficulties they or the child may be experiencing in moving the relationship forward. Certainly the setting, type of child, and educational goals will dictate the stages and variables to be considered.

Kirkland (1964) has developed an approach to be used with multiple-handicapped children from lower socioeconomic families. His "Interpersonal Skills Tutoring" attempts to aid the child, through the relationship with the adult, to acquire and develop more appropriate social and learning skills. Kirkland states, "While the Interpersonal Skills Tutoring approach to disturbed behavior does not directly alter the concrete realities of the child's living environment, it does provide him with new perceptions and newly-learned coping techniques" (p. 7). He goes on to state,

> With an empathic understanding of low socio-economic class group dynamics, the tutor physically enters the child's behavioral (rather than intra-psychic world) to:
> 1. teach *specific* social skills
> 2. *participate* in the process of growth toward interdependence
> 3. lead him through resolutions of *actual* intra- and interpersonal conflict
> 4. *use* the child's peer group as a source of reinforcement for the child's budding growth patterns (p. 9).

Specific Contribution of Teachers to Interdisciplinary Functioning

The repetitious search for specific competencies required by specialized teachers of handicapped children has left prospective teacher candidates in a state of confusion. The early study conducted by the United States Office of Education (Mackie, Kvaraceus, and Williams, 1957) utilized a diverse sample of teacher respondents employed in a number of settings for disturbed children. Their results indicated a basic discrepancy between their felt competencies and perceived needs, in that they felt most proficient in areas they considered relatively less important. One implication was their stated need for understanding of the range of specific techniques and skills which might be applicable in coping with disturbed children.

A more recent study by Dorward (1963) pointed up the need to consider the type of setting in which a teacher is employed as an essential aspect of interpreting competencies valued by teachers. It is significant that one area considered most important by teachers of disturbed children as compared to regular class teachers was experience on a clinical team and knowledge of the competencies and roles expected of other clinical team members. Dorward expresses the view that such competencies could be fostered in the college preparation of individuals preparing to teach.

It is hypothesized that a more fruitful approach both in training and early apprentice training on the job would be a careful analysis of the actual contributions teachers can make to the team process of collecting and integrating data and ultimately making recommendations for modifying behavior. To carry this further, it would be equally advantageous to consider the efficiency level at which teachers operate in terms of comparisons between actual and anticipated contributions.

Only one attempt has been made specifically to detail actual contributions of teachers (and other helping professions) and then determine an efficiency measure (Beller, 1962). In Beller's assessment of interdisciplinary functioning an analysis was made of the specific contributions by teachers, therapy, psychiatric interviews, and other sources, to clinical records. As a second step, he determined the absolute and relative contributions made by each service to specific areas in the clinical record.

His over-all findings indicated that the teachers (in this instance all were nursery school teachers) functioned at the highest level of achievement. This would be interpreted to mean that in the areas in which teachers responded they made quantitatively more contributions than did other aspects or disciplines. Those areas in which teachers contributed on a high level were the developmental history (language, motor movement, constructive play, and reactions to playmates, adults, and self), and in information regarding nursery school (routines, activities, parent-child relationships, idiosyncratic habits and tics, and emotional expression).

Teachers made less of a contribution to family history, intake information, psychological tests, and treatment process. As a general finding, teachers also achieved at an expectation ratio close to the goal set for them by the researchers.

SUMMARY

One cannot keep from being greatly impressed with the complex nature of interdisciplinary functioning. Historically, impetus for such group functioning sprang from medically-oriented approaches. In practice, however, many professional workers point out the many problems and issues surrounding team functioning. A certain amount of anxiety permeates this model of action in that the implicit assumption is one of expecting team members to change, alter, or in some way reach a group consensus. On a slightly different level is the concern many workers experience at having to "give up" a child with whom they are working or at exposing him (and themselves) to approaches and decisions not necessarily in accord with the worker's own viewpoint.

Basically, the resolution of the proper role of teachers and specific skills and information teachers need in order to function effectively on such teams seems to be a matter of *convergence* (Murphy, 1959). By this is meant the necessity for teachers to present themselves as thoroughly well-grounded practitioners in a position to apply appropriate educational and behavioral techniques. At the same time, it may be equally as important for teachers to possess the same parallel skills and knowledges as the other team members possess.

Translated into specifics, this would mean that teachers need a clear conception of their actual and potential contributions to team functioning as well as an articulated role which is in keeping with their own level of sophistication and the requirements of the setting. Also necessary would be their attempt to discover commonalities between their skills and task requirements and those of other team members. As pointed out, such can be accomplished by possessing a sound realization of the roles of other disciplines and the development of process knowledge, which is an attempt to look at relationships and group phenomena as opposed to the crisis application of techniques and the preoccupation with the individual or unique case. The issue of the unique case has tended to encapsulate teachers in their reluctance to utilize and understand other professional groups. This is similar to the perceptions many clinicians harbor, in that they see the role of others as more formal, "scientific," or research oriented, while they profess to be caught up in actual behavior.

Ultimately, it may be necessary for those functioning in interdisciplinary settings to adopt a common psychological and educational grammar which makes available to all participants categories and rules of beliefs and actions. This aspect of convergence as well as those mentioned above may need to find a way into formalized training practices through interdisciplinary practice and responsible supervision by university personnel.

SELECTED REFERENCES

American Psychological Association. *Psychology and its relations with other professions.* Washington, D.C., 1954.

Beller, E. K. *Clinical process: The assessment of data in childhood personality disorders.* New York: Free Press, 1962.

Cohen, R. S. "Some childhood identity disturbances: Educational implementation of a psychiatric treatment plan," *Journal of the American Academy of Child Psychiatry,* 1964, 3, 488–499.

Cumming, M. E., and Ise, M. "Open your mouth and say A-a-h," *Trans-action,* 1965, 2, 42–43.

Devereux, G. *Therapeutic education: Its theoretical bases and practice.* New York: Harper, 1956.

Dorward, B. "A comparison of the competencies for regular classroom teachers and teachers of emotionally disturbed children," *Exceptional Children,* 1963, 30, 67–73.

Kirkland, J. *An interpersonal approach to behavior rehabilitation.* Syracuse: Huntington Family Center, 1964 (mimeograph).

Knoblock, P. "Brain injury and maladaptive behavior in adolescent youth," *High School Journal,* in press.

Konopka, G. *Social group work: A helping process.* Englewood Cliffs, N.J.: Prentice-Hall, 1963.

Mackie, R. P., Kvaraceus, W. C., and Williams, H. M. *Teachers of children who are socially and emotionally maladjusted.* U.S. Department of Health, Education and Welfare, Office of Education, Bulletin 1957, No. 11. Washington, D.C.: Superintendent of Documents, Government Printing Office, 1957.

Mitchell, H. E., and Mudd, E. H. "Anxieties associated with the conduct of research in a clinical setting," *American Journal of Orthopsychiatry,* 1957, 27, 310–323.

Morse, W. C., Cutler, R. L., and Fink, A. *Public School classes for the emotionally handicapped: A research analysis.* Washington, D.C.: Council for Exceptional Children, 1964.

Murphy, M. *The Social group method in Social Work Education: A project report of the curriculum study.* New York: Council on Social Work Education, 1959.

Pepinsky, H. B., and Karst, T. O. "Convergence: A phenomenon in counseling and in psychotherapy," *American Psychologist,* 1964, 19, 333–337.

Rabinow, B. *The training and supervision of teachers for emotionally disturbed children.* New York: State Education Department, 1964.

Comment

KNOBLOCK: There is a remarkable paradox with which you cannot help but be impressed when you start investigating the literature and start looking at team concepts. That paradox revolves around the issue of competency as Dr. Morse found in his CEC study and which some see in working with public school teachers. In many cases, the more competent a teacher is, the less likely is that teacher to be involved in interdisciplinary team approaches or support operations.

The implications may be that since the teacher is doing so well and is such an accomplished person nobody should destroy that. He is often considered as one who doesn't need help like the other teachers do who might not be doing nearly as well. If this is true in practice, as I think it is, then we may wish to look at this issue long and hard.

CRUICKSHANK: We're now concerned with preparation of teachers of brain-injured children, and here we see the teacher as a supplier of information. Often the teacher is assumed to be only the receiver of information. A teacher must be looked upon as a validator of hypotheses, and he must be prepared for this role.

GROSSMAN: One of the things we probably need very much in teacher education is some practicum in learning how to utilize the talents of other people in other disciplines. All too often teachers have not been exposed to other disciplines so that when they go out in the field, they don't know how other people think.

RAPPAPORT: Teams require time and assiduous effort to learn how to communicate. When we talk about teams, we also have to talk about giving their membership the opportunity to learn how to communicate and to have the delegation of responsibility.

GROSSMAN: As far as the educational needs are concerned, there is no question but that the educator has the primary responsibility. Other individuals can give information, but this information in turn has to be used and incorporated into the educator's thinking in conceptualizing some reasonable plan for a particular child.

Chapter 20

A Summary

WILLIAM M. CRUICKSHANK, Ph.D.

Chapter 20

A Summary

WILLIAM M. CRUICKSHANK, Ph.D.

From the preceding chapters the reader will discern that the bases of competency for teachers of brain-injured children are to be found in an interlinking of information which stems from a wide variety of disciplines. Education is one of these disciplines. Education, however, has been hesitant in regard to brain-injured children. The profession of education must rise to meet the challenge of the increasing knowledge of its sister professions. It must devise programs of teacher preparation which in turn will confront the brain-injured child with a teacher worthy of the intricate task to be faced by both of them.

Neurology sinks deep shafts to penetrate the cell and to understand its delicate function. Neurology and psychology together explore the action which takes place at the synapse out of which knowledge of learning will come. Psychiatry and clinical psychology explore the dynamics of the self and the relationship of the self to the society of which the self is a part. Pathology, histology, chemistry, and physics, individually and in concert, provide new dimensions to the understanding of the human organism and how it functions—normally and abnormally. Education as a discipline must do likewise with those techniques and tools which are unique to it.

Not a single profession mentioned herein has reached the apex of its development. No profession claims to have climaxed its development. This fact is, however, not used as an excuse for lack of action. Neurology moves ahead with action programs in spite of the absence of absolutely definitive diagnostic instrumentation. Psychiatry and psychology do not wait for the next developments before engaging in those which are now at hand.

One excuse for lack of activity in the area of education of brain-injured children is that too little is known to do an adequate job with the children. This is not true. Much is known and much can be accomplished immediately. Educators cannot await the arrival of every piece in the mosaic before beginning to assemble the puzzle. Education must, as is the case with other professions, begin to work now, where it is, and with what it has. Success can be achieved for brain-injured children in this approach.

It has often been said that between thirty and fifty years elapse between the development of new understanding and the complete incorporation of this understanding as a commonplace in the classroom with teacher and children. The education of brain-injured children cannot wait for such a lapse of time to take place. A crash program must be developed which will narrow the gap to meet the needs of the present generation of brain-injured children.

Practically every profession concerned with the brain-injured child is in advance of the profession of education in understanding its portion of the problem. This state of affairs is true in spite of the fact that the problem has, in the United States, been *discussed* by educators since before 1940—discussed, but little more than this as one views the issue nationally. This state of affairs is true in spite of the fact that educators hold in their hands the responsibility for this child for more hours each day and for more days each year and for more years in the life of the child than does any other profession. In this respect it is second only indeed to the child's parents themselves. Education must throw off its attitude of *laissez faire* and assume the dynamic leadership role which is expected of it in society. It must strike out with the combined wisdom of other professions and its own creative courage to demonstrate what it can do for this vast number of children with unusual learning problems who are dependent upon its nurture. While there is still much to be learned about brain injury and its impact on human development, enough is known to warrant a massive attack through education on learning and adjustment, on habilitation and amelioration of the problems of the brain-injured child.

This is essentially a problem of habilitation if the issue is viewed, as Rappaport has described it, as one whose etiology is related to impaired mother-child relationships beginning soon after birth. It is habilitation in contradistinction to rehabilitation, because the child has never been a normal entity which has deviated and now requires *re*-habilitation. There is nothing to rehabilitate. The whole life perspective has been distorted. Hence, the problem is one requiring interdisciplinary attack at a point so primitive in the life cycle of the child as to insure total personal habilitation of him and new learning for him as if the psychopathological detour which he may have taken for several years had indeed never taken place. It is more complicated than this, however, for in reality the detour did take place, and the scars which the child has received from it must be healed while at the same time new life direction is being provided for him.

There are two weak links in the chain which must be strengthened ultimately to accomplish this, namely (1) adequately prepared teachers and (2) college professors adequately prepared to implement teacher preparation—teachers of teachers, as Barsch states. The series of discussions herein has been aimed at the first of these two significant issues. Culled from the various discussions, there is in the pages which follow a series of selected statements which summarizes the competencies required of teachers of brain-injured children. Integrated into a logical series, they can constitute the warp and woof of a basic teacher education fabric.*

GENERAL COMPETENCIES AND PERSONALITY ATTRIBUTES

1. Teachers should be aware of the areas or dimensions of development in which the child is to be evaluated and be cognizant of informal methods of diagnosis that will provide some rough pattern of abilities and disabilities of the youngsters (Gallagher).

2. Teachers should know various remedial exercises and methods for meeting specific deficiencies and be able to sequence these exercises in developmental order. Thus, a much greater emphasis on developmental processes in teacher training programs and less concern with group data on development is needed (Gallagher).

3. The educational environment must allow for necessary individual attention and tutoring. Consequently, a "substantially different and, hopefully, an imaginative approach" to educational planning is required. Blindly following a pattern that has been successful with other groups of exceptional children is inadequate to meet the educational needs of these youngsters (Gallagher).

4. A greater emphasis on individual planning, diagnosis and remediation is basic in view of the nature of these children who "have in common, that they are all different" from the average and from one another. The goal of a professional preparation program is to see that a teacher is ready to fulfill his chief responsibility which is determining the nature of the training program for the child (Gallagher).

5. Relationship structure, or the ability of the adult to understand the child sufficiently well at any given moment to relate in a way which

* Appreciation is given to Mr. James Paul for his part in providing the writer with the elements of the summaries.

aids the child's development of impulse control and other ego functions is a basic concept to be understood by teachers. The concept of relationship structure must be added to the concepts of environmental and educational programs and teaching material structure (Rappaport).

6. Teachers must know that the early childhood experiences of the brain-injured child have "fashioned him an ego very different" from the average child. The teacher must be aware of the child's concept of his inner and outer world. From this understanding several predictable expectations of the child and the role of the teacher emerge (Rappaport).

7. Teachers must expect to be an "ego bank" for a psychologically "bankrupt" child (Rappaport).

8. Teachers must know the ego has an extrauterine epigenesis that must evolve through an unhurried and orderly progression of stages (Rappaport).

9. The teacher has certain responsibilities for appropriate understanding and action that derive from the implications of this concept. That is, the teacher's relationship with the child must communicate attitudes, feelings, and content relevant to the ego insufficiency of the child. Teaching, building skills, enabling him to achieve more adaptive behavior and, at times, simply coexistence in the classroom are predicated on the success of such communication (Rappaport).

10. Personality characteristics of the teacher are of primary importance in relationship structure. True self-respect, maturity, proper sensitivity, well-integrated identity, and abundant frustration tolerance are basic characteristics of a teacher who would be an ego bank for brain-injured children. "If an individual does not have the attributes essential to that bank, he should not seek to teach these children, because the venture will fail" (Rappaport).

11. Although most agree as to what a good teacher is, the elements of good teaching and the way to develop these are not agreed upon. Tannhauser suggests a pragmatic approach. Based on her review of teacher training in elementary education, Tannhauser makes the following suggestions for *teacher selection* into training programs for teachers of brain-injured children:

    a. Identify teachers from kindergarten to grade three who everyone agrees are outstanding teachers.

    b. Watch them work with children.

    c. Select those who really enjoy teaching.

    d. From this group select those in whose room you find: children understand what they are doing and why; all children feel reasonably sure they will succeed in the task assigned; children know the resources in the classroom and can use them; behavior problems are anticipated and prevented by redirection; children move from one activity to another without confusion or loss of purpose; children are involved in achieving the task, not in pleasing the teacher; the teacher makes mistakes and the children, with good humor and tolerance, help her rectify them; the children recognize their problems and know the teacher and class understand and are willing to help. Children feel a sense of improving.

e. Finally select those teachers who are: secure in dealing with peers and related professionals; flexible—willing to try and interested in new ways of dealing with old problems; enthusiastic about experimentation; highly motivated to work with children who have special problems.

Given these considerations in selection plus adequate specialized training, the teachers will be successful in classes for brain-injured children if, in their initial adjustment, they maintain good health, have no major family crisis, and do not feel pressured to take courses unrelated to their new work just to meet certification requirements (Tannhauser).

COMPETENCIES SPECIFIC TO EDUCATION OF THE BRAIN-INJURED CHILD

1. Frostig emphasizes the learning and development of specific techniques, i.e. "educational therapy" based on an understanding of the symptomatology of each child.

2. The teacher needs diagnostic and remedial skills aimed at improving the underlying basic abilities as well as the reading process per se; for example, training in auditory perception (e.g., Myklebust); training in language methods (e.g., Kirk); training in visual perceptual materials (e.g., Frostig); training in higher thought processes (e.g., Levi, Peel).

3. Training in other areas suggested by other writers in this book (Getman, ocular-motor skills; Barsch, sensori-motor skills; Hardy, auditory skills; and so forth) are also basic to reading.

4. "Beginning reading can often be introduced before the initial reading readiness training is completed" (Frostig).

5. "It is important for the teacher to realize that optimum remediation depends on careful diagnostic exploration, because remediation has to vary according to the disturbance. No single teaching method can be the correct approach for all children" (Frostig).

6. "A short survey of the range of reading difficulties is one of the requisites in the education of teachers of children with learning difficulties." The survey should include abilities necessary for reading to proceed smoothly *and* an overview of the development of psychological functions from infancy through adolescence. Such an overview should enable the teacher to understand the importance and training implications of the different phases in a child's development for a readiness program, as follows (Frostig): Sensori-motor (0–2)—visual-motor skills and eye movements (e.g., Piaget, Werner, Gesell); language (2–4)—auditory-perceptual skills, language, speech development; visual-perceptual abilities (4–7½); higher thought processes (7½ on).

7. The differentiation between static and sequential perception (auditory and visual) is as basic for the purpose of education as that between the sense modalities. Frostig discusses static visual, static auditory, sequential visual, and sequential auditory perception (Frostig).

8. Teachers should know that there is not a one-to-one correlation between perceptual inadequacy and reading difficulty (Frostig).

9. Teachers should know certain evaluative and diagnostic instruments: (a) sensori-motor skills: e.g., Kephart Scale, Winter Haven Exercises, Cureton Motor Fitness Test, Kraus-Weber Test, and others; (b) visual-perceptual abilities: e.g., Marianne Frostig Developmental Test of Visual Perception, visual-motor sequential subtest of the ITPA, observation of reading errors, careful observation of eye movements; (c) auditory perception: e.g., Wepman Test of Auditory Discrimination, digit span subtest of Wechsler, auditory-vocal sequential subtest of ITPA, word span and sentence span tests, tests of ability to follow verbal directions (Frostig).

10. Training methods relevant to specific dysfunctions or disabilities must be included in teacher training (Frostig).

11. Teachers must be aware of the emotional problems of these children. They must be aware of the importance of so structuring the classroom environment and directing their relationship with the children and their relationships among themselves that both emotional health and school achievement improve (Frostig).

12. In classroom teaching it is not necessary to differentiate between specific reading disability and minimal brain damage since treatment depends on specific symptoms. Teachers need to be familiar with the concept of specific dyslexia as it frequently appears in the literature (Frostig).

13. "No area of development—sensori-motor, language, perception, higher intellectual functions, emotional or social adjustment—should be neglected." The teacher needs to know what area is affected (Frostig).

14. "The teacher should recognize that the majority of remedial reading methods use the phonics approach because the essence of the reading process is the establishment of correspondence between the visual stimuli (letters and words) and the auditory stimuli (the sounds of letters and words)." The teacher should be aware of such methods as I.T.A. and Gillingham. Also, he should be aware of other kinds of methods such as the kinesthetic (Frostig).

15. In the training of higher thought processes, the teacher should be especially aware of the work of Jerome Bruner and Aurelia Levi (Frostig).

16. Teachers should understand the role of etiology; however, the diagnosis and evaluation of symptoms must be the foundation of remedial teaching (Frostig).

17. The teacher should be competent in:
   a. Analyzing into component parts what is involved in being able to master subject matter. For number concepts, "this ability implies a thorough understanding of the structure of our number system and the processes by which it can be manipulated."
   b. Being able to "read children," understanding elements of readiness and the child's habitual approach to his environment.
   c. The ability to assemble an extensive repertoire of teaching methods, learning materials, techniques, skills, games, and other aids, and select those most suited to the situations that arise.
   d. The "ability to create and maintain a classroom atmosphere conducive to learning" using potential strengths of the child's family, related disciplines, and community resources (Freidus).

18. The child needs help "learning how to learn" (Freidus).

19. These children need to base their learning on many more concrete experiences, offered in more detailed steps, than for most children; discovery rather than drill; generalization not rote learning (Freidus).

20. The teacher needs to recognize that "arithmetic is a way of thinking about the quantitative aspects of life, and that it is also a language for expressing and dealing with them" (Freidus).

21. Drill is a "final step based upon a solid foundation of meaning" (Freidus).

22. The criteria for matching and grouping must be established (Freidus).

23. Teachers must know the children who need more experiences in matching in order to operate in terms of sets. They must know how to provide these experiences (Freidus).
24. Teachers must be clear enough about their goals that they can construct their own aids to learning (Freidus).
25. "Teachers need to appreciate the cumulative quality of babies' experiences as they explore their environment," for example, discovering relationships. Teachers must determine the information acquired and how effectively it was received and integrated. Clarity in relationship concepts is basic to the child's understanding number concepts (Freidus).
26. Teachers themselves should experiment with materials offered to children to understand the importance and use of materials for demonstrating the structure of the number system (Freidus).
27. A major weakness in teacher training preparation has been that teachers have not learned the importance of checking back far enough in the child's learning to insure readiness for what needs now to be learned. The teacher must maintain delicate balance between threat and challenge for the child (Freidus).
28. Knowledge of the child and knowledge of the process of learning are both basic (Freidus).
29. Combinations of observation, active participation, discussion, and lectures are important for preparing creative teachers (Freidus).
30. More than learning theory is required. There must be integration with child development concepts. Observation of babies and young children, and interaction with children who are teaching themselves to deal with their environment are needed (Freidus).
31. Study is necessary of the range of primary disorders as well as normal child development. Also, knowledge of secondary disorders is required with awareness of differences in primary and secondary disorders and effects on learning (Freidus).
32. A combination of theory and practice is basic (Freidus).
33. The teacher avoids the jargon of special education and related disciplines and is not content with a superficial, oversimplified meaning behind the words (Freidus).
34. The teacher should be reluctant to accept anything in print without evaluation. He should be exposed to a great variety of printed material for critical evaluation (Freidus).
35. He should avoid convenient stereotypes implied by labels—rather giving due consideration to the complexities of the problem (Freidus).
36. Hearing and listening and ways of helping the child learn through

his auditory difficulties deserve the same emphasis in teacher training programs heretofore given only to such areas as vision and
motor training (Hardy).

37. *How* a child hears is too often ignored when tests reveal *that* he
hears (Hardy).

38. Problems in temporal integration, incapacities in learning, remembering, formulating, and using a symbol code, auditory disorders,
inability to recall a voluntary motor speech pattern, inability to
imitate a motor speech pattern, inability to imitate a motor pattern,
subtle incoordination in fine and/or gross motor movements are
symptoms that appear alone or in combination and interfere with
communication and curriculum learning. All require help (Hardy).

39. These children require imaginative diagnostic teaching in order to
delineate further the problems identified in medical and paramedial
evaluations and, the creation of a tailored program to meet each
child's specific needs (Hardy).

40. Periodic medical reevaluation and continuous evaluation of program effectiveness are critical (Hardy).

41. Broad eclectic background from several disciplines is required.
In the following areas, the teacher needs:

a. Medical and paramedical—knowledge of anatomy, neurophysiology and pathology of the ear and VIII nerve system, eye and
visual system, speech productive system, the brain and CNS;
an understanding of terminology; appreciation of what information is needed in a diagnostic evaluation; the ability to read
and translate reports into a habilitative program; introduction
to psychoacoustics; understanding of etiologic factors; appreciation that some of the children suffered traumatic influences
that caused breakdowns, while others show developmental lacks
or lags, perhaps genetic or biochemical.

b. Child growth and development—firm grounding in all aspects
of child growth and development and normative behavior at
"successive age levels"; knowledge of how children learn.

c. Language and speech—scientific mastery of English phonetics;
understanding of linguistic structure and function; "normative
guidelines for critically evaluating language facility" (oral and
written comprehension and expression); "thorough grounding
in a system for teaching language principles and grammatical
sequence"; experience in analyzing textbooks for vocabulary
and language principles to be taught prior to introducing the
text; the ability to create language drill materials.

d. Communicative disorders—an operational framework for understanding the communicative system as a whole; knowledge of kinds and degrees of hearing, language, and speech disorders; appreciation that interferences that cause communication problems are but part of the total CNS dysfunction that affects other kinds of learning in most of these children; understanding of the concept of "auding"; the ability to create specific exercises and devices aimed at improving auditory memory, span, and sequence; to realize the interrelationships between the visual and auditory systems; the ability of listening critically to the child's oral expression and of analyzing a child's written language; "training in seeing possible relationships between specific reading disabilities and other communicative disorders"; to recognize when a child has a hearing loss and implications for child's functioning; to recognize difficulties with language, memory, and recall and/or formulation and expression of language; to be able to analyze any task failure and especially to separate conceptual breakdowns from language breakdowns; "skill in adapting a task and modifying instructions so the child can succeed"; the ability to make diagnostic observations of the child and share them with the diagnostic team; to keep up-to-date records and progress reports indicating goals, and from these evaluating program effectiveness; to understand therapeutic program of hearing-language-speech therapist and how to reinforce therapy in the classroom.

e. Emotional problems—to understand emotional problems in children; to be able to analyze negative or resistant behavior in terms of the situation that provoked it; to be aware of need for sound teacher-parent relationship; to understand parents and their needs; the ability to help parents understand child; to learn how to be a good clinician.

f. Equipment—a knowledge of the effective use of tape recorder, group amplification, individual hearing aids, teaching machines, language master, and tachistoscope (Hardy).

COMPETENCIES RELATED TO COGNITION, PERCEPTION, AND MOTOR TRAINING

1. The nature of certain control dimensions in the complex cognitive structures and the known or hypothesized effects of mild brain damage should be taught to teachers. Such a framework of understanding may alert the teacher to aspects of classroom behavior that would otherwise pass unnoticed (Gardner).

2. Several problems for research concerning the interaction of teach-

ers and brain-damaged children are indicated that would have direct implications for teacher training (Gardner):

a. Certain teachers may be more suited to the kind of interaction needed with even mildly brain-damaged children *if* these children experience severe anxieties and control difficulties that require special help and understanding for cognitive growth to occur.

b. The cognitive styles of teachers and learners may have important effects upon the learning processes of similarities and differences.

c. Certain aspects of the cognitive styles of teachers may differentiate those who are more effective in teaching these children.

3. The neuropsychologist and special educator must learn to work more closely together and have a greater exchange of information (Gaddes).

4. "The education of the brain-injured child requires the integration of the best judgment and skills of the neurologist, the public health nurse, the special teacher, the educational administrator, the neuropsychologist, and frequently the neurosurgeon, the radiologist, the audiologist, the speech therapist, the social worker, and other professional specialists. When so many professional people are involved, the effectiveness of their communication among themselves, as well as to the teacher, may be determined by the least competent of the group" (Gaddes).

5. A dilemma in teacher training is oversimplification, and hence distortion or overelaboration, and hence confusion (Gaddes).

6. Three areas of learning necessary for teachers of brain-injured children are: "a certain body of knowledge pertaining to neurology, psychology, and education; . . . to communicate successfully with parents, other educators, neurologists, and other medical specialists, social welfare personnel, and all persons concerned with the child's growth and education; . . . specific teaching techniques" (Gaddes).

7. Studies by neuropsychologists are basic to a teacher's understanding of localization and dominance (Gaddes).

8. Research in finger localization and its relation to tactual perception and learning is basic to the teacher's understanding (Gaddes).

9. The broadening of the concept of cerebral dominance to include spatial and temporal dimensions has important implications for the teacher of brain-injured children (Gaddes).

10. Teachers should have awareness of neurology and physiological correlates of learning disabilities or response patterns that are

fairly clearly determined by neurological deficits or dysfunctions, i.e., neural processes underlying perceptual-cognitive-motor performances (Gaddes).

11. Information on handedness, an ignored topic in educational psychology and child psychology textbooks, is a basic area to be included (Gaddes).

12. Specific course work should include one year in clinical neurology with emphasis on brain and brain-stem functions (also exposure to psychometric localization of brain lesions, e.g., Reitan's or Kløve's work) and graduate course work in special education with well-supervised practica (Gaddes).

13. Basic neurological concepts of which teachers should have some awareness are:
   a. The brain reveals little asymmetry of structure.
   b. The brain must be understood in terms of marked and complex differences in function; man has at least two brains.
   c. The two hemispheres operate as a delicate integrated energy system.
   d. Brain lesions may cause chronic behavioral symptoms that interfere with normal learning.
   e. Cerebral dominance may alter depending on the particular function and time of observation; the left hemisphere is usually dominant for speech and language functions; the right hemisphere may have its own sphere of dominance.
   f. Handedness should be carefully defined.
   g. Finger localization has a specific role in classroom learning.
   h. Dominance in hand, eye, and foot may be considered in planning remedial learning programs.

The over-all objective in teacher training is an integrated graduate training program in clinical neurology, research design in neuropsychology, and special education (Gaddes).

14. There are three major principles in teaching the brain-injured child: "teaching should be developmentally oriented"; "teaching should be directed toward the development of generalization"; "attention should be directed toward the establishment of veridicality in the already existing body of the child's information" (Kephart).

15. A training program should enable the teacher of the brain-injured child to: understand basic developmental sequences; be able to observe breakdowns in developmental sequences; understand the learning problems leading to generalization; be able to *interpret* nonveridical responses; be ingenious in devising learning experi-

ences adapted to the child with inadequate space-time structure (Kephart).

16. Teachers need to know that vision, the dominant process of development, is more than sight or acuity which may be measured by a wall chart or other screening devices (Getman).

17. Since visual abilities are learned, the teacher needs to: know those visual abilities and how they are related to academic performance; acquire competency in recognizing visual inabilities in a child which may adversely affect the academic performance; know what performance in certain visual abilities is indicative of need for professional remedial visual care; know how to enhance certain of those visual abilities within his sphere of competency and training (Getman).

18. The teacher needs the following specific and highly related areas of information on vision (symptoms and training implications) related to academic performance (visuomotor skills):
    a. Visual action patterns: eye movement skills (ocular motilities), eye teaming skills (binocularity), eye-hand coordination skills.
    b. Visual performance skills (products or resultants of first three): visual form perception, refractive status of the eyes (Getman).

19. Teachers can make significant contributions by training the first four, making appropriate adjustments in the curriculum, and making referrals when necessary (Getman).

20. "Teachers need to know that, by modern optometric methods, children will be fitted with lenses when they can see without them" (based on the distinction between eye problems and visual problems and use of convex "learning lenses" to satisfy the avoidance urge in response to containing tasks). "Teachers need no longer be fearful of 'over-referring'," since vision is basic to the academic process and teacher observations are most often valid. Teachers should be familiar with visual training theories, procedures, and techniques, and limitations within which improvements of these skills may be effected in the classroom environment (Getman).

21. A rereading of Periere, Montessori, Itard, Sequin, Piaget, and others "through the lenses of current knowledge" will be helpful to the teacher (Barsch).

22. One should substitute "movement-sensitivity" for "sensori-motor" (Barsch).

23. Teachers must understand the concept of triordination as well as coordination and how each sensory modality is important in the proper triordinate alignment (Barsch).

24. For a teacher to understand movement, he must also understand

the "unique manner in which each system of sensitivity contributes to dynamic balance, body awareness, and spatial awareness" (Barsch).

25. "Two courses of teacher preparation are then clearly indicated if 'movement training' is to be considered. First, a teacher must understand movement as transport in space through matching an internalized alignment of triordinates on an external world by projection in space. Second, the systems of sensitivity to information must be studied as interrelated to that alignment. Neither of these basic points of view are generally incorporated in teacher preparation programs at the present time" (Barsch).

26. Teachers must understand the four space meridians—near, mid, far, and remote space (Barsch).

27. Movement orientation in a teacher training program comprises three basic units of preparation:
    a. Developing learning organism—physiologic readiness, postural alignment, grace and ease in transporting body and body parts into space for performance, individual and collective efficiencies of the six processing modes.
    b. Study of environment—physical surround and design of materials. (Since teachers usually must design their own devices, they must learn the principles of design.)
    c. Study of symbolic competency—language as a system of communication, reading as a graphic system of communication and as a stimulant to movement, spelling as a system of visualization of word space, arithmetic as a system of spatial relationships. "Symbolic competency emerges from movement" (Barsch).

28. "Course work must be developed to help teachers perceive the child as a dynamic organism gaining information from energy forms in the gravitational fields of space. The student-teacher must be permitted to explore the space worlds of physiology, anthropology, chemistry, physics, engineering, kinesiology, biology, zoology, and others not with the intent to specialize in any of the fields but always to seek the answer to the same question: 'What specific set of principles does each field contain which have direct pertinence for understanding the dynamics of the individual learner'" (Barsch).

29. Student teachers should study the dynamics of child development in terms of the long-range consequences of each step in the developmental timetable, not as a series of composite norms reflecting an average process (Barsch).

30. Orientation to movement efficiency must involve laboratory experiences with the child as well as "book learning" (Barsch).
31. Personal analysis of the teacher's own movement efficiency should be incorporated in the teacher's training (Barsch).
32. The teacher training program must relate itself to the administrative realities of the ways in which school systems approach the problem, i.e., developmental, corrective, or maintaining (Barsch).
33. The teacher must be able to work with parents (Barsch).
34. A profound understanding of the structure of the human body must precede study of perception and symbolic functioning. "The neurology of impairment is secondary to the understanding of the dynamics of movement." Teacher preparation in this field must have a movement orientation. The teacher "must be truly 'movement oriented' by inclination, collegiate orientation, and experimental validation" (Barsch).

COMPETENCIES RELATED TO PSYCHOLOGY, NEUROLOGY, AND THEIR INTERRELATIONSHIPS

Knowledge and skills necessary for using psychodiagnostic information effectively are:

1. Psychometrics and statistics—more than a general orientation to this area because of concern with a subgroup of the population and specific learning and behavior characteristics of that group (Strother).
2. Psychodiagnosis—identification of behavior to be altered, systematic observation of that behavior, ordering these observations through some conceptual model of the structure of behavior, formulation of an hypothesis, and, ultimately, experimentally manipulating conditions to test the hypothesis. Training in this process would provide teachers with a method of analysis to better understand the behavior and "more powerful techniques of intervention" (Strother).
3. Examples of two programs of training in psychodiagnosis that might be included in teacher training are:
   a. Experimental analysis of behavior based on a Skinnerian frame of reference which involves definition of a class of behavior; tabulation of instances of that behavior; once sufficient reliability in observing the behavior is established, observing the antecedent stimuli and consequences of the behavior; continued observation until a systematic pattern emerges; formulation of hypothesis to change the behavior; testing the hypothesis.
   b. Cognitive approach relating diagnostic information to a con-

ceptual model of cognitive functions. Systematic examination of perception; motor functions; perceptual motor and inter-sensory functions; memory; symbolization, reasoning and concept formation; response formulation; and motor sequencing are involved in psychodiagnosis. A few psychometric tools (e.g., ITPA and Frostig) have been developed which aid in this approach. Teachers must understand the theoretical framework of this approach. They must also understand the relation of these psychological processes to the learning of academic subjects and social behavior. With this background they are prepared for brief formal study of diagnostic procedures utilizing demon-strations and case presentations in order to become familiar with the techniques of the psychologist. Emphasis in theoretical courses and the course in psychodiagnosis should be placed on relationship of these basic psychological processes to school performance which will enable psychologists and teachers to communicate more effectively. Further, knowledge of the methods and materials used to test the child will aid the teacher in informally experimenting with ways of presenting materials to the child and thus using materials more effectively (Strother).

4. Grossman quotes Eisenberg: "Drugs are neither the passport to a brave new world nor the gateway to Hell" (Grossman).

5. Drugs have a definite but limited role in the treatment of disturbed behavior (Grossman).

6. It is important to remember that psychopharmacology is but one aspect of a complex problem (Grossman).

7. "Used carefully they [drugs] can add a significant element to a total plan of management" (Grossman).

8. Grossman would have the teacher introduced to the field of psycho-pharmacology in a manner indicated by the content of his paper with an introduction to taxonomy and an emphasis on the limita-tions as well as potential benefits of pharmacological intervention (Grossman).

9. Thoroughgoing training in psychology with specialized training in neuropsychology and well-rounded training in neurological science is unrealistic as an aim for teacher training. The problem is one of degree, not of kinds of training. Degree of emphasis in neuropsy-chology will vary from one location to another because of definition of the area and other factors (Reitan).

10. Teachers should recognize the complex and variable nature of "brain damage" and the fact that the term is relatively meaningless

because it includes so many diverse and varied neurological conditions (Reitan).

11. Teachers should know that the brain is the principal organ of behavior and the complex implications of such an understanding and that one-word descriptions on the basis of simple observations are inadequate and often misleading. (The child may be passive or "hyperactive.") The concept of false-negatives and false-positives along with appropriate standards for evidence on which to base conclusions must be communicated to teachers. The teacher should know something of the difficulties involved in the diagnosis and description of brain lesions (Reitan).

12. Teachers need to be made aware of studies such as those done by Reitan which take issue with the concept of qualitative differences between the brain-injured and non-brain-injured and the "false impression of hopelessness and despair regarding the potential for improvement of brain-injured children" (Reitan).

13. A meaningful survey of the field of neuropsychology is more realistic than "a degree of training that would permit fulfillment of a complete professional commitment to neuropsychology." Consideration should be given to characteristic types of problems manifested by children with brain lesions and emphasis on illustrations of appropriate and inappropriate teaching (Reitan).

14. Reitan suggests special problems to be included in the instruction of teachers with generalizations and an illustration for each generalization:

    a. Impairment of basic adaptive abilities may be much greater than indicated by conventional intelligence tests.

    b. "Cerebral lesions which cause certain sensory and motor deficits also have definite corresponding consequences with regard to neuropsychological deficits." The entire picture should be a part of program planning.

    c. Failures in adjustment viewed as arising from emotional problems in the child's environment frequently are combinations of psychological deficits resulting from brain damage predisposing the child to maladaptations to problems in living. Teachers need more information regarding "the interactions of deficits caused by brain damage and the special stresses in adapting to environmental problems and interpersonal relationships that result."

    d. Training efforts for some brain-damaged children have been devoted almost exclusively toward development of academic competency which, even when these efforts are successful, still leaves the child with broad areas of deficiency. Teachers must be familiar with the many ways in which brain lesions may impair abilities.

e. With the brain-damaged child variability in psychological test performance, both within a test battery and in the same test administered at different times, is the rule and not the exception. Intraindividual variability in academic performances, especially in accordance with environmental stress, is also to be expected (Reitan).

COMPETENCIES RELATED TO AREAS OF PSYCHIATRY, EGO PSYCHOLOGY, AND EMOTIONAL DISTURBANCE

1. Teachers of brain-injured children should be exposed to "the ideology which asserts that these children have individual developmental and emotional patterns as do all children." Focus should be on the way in which a particular deficit can become a source of emotional difficulty and the steps to be taken in reducing negative effects (Morse).

2. Teachers must be encouraged to "search out emotional, social, and organic factors with equal vigor" (Morse).

3. The content of training of teachers in emotional area can be divided into concepts and skills (Morse).

4. Conceptual systems of developmental psychology, personality formulation, deviant behavior, and behavior alteration are to be mastered by the teacher. Since the focus is on emotional problems, child neurosis, psychosis, the nature of the psychopath, and neglect would be emphasized. The philosophical and psychological concepts of mental health cannot be glossed over (Morse).

5. The special teacher should not be taught a viewpoint about human nature but "earn the right to a viewpoint" by knowing what is rejected and what is accepted (Morse).

6. Areas of content competency (without the assumption of direct application) are:

   a. Normal and aberrant personality development. Background knowledge can be gained through study of major explanations and issues of normal and pathological human nature "in a quest to understand children rather than abstract psychology." This should constitute conceptual information, not skills. Social aspects of behavior should be emphasized since teachers work in group situations. Teachers should master the concepts of the interrelationships of the disability and personality formulated by Rappaport.

b. Personality assessment. "There is to be no special 'psychological test magic' kept secret from teachers."

c. Behavior modification. Teachers should be exposed to theory and observation of psychotherapy. Teachers should understand how each system purports to cause changes in behavior, what is intrinsically implied concerning human nature, and what the critics indicate.

Adequate role and status with co-workers of other disciplines do not develop without knowledge (Morse).

7. Techniques to help the disturbed child in the classroom cope with his difficulties must be developed through supervised practice. The teacher must know how to use other disciplines and draw possibilities for classroom help from their concepts. The following are necessary:

a. Classroom behavior appraisal and the ability to use that information.

b. Adapting and constructing assessment devices for use in a particular classroom setting.

c. Indirect and direct study of the pupil's self-concept, especially school self-esteem. This should provide a "working synthesis of psychological theory for the teacher."

d. Skills in interviewing. "The flexible reality-focused schema embodied in 'life space interviewing' is preferred over derivations of psychiatric or nondirective practice." Interviewing moves the teacher from diagnosing to intervening by serving both purposes.

e. Evaluating social milieu aspects of the classroom. Teachers must translate such evaluation into milieu design specific for the support of individual pupil needs.

f. Using psychological components of activities for therapeutic purposes. Self-expression, success, and opportunities to learn in work and play are examples.

g. Desensitizing the emotional threat of past failure. Small tasks, avoiding overloaded demands through special planning and curriculum alterations, and support at time of acute tension are examples.

h. Using personal relationship for its corrective and identification building potentials.

Consultation, test data, and frank discussion are ways to increase the teacher's self-awareness and thus maximize the helping potential of the teacher-pupil relationship. The teacher training process as well as the academic content is basic in gaining the investment required in the emotional area (Morse).

8. Adamson outlines and discusses information from pediatric psychiatry which he feels is basic to the teachers of brain-injured children, rather than suggesting ideas related to a particular strategy for teacher preparation. Five milestones representing significant conceptualization in the field were discussed:

   a. Bender (1956) reviewed over thirty years of thinking on the subject of psychopathology and emphasizes the problems common to various biological problems.

   b. Strauss and Lehtinen (1947) described the therapeutic educational environment wherein the teacher is viewed as a therapist who must be able to ask the relevant questions in analyzing a child's failure. Other works (Strauss and Kephart, 1955; Lewis, Strauss, and Lehtinen, 1960) described the disability imposed by perceptual disturbance and the implications for performance, personality, and behavior.

   c. Eisenberg (1957) was one of the first pediatric psychiatrists to attempt to correlate emerging neurophysiologic observations with aspects of learning and behavior in brain-injured children.

   d. The work of Moruzzi, Magoun, and their co-workers (1949, 1952, 1963) in neurophysiology resulted in the isolation of the ascending reticular activating system. Awareness of this concept is pertinent for teachers because: a biologic basis for the sensory-modality theory of reinforcement can be described, a partial explanation of the hypothesis that habilitation of brain-injured children is made possible by finding other pathways to do the work of damaged pathways is possible from this conception, one neurophysiologic mechanism by which classroom conditioning may be facilitated has been identified.

   e. Rappaport (1961) dealt with the issue of ego development in brain-injured children and challenged the assumption that damage to neural tissue plays the important role in the brain-injured child's behavior and thought disturbances (Adamson).

9. Adamson suggested several areas of training that merit focus in teacher training which are primarily derived from the literature listed above:

a. Teachers should appreciate the "endless sequence of perceptual errors and misconception"—social as well as sensory—that ensue from perceptual disturbances.

b. Teachers should appreciate the implications of their role as parent substitutes, promoting interhuman relationships and relieving excessive demands on the mother.

c. Teachers interested in the use and theory of drug action on the central nervous system should be aware of Freed's (1962) work.

d. Teachers should be oriented to approaching the child as a whole person—a concept enabled by Rappaport's work.

e. Teachers should appreciate the implications of delays in psychosocial development such as the process of social differentiation. This relates to an issue as basic as the child's awareness of himself as a separate person which has implications for the reality basis of the child's perception of such experiences as failure.

f. There are several direct implications of the concept of "total-life-relationship structure" to which a teacher should be sensitized: the importance of timing in moves or changes; the significance of a climate of mutual trust; the importance of staff availability; and the distinction between collaboration and supervision in the use of other disciplines. This distinction involves using other disciplines to gain understanding of the child, not methods of handling; and having realistic expectations of "the pearls of wisdom on behavioral management." (Teachers need to know that many observations made by the psychotherapist are only harbingers of things to come.) It also involves realizing that teachers (and psychotherapists) must be able to support the development of a strong, healthy counseling relationship between parents and counselor. This relationship can drain off frustrations that might be displaced on the teacher. Such support requires the understanding of the role of parent counselor on the professional team. Teachers should be able to encourage expression of conscious emotions in socially acceptable patterns. Teachers should recognize what Adamson calls "station stops" or psychological problems arising from ego insufficiency (analogy of local versus express trains) in the child's development. Also, he should be able to use other team members to help a child leave "station stops" (Adamson).

COMPETENCIES RELATED TO INTERDISCIPLINARY FUNCTION

1. The proper role and skills necessary for teachers functioning on interdisciplinary teams is a matter of convergence, that is, teachers need to present themselves as "thoroughly well-grounded practitioners in a position to apply appropriate educational and behavioral techniques" (Knoblock).

2. It may be equally important for teachers to have the same parallel skills and knowledge as other team members. The concept of convergence has the following implications which may be encompassed by formalized training practices, including responsible supervision and interdisciplinary experiences:

    a. Teachers need a clear conception of their actual and potential contribution to a team.

    b. Teachers need an articulated role which is in keeping with their own level of sophistication and the requirements of the setting.

    c. Teachers need to discover commonalities of their skills and job requirements and those of other members of the team.

    d. The acquisition of the above is predicated on the realization, by teachers, of the roles of other disciplines and the development of process knowledge, i.e., relationships and group phenomena.

    e. A common psychological and educational grammar may ultimately be a necessity.

    f. The teacher must have independent and interdependent skills for effective team functioning.

    g. Near the middle or end of their training, teachers need supervised practice in a multidiscipline setting (Knoblock).

Several important generalizations can be made from the foregoing summaries. Although every element is important in developing total competency in a teacher of brain-injured children, certain factors stand out as being considered unique by the participants in this Seminar.

It must again be stressed that consensus was not sought in either Seminar discussions or in the working papers which were basic to the discussions. Furthermore, by their nature topics which were raised in certain papers had absolutely no possibility of being mentioned or discussed in other papers. For example, issues of ego psychology discussed by several authors would hardly appear appropriately in a paper which dealt with competencies required of teachers in teaching number concepts, regardless of the orientation of the author of the latter paper. Teaching number concepts, per se, would never appear in a paper dealing with psychopharmacology. Hence it is indeed unfair to discuss the papers as a totality. In spite of this caution, however, it is well to point out those areas where single topics did appear with frequency in several papers.

General Areas of Concern to be Considered in Teacher Education Programs

Eleven of the papers (65 per cent) mentioned the issue of terminology as significant in the understanding of teachers. Twelve of the authors (71 per cent), in spite of the uniqueness of their assigned topics, stressed the importance of teachers of brain-injured children possessing detailed knowledge of specific teaching techniques pertaining to this specialized field of education. Nine of the authors (53 per cent) stressed the importance of basing the teacher's competencies in sound concepts of child development, while 59 per cent (ten persons) pointed out that teachers of brain-injured children must possess competencies which are firmly based on information and concepts from several related disciplines.

Thirty-five per cent of the papers (six authors) stressed such fundamental issues as diagnostic skills, competency in teacher-child relationships, the teacher's role in relating to other disciplines, as well as supervised field experience as being significant in developing competency in working with brain-injured children. It is, of course, safe to state that other authors would also consider these factors as significant and might have included them had their papers been directed to these or closely related areas.

Between 18 and 29 per cent of the writers (three to five persons) included sophistication with diagnostic and evaluative instruments as being basic to teacher preparation. They also stressed such issues as understanding of emotional problems; the stress of social, physical, and psychological environments; process knowledge; psychology of learning; understanding of sensory functions; and capacity to work with parents as being crucial elements in an inclusive program of preparation for teachers of brain-injured children.

Specific Bodies of Knowledge Relevant to the Content of Teacher Education Programs

Because of the disparate nature of the papers, there is obviously less possibility of consensus with respect to the specific areas of knowledge to be included in a program than there is with the general areas just discussed. Psychopharmacology, for example, is likely to be mentioned only in the paper concerned with that topic since it is not related to the content of most other papers. In spite of this, however, three authors (18 per cent) mention this area of knowledge as being significant. Other areas with the percentage of times mentioned by authors are listed as follows:

Developmental psychology	59 per cent	(10 authors)
Psychometrics	47 per cent	(8 authors)
Special education	35 per cent	(6 authors)
General education	29 per cent	(5 authors)
Educational psychology	29 per cent	(5 authors)
Clinical neurology	24 per cent	(4 authors)
Neurophysiology	24 per cent	(4 authors)
Experimental psychology (including learning theory)	18 per cent	(3 authors)
Abnormal psychology	18 per cent	(3 authors)
Ego psychology	18 per cent	(3 authors)
Neuropsychology	18 per cent	(3 authors)
Audiology	18 per cent	(3 authors)
Speech pathology	18 per cent	(3 authors)
Anatomy	18 per cent	(3 authors)
Optometry	18 per cent	(3 authors)
Clinical psychology	12 per cent	(2 authors)
Statistics	12 per cent	(2 authors)
Physical sciences	12 per cent	(2 authors)
Pediatric psychiatry	12 per cent	(2 authors)

The specific areas of competency must not be viewed as entirely separate from the general areas. The two tend to expand and support one another and are basically interrelated. Together these form a basis from which the teacher education program can and must take form. To these must, of course, be added the many details which were mentioned only by the authors assigned to discuss a single aspect of this vital field of professional education. As a whole, teacher preparation programs conceived within this rationale will produce teachers skilled in their profession, knowledgeable in significant content areas, and fully capable of functioning as key members of the interdisciplinary group which must have a vital concern for brain-injured children.